Comedy at the Edge

Comedy
at the Edge

How Stand-up in the 1970s Changed America

Richard Zoglin

B L O O M S B U R Y

Copyright © 2008 by Richard Zoglin

All rights reserved. No part of this book may be used or reproduced in any manner whatsoever without written permission from the publisher except in the case of brief quotations embodied in critical articles or reviews. For information address Bloomsbury USA, 175 Fifth Avenue, New York, NY 10010.

Published by Bloomsbury USA, New York
Distributed to the trade by Macmillan

All papers used by Bloomsbury USA are natural, recyclable products made from wood grown in well-managed forests. The manufacturing processes conform to the environmental regulations of the country of origin.

LIBRARY OF CONGRESS CATALOGING-IN-PUBLICATION DATA HAS BEEN APPLIED FOR.

ISBN-10: 1-58234-624-0
ISBN-13: 978-1-58234-624-3

First U.S. Edition 2008

1 2 3 4 5 6 7 8 9 10

Typeset by Westchester Book Group
Printed in the United States of America by Quebecor World Fairfield

For my father,
who was very
funny, and
for Charla

Contents

Opening Act

In the mid-1970s, when I was a freelance writer living in Greenwich Village, the Improvisation was, pound for pound, the best entertainment value in New York. At this bare-bones, storefront club on the seedy western edge of the theater district, for a few bucks' cover charge and a couple of drinks, you could sit for an entire evening, well into the wee hours, and watch stand-up comedians virtually nonstop. Most were young and unknown; many weren't very good. But a few of them were terrific, and an evening at the Improv always had the excitement of discovery, of getting an insider's early look at the innovators in an art form that seemed to be changing before your eyes.

First times are always the best, and at mine (early in 1975, as best I can figure) the highlight was a trio of comics whom I remember as if they were murderers' row in a 1930s All-Star Game. First came Ed Bluestone, a dour, brainy monologuist who did wry, deadpan wisecracks about his Jewish upbringing. (The only line I can recall—about his Sunday school lessons in Jewish history that played like a weekly soap opera—"Bam! The Jews are enslaved by rabbits!"). He was followed by Richard Lewis, a lean, jittery young comic whose own brand of Jewish angst took the form of nervous pacing and tortured run-on sentences that caught the audience up in the kind of rolling, rhythmic laughter that comedians like to compare to waves crashing onshore. Finally, there was a soft-looking, glassy-eyed weirdo whom I had encountered earlier in the evening—when he barged ahead of a few of us waiting in line at the Improv's tiny restroom, located all too conspicuously in the hallway between the bar and the showroom. He had a pipsqueak voice with a vaguely Eastern European accent, and onstage he nervously told bad jokes, lip-synched to a recording of Mighty Mouse's theme song, and then, just to cross everybody up, did an impression of Elvis that blew the house away. A few months later I saw Andy Kaufman for the second time, on the premiere of *Saturday Night Live*.

Those days now seem both far away and oddly current. After springing up in the 1970s, enjoying a nationwide boom in the '80s, and falling on hard times in the '90s, the comedy clubs are back. New York City alone, as I write this, has nearly a dozen—compared with just three in their '70s heyday. But the sense of adventure has been replaced by the programmed predictability of a General Motors assembly plant. The comics all sound pretty much alike these days, with the same patter to loosen up the crowd ("Anyone from out of town?"—in thirty years no one has come up with a better icebreaker), the same recyclable loop of stand-up topics (sex, New York subways, commercials for Viagra). On weekend evenings, the clubs typically squeeze in three shows, spaced an unforgiving two hours apart: four or five comics, two drinks and the check, and you're out the door in ninety minutes flat. When I took out a pen at one club on a recent Saturday night to make some notes on a comic doing pretty good impressions of Bill Cosby and Dr. Phil, a bouncer suddenly appeared in front of me, ordered me out of the room, and read me the riot act: no note taking without the prior consent of the management and the comics. Just when did the fun go out of stand-up comedy?

For me, and so many others growing up in the baby boom years, stand-up comedy wasn't just fun; it was an obsession. I organized my homework around the stand-up comedians on *The Ed Sullivan Show* and the other TV variety shows that filled so many of the prime-time hours in the 1960s. I communed with them in private on the all-but-forgotten medium of long-playing records. So intent was I on savoring my first comedy album—Bill Dana as José Jiménez—that I held off listening to the entire record in one sitting, saving the B-side for a day just to extend the pleasure. Later came Bob Newhart and Bill Cosby and the Smothers Brothers; collections of Stan Freberg's great song parodies; the novelty hits of the early '60s like *My Son, the Folksinger* and *The First Family*.

Beginning in the late 1960s, however, stand-up comedy began to change. It became somehow more essential. It seemed smarter and more current, and it connected more directly with my generation and the things we talked and cared about. And much of that change was inspired, I realized only many years later, by a comedian whom most middle-American kids like me didn't have in their record collection: Lenny Bruce.

Like Bruce, the comedian-cum-social commentator who challenged the guardians of public morality and died of a drug overdose in 1966, stand-up comedians who reached their artistic maturity in the late '60s and '70s saw themselves as rebel artists. Unlike the comedians of an earlier generation—who, for the most part, told jokes written by others—they wrote their own material and used it to express their personal point of view about what was happening in the country, the culture, and their own lives. They both reflected and helped define the ethos of the counterculture as surely as the troubadours of rock or the protest leaders of the left. They took aim at political corruption and corporate greed, made fun of society's hypocrisy and consumerist excess, mocked the button-down conformity of Eisenhower-era America. By their very presence onstage—alone in front of a mike, telling it like it is—they were advertisements for honesty and authenticity, a rebuke to the phoniness and self-righteousness of your parents' generation. Except when they themselves were phony and self-righteous—and then, of course, they were making fun of *that*, satire of a more devious sort.

They became fixtures in America's living rooms on prime-time variety shows and late-night talk shows, and later they helped pioneer the young medium of cable TV. They released best-selling record albums and drew rock-star-like crowds in arenas and concert halls. They spoke to a new generation, the baby boomers who had grown up with television and the cold war and now jammed into comedy clubs on date night (better than going to a movie—you could talk to each other during the show), finding kindred spirits in these writer-performers who articulated their own political disaffection, social concerns, sexual anxieties, and bad-date experiences. Their voice continues to resonate in the national conversation, from the monologues of late-night TV hosts to the insta-punditry and parodies of the Internet. Their point of view—ironic, skeptical, media savvy, challenging authority, puncturing pretension, telling uncomfortable truths—is the lens through which we view everything from presidential politics and celebrity scandal to the little trials of our everyday lives.

They were heroic figures, who often risked their careers as they reinvented a popular art. Some, like George Carlin and Richard Pryor, went through very public transformations, abandoning their sport coats and ties and recasting themselves as antiestablishment provocateurs. Others, like Albert Brooks, Steve Martin, and Andy Kaufman, turned away from the social-political agenda of Bruce and his followers but were artistic rebels nonetheless—blasting apart the clichés and conventions of traditional show business and turning the satire back on the comedian himself. They were idiosyncratic artists, as different from each other as they differed collectively from the Bob Hopes and Milton Berles of old. There were wildly original, Dionysian performers like Robin Williams, whom nobody could hope to imitate, and more cerebral, equally brilliant ones like Robert Klein, whom nearly everybody did. There were savvy club comics like David Letterman and Jay Leno, who went on to become the toastmasters and tastemakers of the next generation. And there was a clean-cut Long Island kid who pol-ished his "observational" comedy to a fine sheen, domesticated the stand-up revolution, and made it safe for the mass audience: Jerry Seinfeld.

Their rise paralleled a revolution that was taking place across the popular arts, as the nation lurched through the political and cultural ferment of the late '60s. After Dylan and the Beatles, rock artists were no longer satisfied merely to sing other people's songs; now they were writing and performing their own work, expressing the politically rebellious, sexually charged, drug-liberated spirit of the times. The old Hollywood studio system was be-ing challenged by a new generation of film directors who brought stylistic innovations and an irreverent, critical vision of America to the screen. From the Broadway stage to the best-seller lists, artists were speaking with new freedom and frankness; it was the era of *The Graduate* and *Portnoy's Com-plaint*, Ken Kesey and Janis Joplin, *Easy Rider* and *Hair*.

Comedy was hardly left out of this cultural upheaval. Improvisational groups like Second City in Chicago and the Committee in San Francisco were developing a new theatrical style to satirize the mores and manners of uptight '50s-era America. The rude comic book parodies of *Mad* maga-zine spawned the Ivy League irreverence of *National Lampoon*. College kids grooved on the pothead comedy of Cheech and Chong and the trippy, surrealist fantasias of the Firesign Theatre. Counterculture satire even es-tablished a beachhead on network TV with *The Smothers Brothers Com-edy Hour*, which spent two years battling the CBS censors before its premature cancellation in 1969.

The stand-up comics of the late '60s and '70s are the forgotten stars of this cultural revolution. At a time when the youth generation was challenging the power structure and freeing their minds, stand-up comics struck an espe-cially responsive chord. They were great democratic artists, whose power de-pended on forging an intimate bond with the audience—convincing us they were ordinary folks, with the same gripes and anxieties as you and me. Un-like so many of the borscht belt–era comics, who worked the Catskills hotels in the 1940s and '50s, they were not predominantly Jews from New York; they came from the suburbs of New Jersey and the Midwest and California. Some were high school dropouts; most went to college, though rarely top schools. (Not an Ivy League grad among them; those boys wound up writing for *National Lampoon* and later *Saturday Night Live*.)

Even the way they told jokes, the strategy of their humor, was more populist and inclusive. The old-style comics might talk about subjects we all recognized (the wife and kids, airline flights, TV commercials), but they got laughs with the artifice of gag lines—a pun, or a witticism, or a surprise reversal. This emphasized the distance between performer and audience. "I got no sex life," cracked Rodney Dangerfield, one of the old-school comics most admired by the younger generation. "My wife cut me down to once a month. And I'm lucky—two guys I know she cut out completely." No one was expected to actually believe a line like that, or mistake it for a real commentary on marriage. Certainly not the way you believed a Richard Pryor rant about the girlfriend who walked out on him—"I don't mind them *leavin'*, but they tell you *why*!" Or Robert Klein's line about discovering sex as a kid in his father's dresser drawer—"a deck of cards that I went steady with for two years." The old comics made jokes about real life. The new comics turned real life into the joke.

As "in one" performers, with no script or cohorts onstage to provide support, these comedians often had an uphill battle. (Comedy teams, so popular in the 1950s and '60s, virtually died out in the '70s for obvious reasons: they talked to each other, not to the audience.) They had to fight to keep their idiosyncratic talents from being co-opted by a showbiz establishment that likes to foist collaboration on its quirky geniuses. Even at their peak of creativity and popularity, these stand-up innovators were often itchy to move on. They didn't feel validated (or make enough money) until they proved themselves in other fields—movies, TV sitcoms, directing. Stand-up comedy may be the only major art form whose greatest practitioners, at any given time, want to be doing something else.

Many of them had relatively short stand-up careers. Unlike rock stars, they couldn't go on indefinitely with greatest-hits tours. The old jokes had to be constantly refreshed, and that became harder as they aged—as their material became familiar from TV and the cocoon of fame enveloped them, cutting them off from their real-life sources of inspiration. They also faced a predicament common to avant-garde artists in many fields: how to stay on the cutting edge of a culture that has a nasty habit of catching up with them. Carlin's "Seven Words You Can Never Say on Television" were, within a few years, being said all over television (well, at least on cable) and in the movies. Pryor's raw street talk, starring the once radioactive word *nigger*, became common parlance for every black comic or rap artist looking for street cred. Steve Martin dynamited comedy tradition with his "wild and crazy guy" shtick. By the end, fans came to his concerts wearing fake arrows through their heads and shouting "*excuuuse me*" along with him.

By the early '80s, the great days were largely over. Most of the innovators of the '70s were gone—bored, burned-out, or moving on. Martin quit stand-up cold turkey in 1981 and turned his attention to movies. Brooks stopped performing live even earlier, took his comedy into the recording studio, and then gave it up entirely for film work. Pryor kept going, but with diminishing returns, as he succumbed to the lure of Hollywood—and a coke habit that nearly killed him in 1980, when he set himself on fire in a drug-related suicide attempt. Williams—another coke abuser, who was scared straight by his friend John Belushi's drug-overdose death in 1982—was transitioning into movies as well. Klein, by the end of the '70s, had stopped releasing albums and was doing Broadway. Kaufman, whose performance art stunts were growing more bizarre and self-destructive, died of cancer in 1984. Only Carlin, of the era's major innovators, kept his stand-up career going at full speed into the '80s, '90s, and beyond.

Television, meanwhile, was luring away the best and brightest of the younger comics who might have replaced them. Starting in the mid-'70s, when comics like Freddie Prinze and Jimmie Walker became sitcom stars, and accelerating in the 1980s with the success of *The Cosby Show*, TV producers and network execs began scouring the clubs for comedians whose material and comic persona could be repurposed for prime time. Some of them, like Roseanne Barr and Tim Allen, became TV superstars. Others were quick flameouts. But the result was a brain drain that short-circuited the careers of many young comics, who came to regard stand-up not as an end in itself but as a road to sitcom stardom.

No cultural era, of course, has a neat beginning and end. Some comics who came up in the early '60s, like Woody Allen and Bill Cosby, remained stand-up stars through the counterculture years—in Cosby's case, well beyond—and were important influences on many of the comedians in this book. But they reached their artistic maturity, crucially, in the years before the political and cultural upheaval of the late '60s, and their material was essentially unchanged by it. Adventurous stand-up comedy, by the same token, did not disappear with the advent of the '80s. Sam Kinison, the former evangelist from Texas, raised the decibel level and found new ways to offend with his primal-scream comedy. Eddie Murphy, Chris Rock, and other African American comics arrived to colonize the racial territory that Pryor had pioneered. Women like Roseanne Barr, Paula Poundstone, Sandra Bernhard, and Ellen DeGeneres brought fresh female voices to a genre that, even in the heyday of the feminist movement, was still largely defined by testosterone.

But the fertile decade and a half that lasted, roughly, from Bruce's demise in 1966 to Seinfeld's rise in the early '80s was the crucial period when modern stand-up comedy came into being and transformed the culture. They were the peak creative years for a group of brilliant and radical artists who influenced how we see the world, changed the way we talk and think—and made us laugh. This is their story.

CHAPTER 1

After Lenny

If God made the body and the body is dirty, the fault lies with the manufacturer.

—Lenny Bruce

The police paddy wagon was a fitting place for two comedy renegades—one under siege for his "obscene" material, the other just along for the ride—to run into each other.

Lenny Bruce and George Carlin had met before. Indeed, Bruce had played an important role in the younger comedian's early career. When Carlin was still a radio DJ in Los Angeles, developing a comedy act with his drive-time partner, Jack Burns, Bruce came to see them at a Hollywood coffeehouse called Cosmo Alley and liked them well enough to get his talent agency to sign the team. Now, a couple of years later, Carlin was striking out on his own as a solo act, doing a gig at the Playboy Club in downtown Chicago. Bruce was appearing just down the street at the Gate of Horn, a popular folk-music club where Carlin used to buy pot, and after his own show was done, Carlin would walk the few blocks to catch Bruce's late show.

It was just after midnight on December 6, 1962, and Bruce was showing some of the strain of his mounting legal troubles. In just the previous two months he had been arrested three times: once for drug possession and twice for obscenity during an engagement at the Troubadour in Los Angeles. He came onstage that night in Chicago wearing a raincoat over a pajama top and rumpled jeans (he wore the coat, he said, so he'd be ready to go in case the cops arrested him). Just as he was getting into a bit about marijuana, two plainclothes policemen in the audience stood up, announced, "The show is over, ladies and gentlemen," and placed Bruce under arrest.

Carlin, downing beers at a table with a friend from the folk group the Terriers, was pretty loaded by this time, and when the cops, looking for underage patrons, made everyone in the club show ID as they filed out, Carlin mouthed off. The next thing he knew, he was being hustled into the same paddy wagon where Bruce, the club's owner, and a couple of others were waiting.

"What are you doin' here?" Bruce asked when he saw the younger comic.

"I told the cops I didn't believe in ID," Carlin said.

"Shmuck," Bruce replied.

Bruce was convicted of obscenity in Chicago two months later, another chapter in the long-running courtroom drama that, over the next few years, depleted his finances and virtually destroyed his career. Carlin saw him just once more—in the summer of 1966, when Carlin and his wife, Brenda, paid Bruce a visit at his crumbling Hollywood Hills home, where the pool was filled with leaves and the living room strewn with law books. A few weeks later, on August 3, 1966, he was found dead in his bathroom of a morphine overdose.

For most of America, Lenny Bruce's death was not much more than a lurid Hollywood headline. *Time* magazine dismissed him in a twenty-line obituary, describing him as a "leading outpatient of the sick-comic school," who "viewed life as a four-letter word and, with gestures, commented blackly on it." But for Carlin and a new generation of comics who revered Bruce and learned from him, his death touched off a creative explosion that would echo through the 1970s, move stand-up comedy to the very center of contemporary culture, and define the shape of a distinctly American art form.

And it all started with Lenny Bruce.

Or did it? Hailed for his daring social commentary and harassed for his dirty words, idolized by a devoted coterie of fans and beset by paranoia and drug problems, eulogized in books, films, documentaries, stage plays, and the liner notes in countless reissues of his often haphazardly recorded performances, Lenny Bruce, the man and comedian, has long since been obscured by his legend. To understand just why he was the founding father of modern stand-up comedy, that legend needs a bit of cleaning up.

Bruce was, to begin with, just one of a pioneering generation of stand-up comics who in the 1950s and '60s collectively made a clean break with the old one-liner-dominated style of the borscht belt comics. Unlike these old tummlers, with their interchangeable mother-in-law jokes, the new-wave comics—Mort Sahl, Jonathan Winters, Bob Newhart, Shelley Berman, Woody Allen, Mike Nichols and Elaine May, as well as Bruce—wrote their own material, developed highly individual styles, and put stand-up, for the first time, in touch with the real world. From Sahl's political gibes to Nichols and May's pas de deux of modern angst, they showed that stand-up comedy could be hip, personal, politically provocative, and psychologically subtle.

Bruce was hardly (to get this heresy out of the way first) the funniest of the lot. Not during his peak years and certainly not now, when so much of his material sounds dated and heavy-handed. His battles against the protectors of public decency, to be sure, helped knock down barriers to free speech and led the way to a more open popular culture, where four-letter words, nudity, and sexual candor would soon become accepted, even second nature. No other comedian (or any other American entertainer, for that matter) again faced anything close to the legal harassment that Bruce did. But even that does not get at the core of Bruce's impact—the reason why he was the indispensable comedian for a new generation of stand-up comics.

He was born Leonard Alfred Schneider on October 13, 1925, in Mineola, Long Island, the son of mismatched Jewish parents: a conservative, British-born father who sold shoes, and a live-wire showbiz mother who worked as a comedian in burlesque under the stage name Sally Marr. His parents divorced when he was eight, and Lenny grew up mostly with his father, a stern disciplinarian whom he grew to resent, while his mother, who gave him his irreverent point of view, took him on outings to burlesque houses from the age of twelve. After running away from home and spending two years working on a chicken ranch in rural Long Island, he enlisted in the Navy at age seventeen. He served on the cruiser *Brooklyn*, which saw action during World War II, before wrangling a discharge by convincing a Navy psychiatrist that he had homosexual tendencies.

After the war, Bruce began doing comedy in small-time clubs around New York and made his national debut on *Arthur Godfrey's Talent Scouts* radio show in October 1948—introduced by his mother and playing a German mimic doing impressions of James Cagney, Humphrey Bogart, and Edward G. Robinson. After moving to L.A., he worked as an emcee in seedy strip clubs, where he would try anything to get the customers' attention: feigning epileptic fits onstage, making fake phone calls from the stage to the wives of men in the audience, miming getting a blow job from a hand puppet behind the curtain. One night, as a stripper was ending her act, Bruce topped her by walking onstage stark naked.

Eventually he moved up to more respectable, beat-era clubs like Ann's 440 in San Francisco and New York's Den in the Duane and began to gain an underground reputation. A tight-wound, darkly handsome man with a jabbing laugh that punctuated his stream-of-consciousness monologues, Bruce did everything from old-movie parodies (his repertoire of impressions ranged from Bela Lugosi to George Macready) to slash-and-burn social commentary that took aim at society's hypocrisy and hang-ups about sex, morality, religion, and race. He imagined Adolf Hitler getting advice from a Hollywood image consultant and spoofed Lawrence Welk being introduced to drugs by the members of his band. He psychoanalyzed the Lone Ranger, the western hero too proud to wait for a thank-you (suggesting that the Masked Man and Tonto were more than just law enforcement partners), and satirized the way white people condescend to blacks at parties. He envisioned Christ and Moses showing up at St. Patrick's Cathedral and wondering why Puerto Ricans in Spanish Harlem are living forty to a room while Cardinal Spellman "has a ring on worth eight grand." He mused about Eleanor Roosevelt's breasts and suggested that Jackie Kennedy, after the assassination, wasn't trying to save her husband by climbing on that car trunk but simply "hauling ass to save her ass." He tweaked society's fear of nudity, arguing that "if God made the body and the body is dirty, the fault lies with the manufacturer." He got up in front of a nightclub audience and blurted, "Are there any niggers here?" Then, after a silent gasp from the crowd, he explained that "if it was nothing but 'nigger, nigger, nigger,' in six months 'nigger' wouldn't mean any more than 'good night,' 'God bless you,' or 'I promise to tell the truth, the whole truth, and nothing but the truth, so help me God.'" Dick Gregory, the African American stand-up comic, was seeing Bruce for the first time in 1962 when he heard that bit; he turned to his companion and said, "This man is the eighth wonder of the world."

"I'm a surgeon with a scalpel for false values," Bruce once said. Jazz critics like Ralph J. Gleason and Nat Hentoff were early champions. "Others josh, snipe, and rib," wrote the British critic Kenneth Tynan; "only Bruce demolishes." But his raw language and incendiary satire made him a pariah for much of mainstream showbiz. "He airs the lowest thoughts I have ever heard on a stage," wrote one early columnist. He was all but blackballed on television; Steve Allen, who regarded him as a genius, was one of the few who would book him. His career probably hit its peak in February 1961 when he played Carnegie Hall, packing the house for a midnight concert in the middle of a blizzard. It was mostly downhill from there. In October of that same year, he was arrested for saying "cocksucker" onstage at the Jazz Workshop in San Francisco, the beginning of a string of arrests for his allegedly indecent material. He was acquitted of the San Francisco offense, but after three later convictions (in

Los Angeles, Chicago, and New York), nightclubs stopped booking him because they were afraid of getting busted too. Defiant to the end, still getting a few gigs but overwhelmed by his legal problems and money woes, Bruce died a broken man.

For a younger generation of comedians, however, Lenny Bruce became a renegade role model: the comedian who showed the possibilities of an art form that suddenly seemed cool and consequential. George Carlin, who was working as a DJ in Shreveport, Louisiana, when he first heard Bruce on record, was impressed by "the honesty, the fact that he didn't ignore or avoid unpleasant truths or realities. That told me that you could tell your own truth—and you might even think of it as the larger truth—and that you could make it entertaining and interesting and a bit daring." Robert Klein, just graduated from DeWitt Clinton High School in the Bronx and starting to think about a comedy career, saw Bruce's monologues as proof that comedy could "not only make people laugh; it was social criticism. How to entertain your colored friends at parties, his bits about religion—it was so hip for the 1950s. It was an eye-opening thing."

Richard Lewis was "thunderstruck" when he was introduced to Bruce's records by a professor at Ohio State University. "It was so fearless, so insightful," says Lewis, who instantly put Bruce alongside Joseph Heller and J. D. Salinger on his shelf of cultural heroes. David Steinberg, a Yeshiva student in Chicago who would soon join Second City, saw Bruce live at the Gate of Horn and was impressed by his jazzlike verbal riffs—and the way he sprinkled his monologues with Yiddish expressions, even esoteric ones that Steinberg had never heard outside of the family dinner table. Barry Levinson, who was part of a stand-up comedy team in Los Angeles before he began writing and directing movies like *Diner*, was knocked out when he went with his friends to see Bruce at the Lyric Theater in Baltimore. "He started to talk about chipping in for gas money," Levinson recalls. "I remember thinking, he's talking just like we would be sitting around and bullshitting at the diner. Everything we had in our minds would come out of his mouth. It was a defining moment."

Joan Rivers, who was inspired more by Bruce than by any of the few female comics who were around when she started doing stand-up in the early '60s, points out one facet of his appeal that rarely gets mentioned (usually because the mentioning is done by men): in contrast to most of the nebbishy stars of the stand-up world at the time, "he was sexy." Even that least Bruce-ian of post-Bruce comedians, Jerry Seinfeld, dates his discovery that stand-up could be a viable career option to reading a passage in Albert Goldman's biography *Ladies and Gentlemen, Lenny Bruce!!* In a fictionalized reconstruction of a day in Bruce's life, Goldman has Lenny on the phone with his mother, talking about his club gig the previous night. "Show went good," he says. "Did a new piece of material." Seinfeld's reaction: "I said to myself, 'You mean it's not *all* new bits? You mean it's all crafted out and worked on?' It was the lightbulb moment for me."

Heard today, unfortunately, most of Bruce's best-known routines aren't great advertisements for his talent. "Religions, Inc.," his acid re-creation of a Madison Avenue–style meeting of evangelical leaders, was a brave piece of commentary, a swipe at commercialized religion that was years ahead of its time. But as comedy, the juvenile one-liners must have seemed ham-handed even then. (Phone call to the pope: "Billy wants to know if you can get him a deal on one of those Dago sports cars . . . When you comin' to the Coast? . . . Don't worry, nobody knows you're Jewish.") His famous exposé of white liberal hypocrisy, "How to Relax Your Colored Friends at Parties," is another groundbreaking bit whose satire is hammered home without much finesse. ("That Bojangles, Christ could he tap dance. You tap dance a little yourself? All you people can tap dance.") "Comic at the Palladium," his twenty-minute account of a hack Vegas comic bombing onstage in London, is the ur-satire of the old-school Vegas jokesters, the sort of entertainers Bruce set out to bury. But next to the sharper showbiz parody that was to follow from Robert Klein, Albert Brooks, and others, it today seems flabby and obvious.

In his later years Bruce stopped doing most of these scripted routines in favor of more free-flowing, free-association monologues that many compared to jazz improvisations. His celebrated 1961 Carnegie Hall concert, a two-hour stream-of-consciousness splurge on everything from religion and politics to fellow comedians and a recent hip operation, was hailed by Goldman, his biographer, as "the finest all-round performance of his career. Brilliant, vivid, spontaneous, variegated, moody, honest, fantastic, and incredibly candid." To which one could add, a real mess: half-finished sentences, digressions on digressions, hipster lingo, and Yiddish slang so out of control that, at times, Bruce doesn't appear even to be performing for the band; he seems to be talking to himself. (Fred Willard, who was in the audience that night, says many people in the crowd had trouble even hearing him.)

And yet, it was in performances like these that Bruce's real achievement could best be seen. He broke down the old setup–punch line structure of stand-up comedy. And he held back nothing. Everything got tossed into the performance Mixmaster: social criticism, political commentary, pop culture satire, snatches of autobiography, sexual confessions, personal gripes, public hectoring, today's headlines, and yesterday's trip to the laundry. All of it was out there on the stage, raw and unfiltered—everything that he knew, thought, hated, remembered, or could dream up.

This was something new. The old-school comics told jokes that bore little, if any, relation to their "real" lives, feelings, or political views. The new-wave satirists of the '50s were more personal and more connected to the world around them, but they were relatively one-dimensional performers who kept a certain distance from the audience. Mort Sahl, perched on a stool with his ever-present newspaper, came across as an acerbic college professor, lecturing from afar. Bob Newhart, playing such characters as a harried driving instructor or the watchman on duty the night King Kong climbs the Empire State Building, created an instantly recognizable comic persona—the beleaguered Organization Man—but left the audience to wonder just how closely that character matched the real-life Bob Newhart. Nichols and May did biting, beautifully crafted bits about modern relationships, but they were essentially translating sketch material to the stand-up stage. Even Woody Allen, who drew comedy out of his own real-life neuroses and sexual insecurities, had far more of the old-style jokemeister in him than we often remember. ("I cheated on my metaphysics final. I looked within the soul of the boy sitting next to me.")

Bruce, on the other hand, was incapable of separating the comedy from the comedian. Near the end of his career he began exasperating even his fans by filling his sets with long, obsessive accounts of his legal battles. Yet it is these rambling riffs of his last few years—fueled by his rising paranoia, and probably drugs—that show Bruce at his most charismatic and fascinating. In an appearance on a San Francisco radio show in 1963, for example (included on *Lenny Bruce: Let the Buyer Beware*, a six-CD set of his material released in 2004), he offers up, among other things, a discourse on the history of presidential profanity (Truman calling columnist Drew Pearson a "son of a bitch"), defends Norman Rockwell's painting ("the curse is he's prolific"), imitates Eddie Cantor having sex, careens from Fidel Castro to Jimmy Hoffa ("more of a Christian than Bobby Kennedy. Why do I say that? Because Jimmy Hoffa hired ex-convicts, as Christ would have"), and constructs an elaborate fantasy in which he sexually entraps the judge in his obscenity case. Then he shifts into a new gear—racing from idea to idea, damn the segues, full speed ahead, all antennae up, all defenses down:

> Intellectually, I know that a chick that sleeps with fifty guys a year is more of a Christian than the nun. Because she has the capacity to hug fifty guys a year. And I don't care what people say; that's what the act

is—kissin' and huggin'. But that's just intellectually. Emotionally, I don't want to be the fifty-first guy. 'Cause I learned my lesson, man: that's good and this is bad. And in Las Vegas, where they banned *Tropic of Cancer*, where Johnny Mathis got punched out by some Okie mother-fucker who had the chutzpah to—what're you gonna say in front of a Las Vegas waitress to offend her, man? Somebody stuck a pool table up her ass, for chrissake? No, man, he was just drugged by the fact that the guy's colored and he's drinkin' there, that he's *livin'* there, man . . .

He works back to his own legal problems, then takes off for parts unknown:

I'm gonna show you how prejudiced you are. See, the thing is, you have the choice of a judge or a jury. First place, you're a schmuck if you ever take the judge, because the thing is, you're going to tell him a story to convince him— What kind of shit you gonna tell a judge he hasn't heard? You get twelve impressionable people—solid. Now as far as get-ting a goyish attorney—solid. So if you are that prejudiced, who's more likely to murder his daughter in a drunken state—an Irish father, an Ital-ian father, or a Jewish father? Even the Irish know that the Irish would . . . The Irish are the most persecuted minority group ever. Here's what goes down, you see. Everybody is always bitching and would like to thwart authority. Well, unfortunately for the Irish—writing came to Ireland in the fifth century, you know, and so they memorized every-thing and they're genius orators. So when they came over here, they got the gigs in government, they were the heat, they were the rulers. And the people got drugged with that, man. That's why it's such a difference be-tween L.A. and San Francisco. This is a pretty corrupt town, which is cool. The word *corruption* is misused a lot. And the reason L.A. is not is that they haven't had a chance, father to son to son to son, to hand it down. I'll give you the degrees of corruption of cities. Chicago—fantasyland. So corrupt it's thrilling. Honest, man, they can dissolve partnerships, no litigation. It's the only city where the autopsy's cause of death—"He wouldn't listen."

Parse it at your peril—legal advice, civics lesson, paranoid rant, snippets of old bits, seat-of-the-pants social comment. The comics who followed couldn't duplicate this sort of thing (who would want to?). But these vi-brant, manic, free-associating mind games could be dazzling, almost intoxi-cating. Bruce showed that stand-up comedy could be the expression of an engaged, thinking, neurotic, impassioned human being in all his raw, crazy complexity. It was this—and not simply the dirty words, or the First Amendment battles, or any of his particular routines or satiric insights—that made him the revelatory comedian for a new generation.

What the younger comedians who were influenced by him brought was the discipline and craftsmanship that Bruce lacked. They were better actors and more accomplished writers. They knew how to build a routine for laughs—and they didn't see the laughs as a betrayal of their mission as satirists and artists. Bruce could only have envied, say, Carlin's beautifully succinct take on the draft problems that got Muhammad Ali banned from boxing:

> He had an unusual job: beating people up. Government wanted him to change jobs. Government wanted him to kill people. He said, "No, that's where I draw the line. I'll beat 'em up, but I don't wanna kill 'em." And the government said, "Well, if you won't kill 'em . . . we won't let you beat 'em up."

Pryor brought at least as much personal pain onto the stage as Bruce did, and yet he connected more viscerally with the audience. Take his defiant outburst at the start of his 1979 concert film, recorded a few months after his arrest for shooting up his wife's car during a fight on New Year's Eve:

> I don't never wanna see no more police in my life! At *my* house! Takin' *my* ass to jail! For killin' *my* car! . . . And it seemed fair to kill my car to me, right? Because my wife was gonna leave my ass. I say, "Not in this motherfucker you ain't! If you leave, you be drivin' them hush puppies you got on!"

Even the comedians of the '70s who took off in different directions were indebted to Bruce. He liberated stand-up from the old rules and gave them an enormous new sandbox to play in. Bruce made fun of old showbiz and lashed out at Hollywood phonies. Steve Martin satirized the same thing by turning *himself* into the showbiz phony. Bruce uttered forbidden words and dared the audience to walk out. Andy Kaufman, a provocateur of a different kind, read passages from *The Great Gatsby* or did his laundry onstage and dared the audience to sit still for it. Bruce exposed the comedian's private troubles and torment. Albert Brooks turned that into the joke. On his album *A Star Is Bought*, Brooks takes a phone call from a psychiatrist on a radio call-in show:

"I'd like to ask you one question. Are you still trying to show Mother something?"

"Show Mother what?"

"Do you still feel that you can buy your friends with laughter?"

"Let me tell you something, Doctor. I don't have to buy my friends with anything. I don't need friends. I shouldn't have friends. You can't go into this business and expect friends. I am a loner. I must be a loner. That's what an artist is."

"You don't believe that."

"You're damn right I don't believe that. Help me, man, I'm sick!"

Bruce, the original sick comic, would have liked that. He might not have recognized some of the new incarnations that stand-up comedy took in the decade that followed his death. But he would have at least had a measure of satisfaction, had he been able to stick around, in seeing the revolution he started.

CHAPTER 2

Rebellion

There are no bad words. Bad thoughts. Bad intentions.
And woooords.

—George Carlin

Lenny Bruce never played the Copacabana; the swank Manhattan nightclub wasn't his kind of place. It wasn't George Carlin's kind of place either. But in December 1969, Carlin was appearing there under protest, and using it to kiss off old-time comedy.

By the late '60s the Copa was one of the last outposts of a fast-disappearing show business era, a posh room where well-heeled couples in fancy evening dress sat in red-leather banquettes and watched sophisticated entertainers like Tony Bennett and Peggy Lee. Jules Podell, the imposing, corpulent, reputedly Mob-connected boss of the Copa, ran the place with an iron hand. If a table of customers got rowdy, a cadre of uniformed waiters would march over, pick up their table, and simply carry it briskly out of the room, leaving the group to sit there exposed or slink away in shame. "The mirrors are always clean at the Copa," Podell liked to say.

Podell was wary of George Carlin. The hot young comic had played the club once before, but now Podell was hearing about his racy new material, which had just gotten him thrown out of the Frontier Hotel in Las Vegas. Podell called up Irvin Arthur, the agent who handled nightclub bookings at General Artists Corporation (GAC), the talent agency that represented Carlin, and made him promise that Carlin would behave himself. No jokes about religion or fags, Podell insisted, and no making fun of the club. Arthur told him not to worry.

So Podell went ahead with the scheduled two-week engagement. But Carlin wasn't in the mood to cooperate. He was trying very consciously to change his act, reaching out to a younger, hipper crowd, and he told his agents they ought to be booking him in coffeehouses and colleges, not ritzy, old-fashioned nightclubs like the Copa. "I was straining at the leash," says Carlin. "I knew I didn't belong in that place."

Indeed, Carlin's new material—about drugs and sex and the Vietnam War—didn't go over very well with the staid crowd at the Copa. Just to show how bored he was, Carlin took to reading from the yellow pages on-stage or crawling underneath the piano and reciting from the manufacturing sticker. "I don't belong here," he would blurt out in exasperation. "These places went out of style twenty years ago. I see Don Ameche dance past me one more time, I'm getting the fuck out of here."

Craig Kellem, Carlin's chief agent at GAC, came in one night with some of the gang from the agency. All dressed in dark suits, sitting together at what they liked to call the "penguin table," they wanted to see for themselves the comedian who was reportedly flipping out onstage. Kellem adored Carlin. When he was a junior agent, Kellem had taken him on as his first client because no one else at the agency was paying him much attention, and had worked hard to build his career. Now Carlin seemed to be putting all that at risk.

"He comes out and he does about thirty minutes," Kellem recalls. "Then it starts to get hairy. He was pushing it. Tiptoeing over the line. Tiptoeing a lot over the line. I began to hear animal sounds in the room. I turn around and there's Jules Podell at the back of the room, talking to himself, making these guttural noises. He's knocking his ring against the table. He's livid. I'm sitting there watching my adored client, who has promised to be good, trying to compete with these animal sounds coming from the owner of the club. It was disturbing, to say the least."

For Carlin it was liberating. The Copa let him play out his engagement but at the end of his last show gave him a pointed send-off. "It was very artistic, very cinematic," Carlin recalls. "Toward the end of my act, they slowly turned my light off. Instead of the usual thing where the band plays you off, they just brought the light down slowly. And they took the sound down at the same time. Very dramatic. It was almost sweet in a way. And I knew I was free."

George Carlin's career transformation was the defining event of the stand-up comedy revolution that began in the late '60s. He had already established a successful career as a sharp-witted, short-haired comedian who did parodies of commercials and radio DJs and a spaced-out "Hippy-Dippy Weatherman." But as the peace-and-love era blossomed and campus protests mounted, Carlin looked around and decided he was on the wrong side of the generation gap: a thirty-year-old comedian entertaining people in their forties but whose head—helped by quantities of pot and hallucinogens—was with the twenty-year-olds. So he set out to reinvent himself. He let his hair and beard grow, traded in his skinny ties for tie-dyed T-shirts, and began doing comedy that expressed the new, antiestablishment spirit of the counterculture.

He didn't have it easy. The pooh-bahs of showbiz were wary of him—skittish about his new material, cynical about his motives. The younger crowd, too, had to be convinced that this straight-arrow comic whom they knew from *The Ed Sullivan Show* wasn't just an opportunist, cashing in on the hippie fad. And Carlin himself had to come to terms with a career twist that wasn't in the cards when he was plotting out his future as a kid in New York's "white Harlem," figuring that he'd use stand-up as a springboard to a career as a movie comic, like his idol Danny Kaye.

Now Carlin had a new role model: Lenny Bruce, whom he had listened to, seen perform, and met a handful of times before his death in 1966. He channeled Bruce's insurrectionist spirit, his campaign against the hypocrisy and distorted values of white middle-class society, and made it resonate with a new generation—not the beat-era hipsters who were Bruce's chief audience, but the baby boom kids who were protesting the Vietnam War, dropping acid, and listening to the Rolling Stones. If he weathered the crusade a lot better than Bruce did, it was partly because Bruce had already taken most of the heat, but also because Carlin was temperamentally better prepared for it. He was disciplined about his work, a compulsive student of his own career who kept a detailed log of every gig he did (a log that gets spotty only in the years when his cocaine habit spun out of control). In a world of Friars Club conviviality, he was a something of a loner, mixing little with the comedy fraternity or Hollywood's social circles. But his ornery integrity drew admiration, almost veneration, even from the people he left behind along the way. "I'm not sure at the time I appreciated what he wanted to do," says Kellem, the agent Carlin dropped not long after that gig at the Copa. "But he was fighting the good fight. He was incredibly brave and true to himself. And in retrospect, he was right."

Like many heroes of the '60s youth revolution, Carlin was born a little earlier than most of his future fans—on May 12, 1937, near the end of the Depression, in a white enclave near Harlem called Morningside Heights. His father, an ad salesman, was a drinker prone to violent outbursts, and when George was only two, his mother grabbed him and his older brother, fled down the fire escape, and left for good.

Mary Carlin and her boys spent two years shuttling among friends and relatives before finally getting an apartment of their own—with George's father stalking them all the way. "He hounded her," says Carlin. "And he frightened her. When we lived on One Hundred Fortieth Street, we would come back from downtown, get off the subway, and the procedure was, my mother would go to the call box, get the local precinct, and say, 'Hi, it's Mary and the kids. I'm at One Hundred Forty-fifth Street. Come and get us.' And they would drive us home and see us into the house. Sometimes he'd be across the street, just looking." Even when they finally moved into an apartment that his father didn't know the whereabouts of, his mother was still on edge. If they got an unexpected knock, she'd tell George to peek under the door. If he saw a lady's shoes, he could open it. A man's shoes, and they would stay quiet until the visitor went away. This family drama ended only when his father died. George was eight.

His mother had a business school degree and worked as an executive assistant in publishing and advertising, leaving George to spend a lot of time on his own. "Inside, you're saying, 'Where the fuck is everybody?'" says Carlin. "I developed a very strong left brain, to cover my pain and my feelings. I thought, instead of felt. I was alone a lot, and I interpreted it as independence, autonomy, and freedom. I made a life out of it for myself."

Show business was a big part of it from the start. When he was five, his mom taught him to wiggle his hips and imitate Mae West. At eight or nine, he would get on the subway by himself and ride downtown to the big movie palaces on Forty-second Street, where he would hang out and try to get autographs from stars of the stage shows (Danny Kaye on a good day; Durward Kirby on a bad one). When he graduated from eighth grade, his mom gave him a reel-to-reel recorder, and he began taping himself doing parodies of newscasts and sports reports. It was juvenile stuff, but the old recordings show a kid who was already developing his talent for vocal parody:

Stay tuned for Brooklyn Dodgers baseball.

(*Tongue click—crack of the bat. Sharp exhale of breath—the crowd roars.*)

Roy Campanella wins the ballgame!

Carlin inherited his Irish Catholic family's conservative politics and love of language (his grandfather was a policeman who, Carlin says, once copied all the works of Shakespeare in longhand), but he rebelled against his mother's aspirations for him. Instead of going "up the hill," to the nearby bastions of higher learning like Columbia University, he hung out "down the hill," with the kids in his racially mixed neighborhood—smoking pot and generally causing trouble. He went to a relatively enlightened Catholic elementary school, with no grades and no corporal punishment. But in ninth grade he switched to Cardinal Hayes High School, where he got a heavy dose of Catholic discipline. After trying without success to get into the High School for the Performing Arts, he transferred to a public high school in Washington Heights. At age sixteen he dropped out altogether, and a year later joined the Air Force.

Carlin's left brain had already come up with a career plan: he would do his stint in the military, then use the G.I. Bill to go to school to become a DJ, and parlay that into a career in stand-up comedy and ultimately the movies. And things began to happen faster than he could have imagined. Stationed near Shreveport, Louisiana, where he repaired electronic systems on B-47s, Carlin met the town's most popular DJ while acting in a local production of *Golden Boy*. Carlin asked if he could come down to the radio station sometime and watch. The DJ, it turned out, was also the station's owner, and he hired Carlin as a news reader for sixty cents an hour. Before long Carlin was hosting a noontime soft-music hour, then an afternoon drive-time show, *Carlin's Corner*, where he played rock 'n' roll. He became something of a personality in town: "My picture was all over; I could go out to the bars at night and say to a girl, 'Listen, would you like me to play a record for you tomorrow?' It was a nice come-on. I was in clover."

At the Air Force base, though, Carlin was mostly in trouble—talking back to officers, sneaking off when he was supposed to be on guard duty. "I was a fuckup," he says. "I did not like arbitrary authority. I had three court marshals ultimately. No time in the stockade, but I lost rank in a lot of ways. They said, 'Why don't you just get fuckin' snaps on those stripes, George?'" Sometimes trouble just seemed to find him. Once he hitched a ride with a black soldier into town, and they got stopped by a couple of redneck cops, who rousted them and threw them in jail for the night. Carlin had two joints stuffed in his socks, but the cops didn't find them, so he simply toked up overnight and blew the smoke out his cell window.

Carlin's Air Force career ended a year early when he was discharged as part of an Eisenhower-backed effort to downsize the military. He was still only twenty, but with some radio experience under his belt, he landed a job at WEZE in Boston, an easy-listening NBC affiliate. There he made friends with a news reporter named Jack Burns. Like Carlin, Burns was an Irish Catholic who had served in the military. Unlike Carlin, he was a political liberal, who had interviewed Fidel Castro when the Cuban revolutionary visited Boston, and even traveled to Cuba on Castro's invitation. Burns opened Carlin's eyes politically.

"At that time George was fairly conservative," says Burns. "I always had a progressive agenda. I thought it was the duty of an artist to fight bigotry and intolerance. We had long, interesting conversations, good political discussions." "I kind of learned my politics and liberalism from him," Carlin acknowledges. "My mother was part of the Joe McCarthy, Westbrook Pegler, William Randolph Hearst, Francis Cardinal Spellman axis of conservative Catholicism. I was probably more a centrist. But when I watched the Army-McCarthy hearings, I probably rooted for his side. I bought all that because I didn't hear a coherent counterargument anywhere."

In Boston, however, Carlin was a nonideological troublemaker. One Sunday night he was manning the station during the weekly rosary broadcast by Richard Cardinal Cushing, the formidable head of the Boston archdiocese. The live sermon was supposed to last for fifteen minutes, but Cushing gave a windy preamble, and as the rosary droned on, Carlin saw that it was going to cut into the network news at the top of the hour. He knew that if the newscast were preempted, the station would lose ad revenue: "I cut him off, in the middle of the Hail Mary, and I put on Alka-Seltzer. Within a minute, the phone rings, and it was the cardinal. He says, 'I'd like to talk to the young man who took off the holy word of God!'"

Carlin got a pass from his bosses on that one. They weren't so forgiving a few weeks later when Carlin absconded with the station's mobile news van for a weekend jaunt to buy some pot in New York City. That same weekend, there was a prison break at the state penitentiary in Walpole, Massachusetts, and the station had to track him down at his mother's apartment to locate the news van. Carlin wasn't exactly remorseful. Prison breaks were happening with some regularity up at Walpole, he pointed out: "Why don't you just cover the next one?" The station fired him.

Carlin next wound up at KXOL in Fort Worth, Texas, where he was doing an evening show when Burns, his old Boston pal, showed up in a battered car with bald tires on his way out to Hollywood. Carlin convinced him to stay and take a job in the station's newsroom. The two began noodling with comedy bits in their spare time—"vulgar, vile things, but they were funny," says Carlin—and performing them in a local coffeehouse. Then they decided to throw all their belongings into Carlin's new

Dodge Dart and drive to L.A. to see if they could make it as a comedy team.

They got a room together and put a stash of $300 in the sock drawer as insurance, so they wouldn't have to take jobs parking cars or washing dishes. After a few days somebody stole the $300 and they were pounding the pavement. They stumbled on an opening for a morning DJ team at KDAY, a daytime-only 50,000-watt station, and were soon back in radio, working on their comedy bits together in the studio after hours. After a few months they were performing for $125 a week at Cosmo Alley, a coffeehouse in downtown Hollywood.

It was 1960, at the tail end of the beat era, and Burns and Carlin modeled themselves after the new-wave comedians like Bruce and Mort Sahl and Nichols and May. "We were aiming toward people who were sort of hip," says Carlin. "We wanted to be smart and up-to-date and like the comedians we admired who were in the new wave. We aspired to be Blue Angel comedians, which is where Nichols and May played in New York." Carlin did an impression of Jack Kennedy, as well as sharp ones of Sahl and Bruce, and played a character named Herb Coolhouse, a beat poet being interviewed by Burns ("You know, I think we ought to recognize Red China—they grow some groovy stuff over there"). In one of their more outrageous bits, they played Captain Jack and Jolly George, a pair of children's TV hosts who urge the tykes watching to "hide the booze before Mommy gets home" and send away for a "home junkie kit," complete with heroin, hypodermic needle, and bent spoon. "So irresponsible," Burns says now.

Murray Becker, who worked for a music publisher in the same building as the radio station, heard the team rehearsing one night and said he'd try to get his old Navy buddy Lenny Bruce to come see them. Sure enough, Bruce walked into Cosmo Alley one night and, perhaps flattered by Carlin's impression of him, recommended the team to his agents at GAC (which later morphed into International Creative Management). A couple of days later a telegram arrived: "GAC authorizes West Coast office to sign Burns and Carlin in all fields based on Lenny Bruce's recommendation."

Soon they were getting gigs at hip nightclubs like the hungry i, the San Francisco club that had provided an important early showcase for Bruce, Sahl, and other comics. Hugh Hefner saw their act in Chicago and booked them into his Playboy Club. (Hefner, an early champion of Bruce and patron of hip comedy, even helped market the team's first album, *At the Playboy Club Tonight, Burns and Carlin*—lending the club's name to the title even though the record was taped at Cosmo Alley.) They landed a guest shot on

Jack Paar's *Tonight Show*, with Arlene Francis filling in as host. Carlin's head was spinning: less than a year earlier he and Burns had been in an apartment in Texas, watching Paar on TV and fantasizing about being guests. ("How did you guys get together?" "Well, I was fucking Jack's mother . . .") "That was roughly January of 1960," says Carlin. "In October of that year we were *on* the show. I still don't believe it—that's how fast the journey was."

But the Paar spot didn't do a lot for them, and Burns and Carlin spent much of the next year trudging through dreary road dates, doing small-time clubs and one-nighters for groups like the Ford Dealers of Westchester County. Their best bits sometimes came offstage. Once, on a stop in Dallas, Carlin went to pick up their shirts at the laundry and was greeted by a team of armed cops. In one of the shirt pockets, someone had found a newspaper clipping about two men holding up an automobile club. (On the other side was an article about the European Common Market that Burns had clipped.) Both Burns and Carlin were hauled down to the station for questioning. "We play clubs," Burns pleaded. "Ever played this here auto club?" a detective shot back. When they read further down into the article and discovered that the suspects were black, the cops let the pair go. And offered them a lift to the club.

In March 1962, after two years together, Burns and Carlin split up. Both knew it was time. "We had lost some of the inventiveness and creative drive," says Carlin. Burns, in retrospect, felt the team had a basic flaw from the outset: "Most comedy teams are opposites, but George and I were pretty much the same person, two Irish Catholic guys." What's more, they had different career goals: Carlin wanted to do solo stand-up, while Burns thought of himself as an actor and a sketch comic. After the breakup, Burns joined Chicago's Second City improv troupe and later teamed up with Avery Schreiber in a more successful comedy duo.

Meanwhile, Carlin struggled. He adapted some of the old Burns and Carlin bits for his solo act and played dates that had already been booked for the team. He got some good reviews ("Deft, knowing and perceptive [with] an endless fount of new and fresh material," wrote Gene Knight in the *New York Journal-American* of Carlin's gig at the Living Room). But there were also plenty of dispiriting nights at Eagle and Moose lodges in the Midwest, where he got few laughs and learned, the hard way, one of his cardinal rules of comedy: Don't ever be standing on the same level as the tables.

He had gotten married in June 1961 to Brenda Hosbrook, whom he met while appearing at a club in Dayton, Ohio, where she was hostessing.

(Lenny Bruce also worked there, and Brenda had got to know him, driving him to the airport when he needed to pick up certain "packages.") When there were gaps between work, they would stay with Brenda's parents in Dayton or with George's mother in Morningside Heights. Then, after a year on the road and with a new baby daughter, Kelly, they rented an apartment in the building where George's mom lived and decided to see if he could make it in New York.

Carlin went down to Greenwich Village and picked up what work he could at folk clubs like the Bitter End and the Café Wha?. He became something of a regular at the Cafe au Go Go—a jazz club on Bleecker Street, where he would go into the back stairwell to smoke pot with another young comic who had just blown into town, Richard Pryor. The two didn't become close friends, but they watched each other as their careers began to move on parallel tracks. Each worked up a calling-card routine to get the attention of bookers for *The Merv Griffin Show*, which was known for being hospitable to new comedians and was easier to break into than *The Tonight Show*. Each got booked on the show in the summer of 1965: Pryor first, with his Rumpelstiltskin routine; Carlin a few weeks later, with a bit he called "The Indian Sergeant."

Carlin's routine sounds fairly tame and conventional today, but it got laughs and it showed off his knack for pop culture parody. The premise: western movies spend lots of time showing us how the cowboys get ready for an attack, but we never see how the Indians prepare. Carlin then becomes the battle-hardened, New York–accented Indian sergeant, trying to whip the troops into shape:

All right, tall guys over by the trees, fat guys down behind the rocks— you with the beads, outta line . . . There'll be a massacre tonight at nine o'clock. We'll meet down by the bonfire, dance around a little, and move out. This will be the fourth straight night we've attacked the fort. However, tonight it will not be as easy. Tonight there *will be soldiers in the fort*.

The bit scored, and Griffin asked Carlin back for three more shows. Which was a problem, since Carlin didn't have three more routines polished and ready to go. So he suggested to the show's producer that Griffin say he liked "The Indian Sergeant" so much, could Carlin do it over again? Griffin obliged—then Carlin got offered another thirteen-show commitment and really had to scramble. "George and I would get together and he'd say, 'I got nothing,' " remembers Bob Golden, the former house pianist at the Cafe au

Go Go who became Carlin's first manager. "So we would grind out new stuff. Sometimes he'd literally be performing it for the first time on *Merv*." Carlin helped himself out by working up parodies of TV newscasts—which he could constantly update with new material from the headlines and read from a script onstage. "I could write the same day or the day before, and I didn't have to memorize it or test it out," Carlin says. "It gave me confidence. I didn't have to be nervous all day."

Griffin's show led to other TV guest shots, and in the summer of 1966 Carlin joined Pryor as a regular on *The Kraft Summer Music Hall*, a featherweight hour of song and comedy that was a summer replacement for *The Andy Williams Show*. Carlin looked out of place amid the Pepsodent-bright singer-dancers and Ken doll host, John Davidson. (Pryor, who could sing and dance a little, at least looked more at ease in the musical numbers.) But it enabled Carlin to showcase his popular early bits, like the Hippy-Dippy Weatherman Al Sleet, foggily trying to read the radar and distinguish the Canadian lows from the Mexican highs, and a spin-off character he created for the show, Al Pouch, the Hippy-Dippy Postman.

The logical next step for Carlin was *The Ed Sullivan Show*. Though on the downward slope of its twenty-three-year CBS run, Sullivan's Sunday-night variety show was still the premier TV venue for stand-up comedy. ("Johnny Carson gave you the big cities," Joan Rivers liked to say. "Sullivan gave you the country.") But Sullivan had a reputation for being rough on comedians. He would typically watch their act for the first time at a Sunday-afternoon dress rehearsal, in front of a studio audience. If he didn't like their material, he might cut back their time—or even dump them from the show altogether. Even established comics could have a tough time in these run-throughs; Sullivan rarely laughed at anything, and his stone face seemed to cast a pall over the whole audience. Moreover, Sullivan was growing increasingly inscrutable with age. A lot of material seemed to go over his head. Some of the agents and managers—who would gather in a room with the CBS censors on show night and laugh at Ed's gaffes and memory lapses—thought he was going senile.

Sullivan's people began making inquiries about Carlin, but he wanted to hold off doing the show. "I said, I'm new, and they're famous for chewing up young comedians, coming to you a few minutes before you're scheduled and saying, 'The chimpanzees went long; you have to cut two minutes.' I said, I'm not going there until I'm more in a position of strength. Until I can kind of ask for and expect a certain amount of time, and they'll respect that." When he finally was booked on the show, in January 1967, Carlin got a full seven minutes. Still, he had to endure Sullivan's wooden-Indian stare at dress rehearsal, and afterward Golden got a call that Sullivan wanted to see him. Ushered into his presence, Golden sat nervously as Sullivan opened the conversation: "He says, 'George Carlin. He's Irish American, isn't he?' I say, 'Yes, he is.' And he says, 'Well, that's fine.' That was it. I guess because George was Irish, he kind of anointed him. But I don't think Sullivan ever really got him." Carlin appeared on the show ten more times.

In the spring of 1967 Carlin released his first comedy album, *Take-offs and Put-ons*—with a cover filled with dozens of photo-booth mug shots of Carlin, with jacket, tie, and short hair, making faces at the camera. Carlin all but disowned the album later, dismissing his early material as the kind of superficial trivia he later moved beyond. But it is a terrific record, one of the high points of 1960s stand-up. Carlin's media parodies were simply leagues beyond what anyone else was doing at the time. In his signature "Wonderful Wino" bit, Carlin drew on his experience as a radio DJ, nailing the high-pitched Top 40 babble of the era with possibly the fastest dialogue ever spoken on a comedy record:

> We got stacks and stacks of wax and wax, we got the pick to click the ones to watch the oldies but goodies the newies but gooeys, we got the top seven hundred records here in the world of Wonderful Wino—*Wonder-ful Wi-no*.

In a brisk five minutes, Carlin skewers pop-chart fever ("another tune here, this one's brand-new, hasn't even been released yet, it's number one on the charts this week, next week it'll be a golden oldie . . ."), song styles ranging from doo-wop to folk protest (including Danny and the Demonstrators' anthem "Don't Want No War," which ends with a very un-Carlin-like swipe at war protesters: "Don't want no job neither!"), beach movies, acne commercials, and the whole ridiculously peppy Top 40 ethic, where even world crises can't stop the beat:

> *Bulletin, bulletin, bulletin! Bulletin, bulletin, bulletin!* The sun did not come up this morning, huge cracks have appeared in the earth's surface, and big rocks are falling out of the sky. Details twenty-five minutes from now on Action Central News, kids!

Carlin put his absurdist twist on media clichés across the dial. As sportscaster Biff Burns (a name Jack Burns had used in their act), he rattles off the basketball scores: "quickly, because we are running late—110 to 102, 125 to 113, 131 to 127. And in an overtime dual, 95 to 94. That was a squeaker." His parodies of commercials, game shows, and soap operas were quick and lethal, no fat on them. "What have germs got to do with bad breath?" asks the naïve consumer in the old Listerine ads. "Germs *have* bad breath," the pitchman replies. After the *Queen for a Day* contestant pours out her tale of woe—husband out of work, mounting hospital bills, no food for the kids—the emcee asks, momentously, "And if you win, what would you like?" She answers brightly: "A set of golf clubs."

"I didn't realize there was a classification, media parody, until later," Carlin says. "I think I was looking for familiar frames of reference that lend themselves to distortion. Because distortion is one of the most important things in comedy. You look at an ordinary event, an ordinary tableau, and you say, what element can I distort in this? And suddenly you have at least the potential for a joke." But it was more than just a joke. The subtext of his spoofs was how thoroughly pop culture has brainwashed us. Throw any nonsense you like into the familiar formats and formulas, and we're too brain-dead to notice. Carlin's critique of American consumer culture starts here.

That critique was about to get much more overt. It was 1967, and Carlin was having trouble ignoring the counterculture revolution going on around him. The flower children in San Francisco were celebrating the Summer of Love. LSD guru Timothy Leary issued his call to "turn on, tune in, drop out." Dustin Hoffman articulated, with his vacant inarticulateness, a generation's disaffection in *The Graduate*. Protests against the Vietnam War within months would force President Lyndon B. Johnson to abandon his bid for re-election. Carlin, meanwhile, felt trapped in his showbiz prison.

By now he was one of the hottest young comics in the country: getting steady work in nightclubs, appearing regularly on TV, cohosting (with Buddy Greco and Buddy Rich) *The Jackie Gleason Show*'s summer-replacement series, *Away We Go*, in 1967. But he was having trouble reconciling the clash between his "A life," the short-haired comic doing jokes about radio DJs and TV commercials, and his "B life," the backstage Carlin who smoked dope and felt a bond with the protesters. "I hung out with musicians, and I see their hair got longer and their clothing changed," he says. "I started to see people singing protest songs. I hear that people are using their talent to express their point of view, and their point of view is political. And I have all these feelings too. And I'm doing all these superficial things, about the media and disc jockeys and ladies on quiz shows. And I'm doing them for the enemy."

It took a while for him to square this epiphany with the career plan he had sketched out more than a decade earlier. "I was living out this mainstream dream. I was gonna be an actor; I was gonna be like Danny Kaye. Not realizing that I was an outlaw and I didn't have a Danny Kaye gene in my body." Pot and hallucinogens helped him make the break. "These are value-changing drugs," he says. "They change your point of view, especially if you already are kind of bent in one direction."

Starting in 1968, Carlin began to change his looks and his comedy. He let his hair grow. In February 1970 (Carlin noted it in his logbook) he started a beard. He talked about what was going through his mind on daytime talk programs like *The Mike Douglas Show* and *The Virginia Graham Show*. (When he told Graham, the silver-haired doyenne of daytime, that he smoked dope, she responded brightly: "Henry Mancini smokes pot! He said so on the air here.") In clubs he began doing more provocative material—about drugs, Vietnam, corporate America. He tried to ease the transition for his old middlebrow audiences, even making up a poem to demystify his long hair:

Fred Astaire got no hair
Nor does a chair
Nor a chocolate éclair
And where is the hair on a pear?
Nowhere, mon frère

Still, the new Carlin came as a shock to fans who came to clubs expecting to see Wonderful Wino and the Hippy-Dippy Weatherman. At the Frontier Hotel in Las Vegas in October 1969, Carlin was opening for the Supremes when he did a bit about his small ass. "I'm one of these white guys who if you look at me sideways, I go from the shoulder blades right to the feet," he said. "Straight line. No ass. When I was in the Air Force, black guys used to look at me in the shower and say, 'Hey man, you ain't got no ass. Where your ass at?'" An early-evening crowd of golfers and their wives—there for the Howard Hughes Invitational golf tournament—complained to the management afterward, and the hotel cut his engagement short.

The following August, Carlin was back at the Frontier to fill out the remaining dates on his contract. This time, he got in trouble with a routine about the word *shit*. "Listen folks," he said. "I want you to know something I don't say 'shit.' Buddy Hackett says 'shit' right down the street. Redd Foxx will say 'shit' on the other side of the street. I don't say 'shit.' I'll *smoke* a little of it . . ." That got him fired for good.

Onstage, Carlin was taking more and more chances, or simply blowing off gigs altogether. In December 1969 he had had his testy encounter with Jules Podell at the Copa. That same month, he skipped out of a City of Hope dinner, was a no-show for an appearance on the game show *Beat the Clock*, and was high on acid for most of his engagement at Mr. Kelly's in Chicago. The following November, at the Playboy Hotel in Lake Geneva, Wisconsin, he nearly caused an audience riot.

It was the early show on Saturday night at one of the last of the mainline clubs he would play. The audience got riled up as soon as Carlin began making cracks about Vietnam. "I had a very conservative Milwaukee crowd, who were part of the older-generation thought process," Carlin recalls. "One big blond guy who would have made a perfect casting director's dream for one of those Nazi officers, says, 'How would you know about war? You've never been shot at!' I probably did some back-and-forth with him. Then it became an uproar. Some were standing and leaving; some were shaking their fists at me."

Carlin wanted to end the show early, but he was afraid he'd be in breach of his contract and wouldn't get paid. So he bulled through to the end and then, as a show of defiance, walked offstage through the audience. In the near-mêlée around him, he noticed one college-age couple sitting alone at a table applauding him. A couple of hours later, back in his room, Carlin got a telegram—sent by the hotel to its own guest—cutting his engagement short and telling him to vacate the premises: the hotel could no longer guarantee his safety.

Bette Midler, the young singer who was Carlin's opening act, was taken aback when her headliner got canned. "I remember he had these plastic novelties—vomit, poop—and he started talking about this dreadful country where people would actually go and spend money on things like this. He was talking about important things like hunger and social injustice. I was right with him, and I thought it was brave and all that. But they didn't like it. I just remember being so shocked that they would let him go, because I thought what he was doing was perfectly reasonable."

Worse for Carlin, the hotel refused to pay him the $1,300 he was owed for the rest of his weekend gig. He needed the money, so he drove all the way to Chicago to plead his case with Hugh Hefner, his old patron from the Burns and Carlin days: "I figure, here's a guy who stands for freedom of speech, you know? I said to him, that's thirteen hundred dollars, and that may not be much to you or to them, but it's very important to me this week."

"George, there are two Hefs," Hefner told him. "One of them would have enjoyed that show. And the other one is a businessman." Carlin never got paid.

Kellem, Carlin's agent, blanched when he read the reports of the Lake Geneva debacle in *Variety*: "Usually a bad review says your client didn't get any laughs. This one says my client was chased off the stage, the townspeople are coming with torches. That is not a good review." Both Kellem and Carlin's manager, Golden, were feeling increasingly estranged from their client. "It got very tense between us," says Golden. "He just said there's something else I need to be doing with comedy. This isn't it. I could see he was horrendously unhappy. This had become a straitjacket."

It's hard to overstate how courageous Carlin's career reinvention was. He was turning his back on a successful stand-up career and trying to start all over again as . . . what? It was almost as if he were plotting a career path in reverse. His goal was to drop the Copa and the big rooms in Vegas and return to the coffeehouses and colleges, where he thought his natural audience was. The financial gamble was huge. After he got fired by the Frontier Hotel for the second time, he and Brenda had to back out of a deal to buy their first home. "I said good; they did me a favor. I told Brenda, I'm gonna go do the coffeehouses and prove I can do this. And if all I'm ever able to do in my life is fill up a coffeehouse all week long, I'll be fucking happy." Brenda backed him up and even helped put together a press kit explaining his new image. Carlin signed it with his left hand in a childlike scrawl—which did nothing to alter the perception among many that Carlin had flipped out.

Carlin hired new managers, Jeff Wald and Ron De Blasio, who came to see him in Denver when he was working at the Playboy Club and told him he needed an image makeover. "He was a hip guy who didn't look hip," says Wald, a former talent booker for Mr. Kelly's who was married to Helen Reddy. "I saw something underneath. He looked like a guy trying to escape. Yet he couldn't win with the hip crowd because he looked like their accountant." Wald worked hard to convince smaller clubs like the Bitter End and the Troubadour to book Carlin—whom they dismissed as a Las Vegas–*Ed Sullivan* act. The Troubadour finally gave him a one-night gig for $250. "I always say I took George Carlin from two hundred and fifty thousand dollars a year down to about twelve thousand dollars and improved his career," says Wald.

Carlin's log of his tour dates in 1970 and '71 shows his career schizophrenia at the time. A few old-line venues like Mr. Kelly's and the San Francisco Playboy Club ("last straight night club," reads his journal notation in December 1970) are interspersed with smaller, low-paying clubs like the Ice House in Pasadena, the Cellar Door in Washington, D.C., and the Frog and Nightgown in Raleigh, North Carolina. (Carlin drove to that last one all the way from Los Angeles in his new Trans Am, with one hundred rolled-up joints stuffed in a Kleenex box on the front seat next to him.) On May 3, 1971, Carlin collected an unemployment check. A month later he was a last-minute fill-in for Mort Sahl at Santa Monica College. "First standing ovation," reads his journal. It was a heartening milestone. "This is what I aspired to," he says. "This is what I wanted to use the coffeehouses for, to get to the colleges and the concerts. The hair on my arms was probably standing up, it was just so moving. Such affirmation of what I believed about myself."

Still, the transition wasn't easy. For a while *The Tonight Show*, spooked by the reports of his stage antics and drug use, stopped booking him. Dismayed, Carlin requested a personal meeting with Johnny Carson, to try to explain where his head was at. "The word went around the business that I was kind of a crackpot, a risk, and I think it filtered back to Johnny Carson's people. I went over to explain to him that it was a rational choice I had made, and that I was moving in a new direction and that people were buying it, in the colleges and coffeehouses, and that I should be seen seriously again. The trouble was that I was on a coke run when I went over. I was kind of speedy, I had a tie-dyed T-shirt on, and I think it further distanced them from me. The freeze-out continued."

But with Wald's help Carlin got a new record deal—on Flip Wilson's label, Little David—and in May 1971 he recorded a second album, *FM & AM*, at the Cellar Door in Washington. Carlin was so disappointed with his performance that he was in tears after the recording session. But the album, released the following January, was a successful coming-out party for his new career. One side (*AM*) represented Carlin's old style—parodies of TV game shows, lessons on how to imitate Ed Sullivan, a new Wonderful Wino routine. The other side (*FM*) showcased Carlin's new, more socially conscious material, the stuff that had been getting him into trouble at the Copa and the Frontier Hotel. He talked about dope—arguing (as Lenny Bruce had) that the "drug problem" is just as prevalent among the middle class, from coffee freaks at the office to housewives hooked on diet pills to college athletes ("the right wing's last line of defense on campus") hopped up on amphetamines. He tweaked America's puritanical view of sex and Madison Avenue's craven exploitation of it in commercials—birth control pills, he predicted, will one day be marketed with cute brand names like Preg-Not and Embry-No. He riffed on the word *shit*, so endlessly adaptable and yet so frightening to the middle class: "You can't fool me," he said. "*Shoot* is *shit* with two o's."

Carlin had struck the mother lode. He was expanding on many of Bruce's themes, but with more precision and punch. And his timing was better. Bruce's radical critique of society came at the end of the Eisenhower years, and he was never preaching to more than a devoted choir. A decade later, that choir had gathered millions of converts and was starting to change the country: the United States was moving toward the exit in Vietnam, and the sexual revolution was fast obliterating the taboos that Bruce had butted up against. Carlin's *FM & AM*, coming after several years of declining sales for comedy records, was a surprise hit, spending thirty-five weeks on the *Billboard* pop chart. "The album broke everything wide open," says Wald. "It hit a nerve. He was the right guy for the time—sex, drugs, rock 'n' roll, Vietnam. He was the guy who resonated."

Over the next five years, Carlin recorded four more albums, sold out college concerts, and opened up a rich new vein of material, both personal and political. In *Class Clown*, which came out in late 1972, he explored his Morningside Heights childhood, reminiscing about schoolroom stunts like knuckle cracking, arm farting, and cheek popping in obsessive, mock-clinical detail. His vivid account of his Catholic school days was a masterpiece of autobiographical vaudeville and theological criticism. Take his neat summary of the Catholic notion of sin:

It's what's in your mind that counts. Your intentions. *Wanna* was a sin all by itself. If you woke up in the morning, said I'm going down to Forty-second Street and commit a mortal sin—*save your carfare, you did it, man!* It was a sin for you to *wanna* feel up Ellen, it was a sin for you to *plan* to feel up Ellen, it was a sin for you to figure out a place to feel up Ellen, it was a sin to take Ellen to the place to feel her up, it was a sin to try to feel her up, and it was a sin to feel her up. There was six sins in one!"

Around this time Carlin also came up with his famous censor-baiting routine, "Seven Words You Can Never Say on Television." Like Bruce, he attacked society's fear of language head-on. But with no cops waiting to spring the cuffs on him, Carlin brought more mocking good spirit to the enterprise:

There are four hundred thousand words in the English language—and there are seven of them you can't say on television. What a ratio that is! Three hundred ninety-nine thousand, nine hundred ninety-three—to

seven. They must *really be baaa-aaad*. They'd have to be *outrageous* to
be separated from a group that large: "All of you over here, you seven—
bad words!" That's what they told us they are—*bad words*. There are
no bad words. Bad thoughts. Bad intentions. And *woooords*.

Carlin had fun with the list (for the record: *shit, piss, fuck, cunt, cocksucker, motherfucker*, and *tits*). He played with their sound ("*Tits*—such
a friendly sounding word. Sounds like a nickname, right? 'Hey, Tits,
c'mere man . . . ' "). He explained the no-shows (words with dual mean-
ings, for example—"You can prick your finger, but don't finger your
prick"). He gave due consideration to proposed additions (a thumbs-up
for *turd* and *twat*) and criticism of some of his original choices (compound
words like *cocksucker* probably don't belong, he conceded, but it would
upset the rhythm of the list). The message, of course: in the end, they're
just *woooords*.

Carlin was arrested once for doing the routine—at an outdoor Summer-
fest concert in Milwaukee, where children were inadvertently able to hear
it—but the charge of public profanity was dismissed. The routine did,
however, prompt a First Amendment fight that wound up changing prime-
time television. When New York City radio station WBAI played Carlin's
routine on the air in 1973, it was slammed with a reprimand by the Fed-
eral Communications Commission. The station appealed, and a court of
appeals reversed the FCC's order. But in 1978 the Supreme Court upheld
the FCC's right to ban "patently offensive" language during hours when
children are in the audience. That decision led to the creation of TV's
"family hour"—a requirement that the first hour of prime time, from
eight to nine P.M. eastern time, be reserved for family-friendly programming.

The "seven dirty words" routine (as it became popularly known) eventually made it to television—on Carlin's first concert special for HBO, taped at
the University of Southern California in April 1977. The fledgling cable
channel had been airing stand-up concert specials for just over a year (by
old-timers like Henny Youngman as well as younger comics like Robert
Klein), and it would, through the last half of the '70s and the '80s, become
an important platform for the new generation of stand-ups. Yet Carlin's material was considered risky at the time even for HBO. "People in the company were afraid of it, and we sort of muscled it on the air," says Michael
Fuchs, then HBO's programming chief, who scheduled the show on Good
Friday, just to be provocative. "We were warriors in those days."

Still, Carlin's dirty-words routine was controversial enough that HBO felt obliged to include an opening disclaimer, taped by columnist Shana Alexander. "We respect your decision about whether you want to see [the show]," she said. "It contains language you hear every day on the street, though rarely on TV." Even that wasn't enough. Just before Carlin launched into his X-rated bit in the concert's final minutes, HBO froze the frame and added a last-minute cautionary message, like one of those hokey warnings in an old William Castle horror film: "The final segment of Mr. Carlin's performance contains especially controversial language. Please consider whether you wish to continue viewing." The show, in the end, aired without incident.

In the first flush of his counterculture success, Carlin could be gratuitously crude and pandering—with frequent drug references to get the college crowds howling. But as a social satirist, he was more penetrating than ever. He loved dissecting the illogic of language (oxymora like "military intelligence" and "jumbo shrimp") and the social uses of euphemism ("When did 'toilet paper' become 'bathroom tissue'? When did 'house trailers' become 'mobile homes'?"). Bruce had taken on commercialized religion; Carlin tackled the very notion of an omnipotent God:

> How can he be perfect? He's not. It shows in his work. Take a look at a mountain range: Every mountain different. Leaves are all different. He can't even get two fingerprints the same. And everything he ever makes . . . *dies.*

Carlin considered himself a writer first and performer second; he worked out his material carefully in advance and improvised little once he got in front of an audience. But he was far more than just a verbal comedian; onstage he italicized everything with his wiry body, goofy-elastic face, and repertoire of voices (the shrill, tenor-voiced New York cop, the Edgar Buchanan old coot). Some of this was certainly fueled by drugs. Carlin was heavily into coke by the time he recorded his breakthrough records of the '70s. "If you want to see a cokehead, just look at the pictures on *Occupation Foole,*" Carlin told a *Playboy* interviewer years later. (The 1973 album cover shows a scrawny-looking Carlin, wearing a yellow tie-dyed tank top, in a series of contorted poses.) "The body language in those photos tells you everything."

By the mid-'70s, Carlin's drug use was starting to affect his work. He began showing up late to concerts; in some he mumbled nearly inaudibly. At the Westbury Music Fair, a *Newsday* critic reported that many in the crowd couldn't hear him and about a hundred patrons demanded refunds.

At home, Carlin was smoking pot before breakfast, downing twenty beers a day, and going off on four- and five-day coke binges. Brenda was matching him gram for gram and drinking heavily as well. The resulting fights got so bad that when they went on a trip to Hawaii, their daughter, Kelly, then eleven, made them sign a treaty to abstain from drugs. "It lasted all of maybe twenty minutes," says Kelly Carlin-McCall. "I was the only grown-up in the house." After Brenda crashed her car into a hotel lobby, she entered rehab and by 1975 had kicked her habit. Carlin stopped using coke at home but continued doing it on the road.

Carlin admits the cocaine at first had a creative upside. "Onstage, when rapping about a feeling I already owned, I would sometimes get a burst of eloquence," he said in 1982. "For the entertainer, part of the thing you do is just style. And the coke did help me get into great runs of pure form." But then it started to affect his productivity, and his health. In 1978 Carlin suffered a mild heart attack, and it helped prod him to quit. "It was fucking up my family and me," he says, "and it was fucking up my work. I really wasn't being as creative. I lost years. I could have been a pole vaulter in those years, and instead I was kind of like doing hurdles."

Carlin's drug use was at a high point in 1975, when Lorne Michaels booked him as the first guest host for NBC's new late-night comedy series *Saturday Night Live*. Craig Kellem, Carlin's former agent, then working as *SNL*'s talent coordinator, had suggested Carlin for the show. But Michaels saw the comedian as a compromise choice (he preferred Richard Pryor or Lily Tomlin, both of whom he had worked with before), and it was not a happy collaboration on either side. Michaels thought Carlin wasn't in tune with the new-style comedy he wanted his show to represent. "He was slightly older than us, a little more jazz influenced, a little different music," says Michaels. More problematic for Michaels was Carlin's lack of experience as a sketch performer. He was the lead in one sketch written for the first show—playing Alexander the Great at his high school reunion—but it was cut before airtime. "It just didn't play," says Michaels. "He couldn't do it."

"There was a distance from the get-go," says Kellem. "Carlin came in with a very independent attitude. He had definite ideas about what he was going to do and not do. And Lorne was pissed off. He just tuned out." Carlin was at the center of one of the big disputes that gave Michaels grief during that first tension-filled week. The network insisted that Carlin wear a suit and tie on the air; Carlin wanted to wear a T-shirt. After a blowup just before dress rehearsal, they finally compromised on a suit jacket over a T-shirt. To complicate matters, Carlin was in a drug haze for much of the week. "I'm grinding my jaw and clenching my teeth," Carlin would say years later, after watching a tape of the show. "I remember the amount of cocaine I did that week and it sort of fills me with a feeling of a lost opportunity." (Michaels claims he didn't notice the drugs and says Carlin "couldn't have been nicer.")

Carlin remains the forgotten man in the oft-told tale of *Saturday Night Live*'s birth. Michaels never asked him back (though Carlin did host the show one more time, in 1984, after Michaels was gone), and he was pretty much written out of *SNL*'s seemingly endless retrospectives and tributes. Yet on that first show, when the Not Ready for Prime Time Players were unknown and barely visible in a handful of brief sketches, Carlin did three separate monologues, which gave the show some needed comic ballast. What's more, on a show vowing to revolutionize TV comedy, Carlin was responsible for its only moment of real controversy: his final monologue, on the omnipotence of God, caused the network switchboard to light up with complaints and prompted an angry network rebuke.

As *Saturday Night Live* took off in the late '70s, Carlin's career hit a wall. The Vietnam War protests were long over, the Bee Gees had replaced the Beatles on top of the pop chart, and Carlin's counterculture image, which had caused such a stir just a few years earlier, was looking dated. The hot new comic on the block was Steve Martin, whose balloon animals and happy feet seemed a repudiation of all the social relevance that Carlin had brought to stand-up. Carlin's record sales and concert attendance were dropping, and he seemed to be coasting creatively—playing Vegas again, guesting on *Welcome Back, Kotter*. "I think people were jumping off my bandwagon," he admits. "I wasn't the talk of the town. Creatively I really had nothing new and different to say."

Unlike other stand-up comics who forged second careers in acting or directing, Carlin had little else to turn to. His few forays into movies (small parts in the 1968 Doris Day comedy *With Six You Get Eggroll* and 1976's *Car Wash*) were barely noticed. He thought about doing a concert film, then watched as Richard Pryor released one first in 1979. Carlin tried to develop his own movie, *The Illustrated George Carlin*, which would mix concert footage with live-action and animated scenes. But it never worked out and only drained his finances. The IRS hit him up for back taxes. On a drive back from Toronto to Dayton, he had too many beers, got into an accident, and broke his nose.

Then Carlin staged an unexpected comeback. In the late '70s he gradually weaned himself off coke, and in November 1981 he released his first album in four years, *A Place for My Stuff*. A year later he taped a concert at Carnegie Hall for HBO, his first for the cable channel in four years. Pulling it off was "a major high-wire act," says Jerry Hamza, a concert promoter who became Carlin's new manager and business partner. The hall was available for only one night, which meant there was no chance to tape a backup dress rehearsal, as is customary. The crew couldn't even get into the auditorium to set up in the afternoon because of a cello concert. Carlin himself, still recovering from a second heart attack, was a little shaky onstage. But wearing a long-sleeve green T-shirt and with neatly trimmed hair and beard, he was more mellow and reflective, opening with a rare reference to his personal problems:

Been taking a little time off. Had a heart attack . . . I would like to bring you up to date on the comedians' health sweepstakes. As it stands right now, I lead Richard Pryor in heart attacks, two to one. However, Richard still leads me, one to nothing, in burning yourself up.

After the concert, Carlin was disappointed; he thought the hall was cold and the crowd detached and unresponsive. But when the Carnegie Hall concert aired on HBO in January 1983, it revitalized his career. Attendance at his shows, which had dipped below one thousand in some markets, bounced back up to more than four thousand. HBO signed him for more specials. Given a second wind (and shorn of his coke habit), he resumed a busy touring schedule that continued without letup for two more decades. He branched out with books—collections of his random musings like *Brain Droppings* and *Sometimes a Little Brain Damage Can Help*— and even costarred in a short-lived sitcom in 1994.

In the Reagan years, he shifted his focus to antic, small-bore observations ("Have you ever noticed that you never get laid on Thanksgiving? I think it's because all the coats are on the bed"). Then, in the early '90s—realizing he had to raise his voice to compete with younger comics like Sam Kinison—he tacked back toward angrier political material, attacking America's war culture, the environmental movement, and the middle-class obsession with golf. His comedy grew increasingly dark, so that by 2005 he was cheerleading for suicide and mass ecological disaster. "I sort of gave up on this whole human adventure a long time ago," Carlin says. "Divorced myself from it emotionally. I think the human race has squandered its gift, and I think this country has squandered its promise. I think people in America sold out very cheaply, for sneakers and cheeseburgers. I think they lost their way, and I really have no sympathy for that. And I don't think it's fixable."

That cerebral, aloof, rather chilly stand-up persona may be one reason

Carlin was more admired than copied by the comedians who followed him. Richard Pryor, among his major contemporaries, was hailed as the more instinctive genius. Robert Klein's looser, more improv-based style drew more imitators. But for a generation too young to have seen Lenny Bruce, Carlin was the indispensable role model. Comics from Jay Leno to Bill Maher saw him as a major inspiration. An engineering student at the University of Arizona in Tucson named Garry Shandling drove up to Phoenix two nights in a row to show his idol Carlin, appearing at a club there, some monologues he had written. "He sat there with the pages, like a teacher. He said, you're very green, but if you're thinking of pursuing this, I would," says Shandling. "It played a big part in me moving to L.A. to pursue a career in writing. Carlin was breakthrough at the time. Talking to my generation. His sense of humor was extraordinarily on the money. I think he is still underrated."

Carlin's longevity as a stand-up was virtually unique among comics of his era—a top touring comic for four decades with virtually no boost from Hollywood, Broadway, or a hit TV series. It was a testament to his ability to stay on the edge, even as the hair and beard went gray. He evolved from white-bread media parodist to counterculture provocateur to curmudgeonly uncle to apocalyptic pessimist; but what remained constant was his eye for the world's inequities and absurdities, and the caustic eloquence with which he called them to our attention. Even in his late sixties, Carlin was able to distill an entire new vocabulary of Internet-era jargon into one extraordinary "Ode to a Modern Man":

I've been uplinked and downloaded. I've been inputted and outsourced. I know the upside of downsizing; I know the downside of upgrading. I'm a high-tech lowlife. A cutting-edge, state-of-the-art, bicoastal multi-tasker, and I can give you a gigabyte in a nanosecond . . .

Carlin's impact was broad and deep. He carried on Bruce's crusade against hypocrisy, cant, and social injustice—for a generation that was more receptive to it and willing to turn it into action. His early takeoffs of DJs and TV commercials set a gold standard for scores of media satirists to follow, and his jokey newscasts provided the template for news parodies from *Saturday Night Live*'s Weekend Update to Jon Stewart's *Daily Show*. His riffs on schoolroom pranks and bodily functions and the little absurdities of language showed the next crop of "observational" comics that nothing was too trivial or mundane—or tasteless—to become fodder for smart comedy.

Just as important, he showed that stand-up comedy could be a noble calling, one that required courage and commitment and that could have an impact outside of its own little world. And you could make a lifetime career of it, without burning out or self-destructing. That was an achievement Richard Pryor—whose career took a much different trajectory after those days smoking dope with Carlin at the Cafe au Go Go—couldn't quite match.

CHAPTER 3

Race

*One thing I found out. When you're on fire and runnin' down
the street, people get out of your way.*

—Richard Pryor

Even as George Carlin was transforming stand-up comedy in the late
1960s and early '70s, the old guard was still a force to be reckoned with.
Bob Hope's polished one-liners about the president defined topical stand-
up comedy for most Americans well into the '70s. Ed Sullivan might occasionally bring on young turks like Carlin, but his tastes ran mainly to
old-school comics like Jack Carter and Alan King. Pushing the envelope in
Las Vegas, for most of Middle America, didn't mean Carlin's drug jokes,
but the risqué one-liners of Buddy Hackett and Shecky Greene.

Yet the times were changing, and the old gagmen knew it. During the up-
heavals of the late '60s, Las Vegas was struggling to stay relevant, and hip
young comics like Carlin were seen as a key to attracting the younger
audience—most of whom were going off to rock festivals, not booking
rooms at the Riviera Hotel. But Carlin was thumbing his nose at traditional
Vegas comedy. "In an instant he made them old-fashioned," says Dennis
Klein, who wrote for Shecky Greene and other Vegas comics in those years
(and later created TV sitcoms like *Buffalo Bill* and *The Larry Sanders
Show*). "He was seen as a turncoat. He was slapping them in the face."

But if Carlin was a turncoat, Richard Pryor was a threat. His raw,
racially provocative comedy seemed an emblem, not just of the changes
comedy was undergoing, but of the turmoil gripping the whole country—
the rising tensions of an era when peaceful civil-rights demonstrations
were giving way to the militant rhetoric of the Black Panther Party. That
generational clash surfaced in a rare public way one afternoon in 1974,

when Richard Pryor and Milton Berle had a strange interlude on *The Mike Douglas Show*.

Berle, the old TV shtickmeister, had just published an autobiography, which, in the confessional mode of the day, revealed that during the 1930s he had fathered a child out of wedlock, the result of an affair with a Hollywood starlet. Berle was soberly telling Douglas and the daytime TV audience about the agony it caused him—the girl wanted an abortion, his mother insisted they get married—when Pryor, an earlier guest on the show who was sitting just off-camera, began to snicker audibly.

Berle at first tried to ignore him. Then he abruptly stopped telling his story and began lecturing the younger comedian. "I told you this nine years ago and I'm going to tell you on the air in front of millions of people," he said, barely containing his rage. "Pick your spots, baby."

"All right, sweetheart," Pryor replied, with a mocking hint of Bogart. Then he caught himself and groped toward an apology. "I'm sorry—honest. I'm crazy, and I'm just having fun here."

Berle persisted. "I want to ask you why you laughed."

"I laughed 'cause it's funny, man," Pryor said. "It's funny to me. It ain't got nothing to do with you . . . I apologize because I don't want to hurt your feelings. I respect what you do. But I don't want to kiss your ass."

Steam rising, Berle looked offstage and asked that the director stop the tape. "I'd rather not discuss it anymore," he said to Douglas, then turned to his cigar: "Can I have a match?" Pryor offered him a light. "No thanks," Berle snapped. "I don't smoke that."

There it was—comedy's generation gap, bursting uninvited into one of television's soothing afternoon house parties. The moral self-righteousness of the older generation versus the nose-thumbing irreverence of youth. The politburo of old Hollywood, doling out stage-managed glimpses of the "real life" of stars, versus the uninhibited new comedians who let it all hang out onstage. The cigar-smoking legend from TV's golden age versus the angry African American comic with the Black Panther mustache, throwing grenades at everything the legends had built.

Of course, it wasn't so black and white. Berle, even on his moralistic high horse, was exposing a chapter of his life that had obviously troubled him deeply. Pryor, possibly high on drugs, was rude without provocation. But then, Pryor never made things easy. The comedian of the post–Lenny Bruce era most often hailed as its greatest genius could also be its most infuriating. Like Carlin, he reinvented himself in the late 1960s, rejecting his early, safe-for-whitey comedy and setting out to tell the truth as he saw it—about race, sex, and his own baroquely dysfunctional life. Unlike Carlin, he didn't plot out his career like a field general, but he seemed to careen through it on instinct, battling drugs and his own private demons all the way. His success was a happy confluence of artist and era: a brilliant wild child who was perfectly suited to a time of cultural upheaval, when revolution and craziness weren't all that far apart.

Pryor grew up in the years of segregation and began doing comedy in the early 1960s, at the height of the civil rights protests. He wasn't the first crossover black comedian to talk openly about race. Dick Gregory, before him, had broken through in white nightclubs, sitting on a stool and serving up mordant commentary on the civil rights conflicts of the era. ("I sat-in six months once at a Southern lunch counter. When they finally served me, they didn't have what I wanted.") Godfrey Cambridge, a portly off-Broadway actor turned comedian, delivered satire of America's racial divide in a more traditional storytelling–punch line package. Flip Wilson progressed from the Apollo Theater to a popular TV variety show with a repertoire of characters that, if they didn't quite amount to racial commentary, were at least unapologetically black.

The most popular black comedian of the '60s, however, didn't talk about race at all. Bill Cosby, a former physical education major at Temple University, had begun working in Greenwich Village clubs in the early '60s with an act that imitated Gregory's. (Playing the first black president, for example, Cosby tells a friend about his new job: "Yeah, baby, everything's fine, except a lot of For Sale signs are going up on the block.") But he quickly dropped his racial material and switched to more universal, color-blind comedy about his Philadelphia childhood—stand-up that made a statement about race by simply ignoring it. He struck a chord in a country that longed for reassurance that blacks and whites had more tying them together than tearing them apart. Cosby became the first black star of a network TV drama series, CBS's *I Spy*, and won Grammy Awards for best comedy album an unprecedented six years in a row, from 1964 to 1969.

Pryor was only three years younger than Cosby, but he seemed of another generation. He didn't ignore race, as Cosby did, or approach it as a social-political issue, like Gregory, but treated it as an unavoidable part of what made him who he was. He presented a slice of the African American experience that had rarely, if ever, been seen by mainstream white audiences—the hustlers, pimps, junkies, winos, and street preachers he had grown up with—and did it in a way that rang true for black audiences yet was so piercingly human that whites didn't feel excluded.

But Pryor's comedy went beyond race. He plunged without restraint into his own messy personal life: the drug problems, the run-ins with the law, the turbulent relationships with women (seven marriages to five differ-ent women, three black and two white), the health problems, and most fa-mously, the self-immolation that nearly killed him in 1980. And he did it with such confessional intensity, unsparing honesty, and performance brio that no one could look at stand-up comedy the same way again.

At first he didn't like to talk much about his childhood. "You know, my life really ain't been too interesting," he told a reporter from *Ebony* mag-azine, which ran one of the first profiles of him in 1967. Later, he may have embellished the grim details of his early years. The facts are that he was born Richard Franklin Lennox Thomas Pryor, on December 1, 1940, in Peoria, Illinois. His mother, who appears to have been a prostitute, and his father married when Richard was three and split up when he was ten. He then went to live with his grandmother, who ran a chain of whore-houses in town. In his autobiography, *Pryor Convictions*, Pryor describes learning about sex by peeking through keyholes to watch the prostitutes at work, and soaking up neighborhood lore at a bar called the Famous Door, where "people came in to exchange news, blow steam or have their say." He was kicked out of Catholic school when they found out about the fam-ily business, and he moved to an integrated elementary school. There he got an early taste of racism when he gave a scratch pad as a gift to a little white girl he had a crush on. The next day, as Pryor tells it, the girl's an-gry father came to school and berated him in front of the class: "Nigger, don't you ever give my daughter anything."

At age twelve he transferred to a predominantly white school, where a teacher got him to come to class on time by promising him a few minutes every morning to tell jokes in front of his classmates. He began dropping by the Carver Community Center, where a supervisor named Juliette Whit-taker took an interest in him, giving him a small role in a production of *Rumpelstiltskin* and casting him regularly in talent shows. After getting thrown out of school at fourteen—for taking a swing at a science teacher who was trying to discipline him—he did odd jobs shining shoes and clean-ing up at strip clubs before getting hired at a local meatpacking plant. Itchy to get out of Peoria, he enlisted in the Army when he was eighteen and was sent to Germany. After he stabbed a white soldier in the back during a race-related brawl, he was discharged early and wound up back home.

He got a job singing and doing comedy at a local nightspot called Harold's Club. Some of his material already had a racial edge: he did a takeoff of Edward R. Murrow's *Person to Person*, playing a dirt-poor Mississippi black family giving Murrow a tour of their house. ("Hi, Mr. Murrah. Just step over the chickens. Yes, sir, that's our chair. And our

TV . . .") He became the emcee at another club, Collins Corner, where he met entertainers who traveled the "black belt" circuit of nightclubs across the Midwest. Soon he was traveling with them, developing his comedy act in cities like St. Louis, Pittsburgh, and Youngstown, Ohio. Then, in 1963, he read a story about Bill Cosby; said, "Goddamn it, this nigger's doing what I'm fixing to do"; and moved to New York City.

Like Carlin around the same time, he gravitated to the Village folk and jazz clubs. He got regular spots at the Café Wha? on MacDougal Street, whose owner, Manny Roth, became his first manager. Cosby was the hot black comic in the Village at the time, and Pryor began copying his genially race-neutral comedy. The shy kid from Peoria "initially was a lot intimidated" by Cosby, says Roth. "Cosby was college educated, a big guy, a different bearing, really impressive. Richie was a scared little kid. He was doing generic material. He wasn't very consistent onstage. One time I walked downstairs because I thought I heard Cosby on the stage. It was Pryor, doing an imitation of Cosby. I told him, you gotta be yourself."

Roth helped spruce him up, bought him a suit when he got a gig uptown, and went with him to Harlem to get his hair conked. A *Variety* reviewer saw his act at the Living Room in March 1964 and praised the young comic's "avant-garde viewpoint" and his "healthy instinct for irreverence," while noting that he "still has much to learn" before being ready for the bigger clubs. After Rudy Vallee, the old '30s crooner, caught his act, Pryor landed a guest spot in August 1964 on Vallee's summer show *On Broadway Tonight*. The next year he began making regular appearences on *The Merv Griffin Show*, whose gushy host—who gave early TV breaks to so many of the young comedians of the era—became a big fan. Griffin would introduce him as "our own little Richie Pryor," and frequently give him the favored cohost's seat next to him. "He was childlike, so adorable," said Griffin. "I would book him on with older comedians, and they were all stunned by him. Bill Cosby called me one day and said, 'Have you heard him do any of my material?'"

Pryor's early TV bits, however, were as much indebted to the physical clowns he had grown up watching in the movies and on TV, like Red Skelton and Jerry Lewis. He played a bowling pin, for instance, that was the last on the lane left standing, and a weight lifter nearly busting his veins trying to pick up 750 pounds. He would announce his impression of the "first man on the sun"—and then jump around with a hotfoot. His most elaborate early bit was an homage to his own showbiz start in Peoria—a re-creation of a children's production of *Rumpelstiltskin*, with Pryor impersonating all the kid actors, nervously trying to remember their lines and impress their parents: "Hocus-pocus, ab-fer-a-da-bra! Vanish from the land for-*ever*!" (*Confused pause, then sotto voce*) "You better vanish—my mutha's here."

Sometimes he would sneak a few firecrackers into the box of sweets. He introduced one routine as "my impression of mankind," then did a fast-forward highlight reel of human history—Adam and Eve, Julius Caesar, Benjamin Franklin—each vignette punctuated with a quick verbal or visual gag. At the first Thanksgiving, someone asks, "Aren't you thankful?" The reply: "Yeah, massa." But mostly, Pryor, with his lithe body, rubbery face, and big, worried eyebrows, was cute and eager to please. In the summer of 1966, he got a regular spot on *The Kraft Summer Music Hall*, along with Carlin, and he looked comfortable even in the corny, summertime medleys of "Up a Lazy River" and "Down by the River Side."

But as he gained more confidence and developed his act in hip night-clubs like San Francisco's hungry i, his material grew more personal and more race-conscious. Talking about his Peoria childhood, he'd say he had a Puerto Rican mother, a black father, and lived in a Jewish tenement building in an Italian neighborhood: "I would go outside to play and the kids would say, 'Get him! He's *all* of them!' " He did a Lenny Bruce–style riff on a superhero for black people: "Super Nigger! Disguised as Clark Washington, mild-mannered custodian for the *Daily Planet* . . . with his X-ray vision that enables him to see through everything except whitey." In another early bit, Pryor did an elaborate reenactment of a traveling theater troupe's visit to a Southern chain gang. When the effete theater director announces the play, about a Southern belle who falls in love with a black blacksmith, the redneck jailer objects. "It's quite all right," the director re-assures him. "The nigger gets killed."

The top TV shows began calling—*The Ed Sullivan Show*, *The Tonight Show*. But cleaning him up for television was a challenge. Sandy Gallin, then a young agent at GAC, the agency that also represented Carlin, dis-covered Pryor at the Cafe au Go Go in 1963 and represented him through the '60s. "It was always a big discussion for us to find what was suitable for TV," says Gallin. "To get three or four minutes for *Ed Sullivan*—it was work. He did not like playing the game of conformity. But he was bright enough to know that this was gonna help him advance his career. It was difficult for him. He felt like he was selling out."

Pryor's volatile behavior, both onstage and off-, could be as much of a problem as his material. Even in the Café Wha? days, Roth remembers seeing Pryor get so enraged at a heckler that he stabbed the guy with a fork. At a club in Los Angeles, when Pryor noticed a woman in the front row who wasn't laughing, he suddenly unzipped his fly and peed in her direction: "Do you think *this* is funny?" Unhappy about having to open for Trini Lopez at Basin Street East in New York, Pryor did most of the show lying on the floor behind the bandstand. When he opened for Steve Lawrence and Eydie Gorme at the Sands Hotel in Las Vegas, Gallin got a panicked call from the hotel's manager, complaining that Pryor was out of control, "swinging from the chandeliers."

At the Improvisation in New York, the new showcase club for comedians where Pryor would drop in occasionally, owner Budd Friedman remembers him as a charming cutup, who once tried to distract a girl singer onstage by parading around dressed only in shoes, socks, and a hat. ("Well, there goes another myth," shouted Budd's wife, Silver.) But his mood could turn dark just as quickly. One night Pryor came into the club loaded and complained to Friedman that he was being taken advantage of because he was black. Friedman was hurt and taken aback; he paid Pryor the same as he paid all the comics who worked in his club—nothing.

Pryor would show up late or not at all for some gigs and had a thing about money. "He was very paranoid about signing contracts, very suspicious that people wanted to take advantage of him." says Gallin. "I think he thought I was the only white man who wasn't trying to cheat him." After getting sued for child support by a girlfriend, Maxine Silverman, with whom he had a daughter, Pryor claimed he threw away his driver's license, closed his bank account, and stopped paying taxes. (In 1974 the IRS caught up with him and sent him to jail for ten days.) Even when he was getting top dollar on *The Ed Sullivan Show*—$7,500 per appearance—he wanted to be paid in cash. When he got a check instead, he would go downtown to cash it immediately at Sullivan's own bank.

Craig Kellem, Carlin's agent at GAC, used to babysit the agency's clients when they appeared on Sullivan's show. Anytime Pryor was a guest, Kellem knew he'd earn his money. "There was always a danger, a subtext," says Kellem. "Is he gonna get mad? Is he gonna show up on time? The big question was, who was going to get Richard Pryor out of bed to go to dress rehearsal? Usually, you'd try to get the most naïve guy in the office to do it. Nobody else wanted to face his wrath." Pryor was a no-show on Sullivan at least once. Amazingly, Sullivan didn't blackball him. "It was so unlike them to let him back," says Gallin. "Ed would say, 'I don't know why I book him.' But they absolutely loved Richard. They understood his talent, and he got away with murder because of it."

His unrestrained appetites, violent temper, and mounting drug use (Pryor says he began snorting coke around this time) made for a combustible mix. When he was still playing the "black belt" circuit, Pryor had served jail time for assaulting a nightclub singer in Pittsburgh. Now, Gallin became used to late-night phone calls to bail his client out of jail. In early 1967 Pryor was arrested in California for carrying pot across the border from Mexico. Later that summer he got in a fight with a desk clerk at the motel where he was living on Sunset Boulevard and nearly blinded the clerk with a punch that broke his glasses; Pryor was charged with assault and sentenced to probation. Gallin witnessed some of this firsthand; in Gallin's office, Pryor once pulled a gun and slugged a record producer whom he thought was cheating him.

Pryor, meanwhile, was heading into the same sort of career crisis that was about to hit Carlin, his old colleague from the Village and summertime TV, feeling increasingly hemmed in by the compromises he had to make for mainstream showbiz. Like Carlin, he felt it most acutely in Las Vegas, where he was trying to make his comedy work for the high rollers. "I was doing material that was not funny to me," he explained. "It was Mickey Mouse material that I couldn't stomach anymore. In Vegas, my audience was mostly white and I had to cater to their tastes. I did a lot of that in those days. I wanted to do more black material, but I had people around me telling me to wait until I had really made it and then I could talk to the colored. I knew I had to get away from people who thought like that and the environment that made them think like that."

His frustrations came to a head in September 1967, when he abruptly walked offstage during a gig at Vegas's Aladdin Hotel. It became the legendary turning point of Pryor's comedy—the story retold often, the dates frequently confused, and the details sometimes embellished. (*Newsweek* reported that after he walked off the stage, Pryor took off his clothes, jumped on a gaming table, and yelled, "Blackjack!" Pryor later said the story was a joke, and the reporter apparently took him seriously.) In his autobiography, Pryor describes the walkout as something between an epiphany and a nervous breakdown. He came out onstage "completely fucked up," saw Dean Martin staring at him in the audience, and froze up. "I imagined what I looked like and got disgusted. I grasped for clarity as if it was oxygen. The fog rolled in. In a burst of inspiration I finally spoke to the sold-out crowd: 'What the fuck am I doing here?' and walked off the stage."

Whatever motivated it, his walkout in Vegas cemented his reputation as a loose cannon. Some mainstream clubs like Mr. Kelly's in Chicago stopped booking him. Fans of the old, cute Richie Pryor were taken aback to see the unleashed new Pryor onstage. Merv Griffin went to see Pryor's club act in Baltimore and brought along his fifteen-year-old nephew. "It was the filthiest act I'd ever seen in my life," Griffin said. "I was stunned. I went backstage and I said, 'Richard, what are you doing?' He said, 'I'm doing my act.' And I said, 'But, Richard, it has nothing to do with your fans.' And he said, 'I got visited.'"

Pryor always resisted efforts to link his comedy to the black political movement. But he was certainly affected by what was going on in the country. By 1967, the integration battles of the early civil rights days were being replaced by calls for revolution and black power. Race riots in Detroit and Newark added a sense of urgency to the problems of the black underclass. In early 1968, Dr. Martin Luther King was assassinated. Amid all this Pryor, now living in Los Angeles, married Shelley Bonus, a white Jewish hippie from a Brooklyn show business family (her father was Danny Kaye's manager) who had marched with Dr. King and who encouraged Pryor to do more radical material. "She came from a middle-class Jewish family and thought she was a black militant," says Rain Pryor, their daughter. "She was down for the cause. She told him not to be so safe, pushed him to be more truthful. Not to be a revolutionary, but to speak the truth."

Pryor also got friendly with Paul Mooney, a black improv comic from the San Francisco Bay area who idolized Lenny Bruce ("He was definitely for blacks; white people hated him") and pushed Pryor to do harder-edged racial material. "Richard was really into Bill Cosby. I was pulling him away from Bill Cosby," says Mooney, who became a writer for Pryor and one of his closest friends. "Richard was in awe of me because I wasn't afraid of white people. I added kerosene to the fire."

By the end of the '60s, Pryor had recorded one album (*Richard Pryor* in 1968) and was nursing a fledgling movie career (a small role in the 1968 youth-cult fantasy *Wild in the Streets*, among other films). But his personal life was a mess. He had split up with Shelley and was facing an arrest warrant in his child-support battle with Maxine. To escape, he did what a lot of young people at the time were doing: he dropped out and moved to Berkeley. Mooney drove him there, telling him he had to get away from the phonies in Hollywood and see what was happening on the campuses.

For much of the decade, the U.C. Berkeley campus had been the scene of almost unrelieved turmoil—from the 1964 free speech movement, which kicked off the era of '60s student protest, through anti–Vietnam War demonstrations and the 1969 street battles over People's Park. Berkeley was also the center of a circle of progressive black intellectuals and writers, among them Claude Brown (*Manchild in the Promised Land*),

Cecil Brown (*The Life and Loves of Mr. Jiveass Nigger*), and Ishmael Reed (*The Free-Lance Pallbearers*). Pryor, living in a $110-a-month apartment, hung out with them. He read *The Autobiography of Malcolm X* and listened to Marvin Gaye's *What's Going On*. He continued to work on his comedy too, in small clubs on both sides of the bay, experimenting with more improvisational, overtly racial material. "I was working very hard and wasn't making great money but I loved it because I was doing the material I wanted to do," he said. "I learned what freedom is." When he came back to Los Angeles a year later, he was a changed comic.

He began working at Redd Foxx's club in central Los Angeles, where the largely black audiences responded enthusiastically to his new material. The transformation is apparent in his second album, *Craps (After Hours)*, taped at Foxx's club and released in 1971. The last restraints on his language and racial grievances were gone. He recounted being hauled into police lineups in Peoria because "all the ugly white girls that couldn't get any said niggers raped 'em." He talked about watching black and white boxers—"Niggers and white people fight, I always be rootin' for the nigger, even if he bad. Please, whip the white folks, I don't want white folks to win nothin'." Just ten years after Lenny Bruce was busted for saying *cocksucker* onstage, Pryor used the full complement of X-rated words with abandon—and even delivered a little Bruce-ian lecture on obscenity: "You can't talk about fuckin' in America; people say you're dirty. But if you talk about killin' somebody, that's cool. I don't understand it. Myself, I'd rather come."

The album also shows Pryor beginning to really explore his Peoria past, not with wisecracks but by re-creating the characters who populated his world, like the street preacher who rhapsodizes about meeting God "outside a little hotel in Baltimore: I was walking down the street eatin' a tuna fish sandwich . . ." And the regulars at the local bar, like Big Black Bertha, whose "ass weighed 280; Bertha weighs 300." And the irascible father of a girl he wants to go out with, shooing him off the front porch: "I works *too hard* to send my girls to school to get an education—and not the kind *you* wants to give 'em." He replays an encounter on the street with an old acquaintance during a trip back home, so revealing of Pryor's insecurity about his own fame:

> I like goin' home, 'cause I can show off. But some brothers break my face: "Nigger, you ain't shit. You wasn't shit when you was here. That's the same shit you was doing around the poolroom, nigger. It ain't nothin' . . . Lemme have a dollar."

Craps (After Hours) was an underground success, but primarily reached a black audience. Most of the rest of the country knew Pryor during those years mainly as a rising young movie and TV star. In 1972 he won critical raves for his jittery, charismatic performance as Piano Man in *Lady Sings the Blues*, the biography of Billie Holiday starring Diana Ross. He was furious at being passed over for the lead role in Mel Brooks's *Blazing Saddles*, a film he helped write. (The studio considered Cleavon Little less of a risk.) But he got high-profile guest shots on TV in Flip Wilson's variety show and, most memorably, on Lily Tomlin's Emmy-winning 1973 TV special, *Lily*—whose highlight was a sketch in which Pryor played a reformed junkie and Tomlin the greasy-spoon waitress with whom he strikes up a poignant friendship.

By his next album, 1974's *That Nigger's Crazy*, Pryor's stand-up comedy had reached full maturity. Much of the stridency of *Craps* was gone—the racial satire less forced, more organic, drawn from experience. He explained, for example, how he reacts when white cops stop him on the street—with a loud, clearly enunciated "'I AM REACHING INTO MY POCK-ET FOR MY LI-CENSE.' 'Cause I don' wanna be no fuckin' accident." (Two Detroit policemen later told Pryor that a black suspect they picked up used the same line.) He talked about the difference between how white people and black people react to horror movies ("Niggers make *noise*"), or get ready for sex (delivered in that bland, uptight, Dudley Do-Right voice that constituted his most acid satire of whitey: "Pass the potatoes; think we'll be having sexual intercourse this evening?").

His vivid character vignettes were little masterpieces of autobiographical comedy. In a bit on how his father used to quiz him before letting him go out for the evening, you cringe along with him under the bullying assault:

Say, where you goin' Richard, huh? I don't give a fuck where you go, *be home by eleven*. You understand eleven, don't you, nigger? You *can* tell *time*, can't you? . . . Eleven o'clock, bring your ass here. I don't mean down the street singin' with them niggers either. I ain't gettin' your ass outta jail no more, motherfucker. That's right . . . And bring me back a paper.

He showed empathy but no sentimentality toward the down-and-outers, each fighting for his own bit of turf or measure of self-respect. A meeting on the street between an old wino and a young junkie pirouettes from comedy to pathos so quickly that the audience literally gasps:

Wino: Look at that nigger, look at him in the middle of the street. Junkie motherfucker, look at that. Nigger used to be a genius, I ain't lyin'. Booked the numbers, didn't need *paper or pencil*. Now the nigger can't remember who he is . . . [*Shouting*] Better lay off that narcotic, nigger! That shit done made you null and void . . . I'm just ashamed to see you like that.

Junkie [*flying*]: Ashamed to see me? What about the shit out here? Niggers fuckin' with me, baby. I went to the unemployment bureau, bitch sittin' behind a desk—"You have a criminal record." I said, "I know that, bitch! I'm a criminal! Just tell me where I can get a job!" Ugly bitch. I seen better faces on an iodine bottle . . . I went home, my dear called me a dog, you dig that? My father say he don' wanna see me in the vicinity, just 'cause I stole his television. That's the politics, baby. I'm sick, Pops, can you help me? My mind's thinking about shit I don' wanna think about. I can't stop the motherfucker, baby. Movin' too fast for the kid. Tell me some of that old lies of yours, make me stop thinking about the truth. Will you help me?

Wino: Yeah, I'm gonna help you boy. Because I believe you got potential.

These portraits were wonderfully specific, yet evocative of a whole community—unmistakably black yet too recognizable to be mere instruments of a racial agenda. Pryor's amazing versatility and focus as an actor brought them alive, but so did his writing—the punchy single syllables ("that shit done made you null and void"), the woozy non sequiturs ("that's the politics, baby"). It was funny, truthful, unbearably sad. Stand-up comedy had never seen anything like it.

Unlike *Craps (After Hours)*, *That Nigger's Crazy* was a crossover hit. It spent more than a year on the *Billboard* pop chart and won a Grammy Award for Best Comedy Recording. The hip critics discovered Pryor, hailing him as they had no comedian since Lenny Bruce. "He has expanded stand-up comedy to the dimensions of pure theater," exulted David Felton in *Rolling Stone*, "and has accurately presented the times we live in, perhaps in the only way the times we live in can be presented accurately." "Almost singlehandedly," wrote James Alan McPherson in the *New York Times Magazine*, "he is creating a new style of American comedy . . . which must be observed and heard at the same time in order to be completely understood and appreciated."

One reason it seemed new is that Pryor had stripped his stand-up comedy almost entirely of jokes. "I know all the tricks," he said. "I assume that everybody does. But people like me because I won't use them, and if I do, they can tell." The few snippets of verbal cleverness in Pryor's mature comedy stand out for their rarity. "They give niggers time like it's lunch down there," he said in a bit about prisons in the South. "You go looking for justice, that's just what you find—just us." (A note on the album where the routine appears, *Is It Something I Said?*, reports it was "stolen from Paul Mooney.") He drew comedy from the profane bluster of his characters' street talk and the gulf between their puffed-up view of themselves and the sad reality of their lives. It was a classic comic strategy—poking fun at vanity and self-delusion—but Pryor made it resonate with the thwarted dreams of a whole culture.

And America was ready for it. By the mid-'70s, the militancy of the late '60s had faded, and the urban ghettoes had quieted down. White Americans now seemed less afraid of blacks starting a revolution than of a white president, Richard Nixon, compiling an enemies' list and committing criminal acts. They didn't want to be yelled at, but they were willing to meet Pryor more than halfway—to enter his world, not just to hear what he had to say about theirs.

One person who thought Pryor was the right comic for the times was Lorne Michaels, who was busy putting together his new comedy series *Saturday Night Live* for NBC. Michaels had worked with Pryor on the Tomlin special and thought he was the "funniest man on the planet"— cooler than Carlin, hip and dangerous in a way he wanted his new show to be. "He was the guy who had done *Rumpelstiltskin* on *Ed Sullivan* and had walked away from that," says Michaels. "To me he was as significant in comedy as Bob Dylan and Paul Simon, or the Beatles or the Rolling Stones, were to me in music, as powerful as anybody who was making films at the time. It elevated the seriousness, the importance, of what we were doing in comedy."

Pryor was at the top of Michaels's wish list of guest hosts for *Saturday Night Live*, but NBC had a problem with him. A few months earlier, working on a Flip Wilson show in Burbank, Pryor had beaten up an NBC page who wouldn't let a friend of Pryor's backstage. The page sued Pryor for one million dollars (the case was later settled out of court), and the network barred Pryor from its studios. Michaels threatened to quit—even walking off his show for twenty-four hours—until NBC relented and let Michaels hire him.

Pryor, typically, didn't make Michaels's life easy. First, Michaels and his talent coordinator, Craig Kellem, had to fly down to Miami to meet him at a jai alai arena to talk him into doing the show. Before he agreed, Pryor insisted on his own writers (among them Paul Mooney), a big block of tickets for friends, and a spot on the show for his ex-wife, Shelley (who did an ill-fitting performance piece on the show about a pair of carousel horses, told in rhyming couplets). Having all but commandeered the show, Pryor refused to come to the studio until rehearsals started, forcing the show's execs to troop over to his hotel, where he was holed up with his vaguely threatening entourage. NBC, worried about what Pryor might do on live TV, made Michaels agree to a several-second tape delay for the show. Michaels kept it a secret from Pryor, afraid his star would walk off if he found out. (Pryor wrote later in his autobiography: "If I'd known, I never woulda shown up.")

But his guest appearance on *Saturday Night Live*'s seventh show, in December 1975, was a triumph for both Pryor and the young program. He reprised some of his best monologue material (including the wino-and-junkie routine), kept his language in check, and meshed easily in sketches with the Not Ready for Prime Time Players. The most celebrated was a two-hander in which he played a job applicant being given a word-association test by Chevy Chase, a session that degenerates into racist name-calling:

Chase: Spearchucker.

Pryor: White trash.

Chase: Junglebunny.

Pryor: Honky.

Chase: Spade.

Pryor: Honky honky.

Chase: Nigger.

Pryor: *Dead* honky.

Pryor was happy enough with the *Saturday Night Live* experience that, when Universal signed him to a movie deal the following year, he asked Michaels to come out to L.A. and be his producing partner. (Michaels says he considered it, but opted to stay with the show.) Pryor's *SNL* episode did better in the ratings each time it was rerun, demonstrating his growing popularity. Less than two years after blackballing Pryor from the network, NBC offered him his own series.

The Richard Pryor Show, which aired in the fall of 1977, was a legendary missed opportunity, scuttled by the network's timidity and Pryor's erratic behavior. NBC originally wanted ten episodes, but Pryor agreed to do only four. The network wanted to use old-timers like Sid Caesar and Imogene Coca in the cast, but Pryor nixed the idea. Instead, the show featured an ensemble of newcomers, many of them culled by Mooney from the L.A. comedy clubs (among them Sandra Bernhard and a pre–*Mork and Mindy* Robin Williams). Pryor was away for much of the preproduction period and took time off to get married (for the third time) just before the show went on the air. Rocco Urbisci, a young producer brought in to run the show because he had worked with Pryor on a *Midnight Special*, ordered a wedding cake for Richard and Pam Grier, whom he had been dating. When Pryor came in with his new wife, a model named Deboragh McGuire, Urbisci had to throw away the cake.

Pryor tested the limits with the network wherever he could. NBC insisted that Pryor do an opening monologue, and Pryor sabotaged it with obscenities. "Everyone from the network was there in the booth to watch," says Urbisci. "He starts the monologue: 'White bitch sucked my dick.' There wasn't one section of it we could use." In a question-and-answer session with the audience, a woman said to him, "Tell me one of your wildest dreams." Pryor's reply: "To be able to fuck a white woman and y'all don't fuck with me." The question-and-answer session also wound up on the cutting-room floor.

The worst clash with the network came over the opening for the first show. Pryor came out to introduce his new series and made joking reference to NBC's concerns about his raw material. "Look at me, I've given up absolutely nothing," he said, as the camera pulled back to reveal Pryor in a flesh-colored body stocking, with no genitals. Four days before the show was to air, NBC told Urbisci to cut the scene. He refused to without Pryor's approval. When Pryor found out, he complained in the press that NBC was "stifling my creativity" and quit the show. In the end, the network aired the four mostly completed episodes, which got trounced in the ratings by *Happy Days* and *Laverne and Shirley*. That was that.

Mooney contends the NBC suits were less to blame for the show's meltdown than Pryor's inability to handle the pressure. "It wasn't the network," he says. "The network loved him. They all had jobs because of him. It was Richard. The drugs, the drinking, and the everyday drama were too much for him." Urbisci, for his part, says he had no problems with Pryor: "It wasn't a walk in the park. There were sometimes delays. But he was always there." The show itself was a mixed bag. The attempts to showcase Pryor's improvisational skills with the overpopulated ensemble cast mostly fell flat. But a few sketches had some bite. In one, Pryor is part of a team of archaeologists who discover the Book of Life in an ancient crypt. Pryor enters the crypt to examine the volume and excitedly tells the rest of the (white) archaeological team that it reveals the black race was responsible for all of mankind's great discoveries. They seal him up inside the crypt and quietly sneak away.

The Richard Pryor Show was hardly a setback for Pryor's career, however. In 1975 he had hired a new manager, David Franklin, a black entertainment lawyer from Atlanta, who also represented Miles Davis and Roberta Flack. Flack had recommended Franklin to the comedian because she thought Pryor was getting ripped off. "She said, David, we gotta save Richard Pryor," says Franklin. "Save him from the vultures." Franklin took a look at Pryor's financial records and was surprised to see that he had made only $100,000 in 1974, despite the success of *That Nigger's Crazy*—partly because bootleg copies of the record were circulating freely. (Pryor wasn't happy about the situation either. On a wall in his house he kept a copy of his gold record—with a bullet hole through it.) When Pryor's record label, Stax, was about to go out of business, Franklin bought up the master recordings and made a new deal to rerelease them with Warner Bros.

Meanwhile, Franklin set out to make Pryor a crossover star. He told him to stop advertising his concerts as "X-rated." (Pryor had been spooked by an arrest for obscenity in Virginia and "thought it was just fair to warn people," Franklin says.) Franklin felt his act would work in much bigger venues, so he booked him into places like New York's City Center and Pittsburgh's Heinz Hall, where Pryor did sellout business. Franklin read movie scripts for him (Pryor was dyslexic and had trouble getting through anything of length) and put him in a mix of lightweight comedies, like *Greased Lightning* and *Silver Streak* (where he stole the picture from nominal star Gene Wilder), and dramatic films, like Paul Schrader's *Blue Collar*, which gave him a chance to show his range. By the end of the '70s Pryor was the most bankable black star in Hollywood.

His stand-up was evolving as well. On his 1975 album, *Is It Something I Said?* (which went platinum and won him another Grammy), he introduced Mudbone, the garrulous street philosopher from Tupelo, Mississippi, who became his most famous creation. He began talking more frankly about his fraught relationships with women—his misogynist rants (*bitch* rivaled *nigger* as Pryor's favorite epithet) always tempered by a recognition that he couldn't live without them. Reenacting the scene when his girlfriend tells him she's leaving, he tries to stifle the pain and be cool:

Fuck all the arguing, just take your time and pack your shit. Is that bag gonna be big enough? 'Cause if not, you can use one of mine. You cool? You got money and everything? I can't make you stay if you wanna leave. All you have to do is [*suddenly bursting into a sobbing rage*] *find another way outta here other than that door! 'Cause you try to leave me, bitch, I'm gonna kill your ass!*

In 1976's *Bicentennial Nigger*, Pryor offered his most overt and bitter commentary on America's racial history, adopting the guise of a two-hundred-year-old slave who turns his life story into a sarcastic, pageant-like recapitulation of the black experience in America, accompanied by patriotic underscoring and Stepin Fetchit–like laughter:

They brought me over here in a boat. It was four hundred of us come over here (*hyuk hyuk*). Three hundred and sixty of us died on the way over here (*hyuk hyuk*). I love that. That just thrills me so. I don't know why you white folks are just so good to us (*hyuk hyuk*). Then they split us all up, yessiree. Took my mom over dat way, took my wife dat way, took my kids over yonder (*hyuk hyuk*). I'm just so happy (*hyuk hyuk*). I don't know what to do if I don't get two hundred more years of this . . .

Pryor's racial anger made more spontaneous appearances onstage as well. On *The Phil Donahue Show*, when a white woman in the audience asked him what black people had against *Amos and Andy*, Pryor responded: "You're old and you're going to die soon, so why should you care?" On *The Tonight Show*, Pryor startled Johnny Carson's audience with a call to arms: "If you're black and still here in America, get a gun and go to South Africa and kill some white people." Appearing at a gay rights benefit at the Hollywood Bowl in November 1977, Pryor got angry at what he thought was shabby treatment of a black dancing group backstage, and made what some in the audience thought were disparaging cracks about gays. "When the niggers was burnin' down Watts, you motherfuckers was doing what you wanted to do on Hollywood Boulevard," he said. As the boos mounted, he walked off the stage with a defiant: "You can kiss my rich, black, happy ass."

Then the media psychoanalysis began. "His life vacillates between sweet appeasement of the people he knows he must deal with in order to make it—producers, studio heads, writers, fans—and the opposite, the point at which he begins to feel he has become the nigger clown for all of them. Then he explodes and feels the need to do some outrageous, anti-white antic," wrote William Brashler in a *Playboy* profile titled "Berserk Angel." Others simply blamed the coke. "There was bags of it," says Mooney. "They used to pass around hundred-dollar bills, thousand-dollar bills. It was everywhere. You know why I knew Richard liked me as a friend? He would never offer me drugs. When those people would come around, he'd say, 'Paul doesn't do drugs. Give me Paul's share.' " Yet Mooney learned to tread carefully around his friend, always alert for the next blowup. "I could sense it, see it coming. He'd be very quiet and he would start talking real weird—he would get into that maniac character. I would always leave."

Women got the worst of it. In the early-morning hours of January 1, 1978, the police were called to his Northridge, California, home when Pryor, in a rage after an argument with his wife Deboragh, peppered her car with gunshots and rammed it with his Mercedes. He was charged with assault and sentenced to probation. His fourth wife, Jennifer Lee, whom he dated for several years before marrying in 1981 (they were divorced after a few months and remarried in 2000), wrote a memoir, *Tarnished Angel*, in which she chronicled the jealous rages, coke binges, three-way sex parties, and furniture-shattering fights in awe-inspiring detail. Wedding day for Richard and Jennifer: "He jumps out of bed, runs toward me, grabs me by the neck, smashes my head against the wall, then throws me onto the floor. 'Believe this, bitch, I'll fucking kill you.' I run outside and fall weeping on the ground, crying into the wet grass in my torn white wedding night-gown." Says Rain Pryor: "He had terrible, terrible fears of women. He grew up in a whorehouse. Women were powerful. The way for him to be power-ful back was through money, and physically."

Yet Pryor could also be sweet, disarmingly childlike, generous with friends. When they were working together on *The Richard Pryor Show*, Urbisci says he got a call from Pryor asking him to come over and keep him company. When he got to Pryor's house, the comedian put on a video-tape and they sat together in silence watching *The Wizard of Oz*. Pryor was always a soft touch for family members and friends, putting them on the payroll and bailing them out when they got in trouble. Franklin once got a tearful call from Pryor, telling him that his uncle Dickie—a three-hundred-pound hustler from Peoria who, in Franklin's words, "spent every waking hour trying to rip Richard off"—was in jail and needed someone to arrange a $25,000 bribe for the judge. Franklin told Pryor to wire Uncle Dickie the money and stay out of it.

In the late '70s, Pryor was on top of the stand-up world, a rock star to the younger comics in L.A. who gathered to see him work out at the Comedy Store, the showcase club run by Mitzi Shore. "He would go on last," Robin Williams recalls. "Everyone would come and watch. It was like an audience for the pope. I saw him do stuff that he would never do again. People would yell out, 'Do Mudbone!' and he'd say, 'You do Mudbone, motherfucker. You know it better than me.' It was kind of a transformative thing, seeing him just trying stuff and going so far out, the most personal, painful stuff you could ever see in your life." Williams, one of the few comics in Hollywood who could match Pryor in coke use, saw the effects of the drug and the drinking. "Coke would get him going, but alcohol would give him just enough buffer between him and the audience to kind of let it out," says Williams. "You could see when he was off of it. Then it was hard because he was getting too much feedback. The fear would kind of take over. But when he had a couple of Courvoisiers, he was like fuckin' flyin'."

Through much of 1978, Pryor, unusually focused, was using the Comedy Store to work on new material—improvising, getting notes from Jennifer during the day, honing his routines into what he called "the best comedy of my career"—for a concert tour in the fall, which was the basis for *Richard Pryor: Live in Concert*. Shot without frills at the Terrace Theater in Long Beach, California, in December 1978 (and released just two months later), it was the first time a comedian's stand-up material had been turned into an entire feature film. Pryor was at his most energized and intimate, prowling the stage in a red silk shirt, putting the audience on notice that nothing would be off-limits from the outset, starting with his well-publicized New Year's Day arrest for shooting up his wife's car. He tweaks the white people in the audience who wander in late ("You ever notice how nice white people get when there's a bunch of niggers around?"); reminisces about being beaten by his grandmother and going hunting with his father; and obsesses about his sexual prowess: "You can tell when you've made good love to your woman, because she will go to sleep. But if you finish fuckin' and your woman want to talk about computer components, you

got some more fuckin' to do." He even re-creates the heart attack he had
suffered during a visit to Peoria in 1977—writhing on the stage and ani-
mating the attack as a merciless street thug:

> I was walking in the front yard and someone say, "Don't breathe no
> more!" I say, "Huh?" "You heard me, motherfucker, don't *breathe*!"

Comedy could hardly get any more painful or penetrating. Yet Pryor
showed other, more surprising colors as well—for example, in a long riff
on the death of his pet squirrel monkeys, which ends with a ruefully
whimsical visit from the vicious German shepherd next door:

> "Whassa matter, Rich?"

> "My monkeys died."

> "Say what? Your monkeys died? Ain't that a bitch. You mean the two
> monkeys used to be in the trees, they died?"

> "Yeah, they died."

> "Shit. I was gonna eat them, too. Don't linger on that shit too long, you
> know. It fuck wi' ya."

> "I'll try."

> "Yeah, you take care." [Then, before jumping back over the fence to go
> home] "Now, you know I'm gonna be chasin' you again tomorrow."

Richard Pryor: Live in Concert cost almost nothing to make and
grossed fifteen million dollars at the box office, becoming the model for
virtually every comedy concert film to follow—often copied, but never
equaled. Pryor himself may have come the closest with a follow-up three
years later, *Richard Pryor: Live on the Sunset Strip*. In between, however,
he generated some of his most harrowing real-life material yet.

In 1979, Pryor began freebasing—in which cocaine is dissolved in ether
and then heated to make a more potent and purified form of the drug—
and his erratic behavior grew worse. Franklin, whom Pryor tried to shield
from his drug use, noticed the change. "Back in '77, '78, when Hollywood went through freebase heaven, Richard used to say, the one thing

about him, he would never freebase," says Franklin. "He would see people freebase and be holed up in a corner, on the floor, out—and he didn't want to wind up like that. But then he started telling me that freebasing was simply cocaine that is free of contaminants. That was the first time I noticed that something was going on."

Pryor failed to show up for the start of a three-day shoot for a cameo role in Mel Brooks's *Wholly Moses!* Later, on the Arizona location for *Stir Crazy*, his second teaming with Gene Wilder, he rented a house miles away from the rest of the crew and often showed up hours late for shooting. When a crew member horsing around accidentally tossed a slice of watermelon in his direction, Pryor thought it was a racial insult and walked off the set. Franklin managed to negotiate his return—even getting the studio to cough up an extra $500,000—but it was clear Pryor was in bad shape.

On June 9, 1980, Pryor was locked in the bedroom of his Northridge home, depressed and desperate. After smoking all the cocaine he had, drifting into what he later described as a state of "serious dementia," he poured cognac all over himself and lit a Bic lighter. An aunt and a cousin, who were in the house, tried to smother the flames, but Pryor ran outside in a panic. By the time an ambulance got him to the hospital, third-degree burns covered the top half of his body. The police initially reported that the ether he was using to freebase had accidentally blown up in his face. Franklin, knowing that possession of cocaine would be a violation of Pryor's probation, told the press Pryor had accidentally set fire to a bottle of rum he was drinking. Only much later did Pryor admit that it was a suicide attempt.

The conflagration nearly killed him. But with six weeks in the Sherman Oaks Community Hospital Burn Center, he began a slow recovery, and a year later he reemerged with a vow to clean up his life and restart his career. He shook up his inner circle, bringing in Jim Brown, the former NFL running back turned Hollywood star, to manage his new production company and parting ways with Franklin, whom he sued for embezzlement. (Franklin says he left voluntarily after the accident because Pryor refused to take a year off and go into therapy. He denied the embezzlement charge and blamed it on Pryor's paranoia. The lawsuit was settled out of court, and Franklin was sanctioned by California's Labor Commission for acting as an unlicensed talent agent.)

Pryor used all this as the inspiration for his last great stand-up performance. *Live on the Sunset Strip* was filmed at the Hollywood Palladium in December 1981, just a year and a half after his self-immolation. Pryor, who was using coke again, was nervous about being back onstage and didn't do the long preparation work he had done for the first concert film. To some intimates, he seemed off his game. Halfway through the first of the two performances that were to be filmed, he walked off the stage. He pulled it together the second night, but he still needed to come back afterward for reshoots. He acknowledged later that the film "wasn't as great an overall performance as the first concert movie."

Still, it has some of Pryor's most fearless and self-revealing comedy. Dressed in a flashy red suit with a black tuxedo shirt, looking fit, if a bit more subdued, Pryor relives his infamous brush with death, turning the freebase pipe into another of his characters:

> "Time to get up, time for some smoke, Rich. Come on now, we're not gonna do anything today. Fuck your appointments—me and you are just gonna hang out in this room together."

And he turns the accident itself into the blackest of black comedy:

> When that fire hits your ass, that will sober you up quickly. One thing I found out. When you're on fire and runnin' down the street, people get out of your way.

The most surprising revelation in the concert, however, was Pryor's account of a trip to Africa he had made in 1979. The back-to-his-roots journey, he said, had ended with an epiphany about the racial epithet that had become a trademark of his comedy:

> I was leaving, sitting in the hotel lobby, and a voice said, "What do you see? Look around." And I looked around, and I saw people of all colors and shapes. And the voice said, "You see any niggers?" I said, "No." It said, "You know why? 'Cause there aren't any" . . . And it started to make my cry, man. All that shit. All the acts I've been doing. As an artist and comedian. Speaking and trying to say something. And I been saying that. That's a devastating fucking word. That has nothing to do with us. We are from a place where they first started people.

Pryor vowed to stop using the word *nigger* in his comedy from then on. Some of his old friends, like Mooney, thought it was a sign the white people had gotten to him. By all accounts he stuck to his promise. Yet it seemed irrelevant to Pryor's slow fadeout as a force in stand-up comedy. He did one more concert film, *Richard Pryor: Here and Now*, in 1983, but his material seemed warmed over and his newly reformed persona didn't play as well. (When Pryor said he had stopped drinking, someone in the crowd yelled out, "I don't believe that shit!") "I don't think I'm as funny as I used to be," he admitted to Gene Siskel in a 1983 interview. "I'm finding it hard imitating Richard Pryor." He continued to make movies—getting paid four million dollars for a role in *Superman III* (more than star Christopher Reeve) and directing the autobiographical drama *Jo Jo Dancer, Your Life Is Calling*. But in 1986 he began experiencing periods of sudden weakness and loss of balance. He looked so bad during a *Tonight Show* appearance that rumors spread he was sick with AIDS. The diagnosis turned out to be multiple sclerosis. Pryor gamely continued to make films, and occasional stand-up appearances, for several more years before the disease finally silenced him.

The gush of tributes after his death in December 2005 confirmed Pryor's legacy. Among his contemporaries, he was widely acclaimed as the most brilliant stand-up performer of his generation. Virtually every black comic who followed, from Eddie Murphy to Chris Rock, took from him—the racial satire, the autobiographical candor, the four-letter words (and a six-letter one, *nigger*, that they quickly restored to the vocabulary), even the way he strolled the stage and related to the audience. "Pryor started it all," said Keenen Ivory Wayans. "He made the blueprint for the progressive thinking of black comedians, unlocked that irreverent style." Watching him on *The Ed Sullivan Show* when she was growing up in New York City, Whoopi Goldberg experienced her own comedic epiphany: "The characters he introduced I had never seen onstage. He was talking about real stuff that was happening. We all had junkies in the streets; we all had Mudbone; we all had these folks in our realm." For white America, emerging from an era of racial strife, Pryor's comedy was harsh but healing. The black comics who reached out to white audiences before him tried to foster racial understanding by stressing how much alike we are. Pryor rubbed our noses in the differences—and yet made us feel their universality.

The power of Pryor's comedy had its drawbacks as well. Plenty of comedians, white and black, emulated his rough language and in-your-face style but missed the empathy and vulnerability that informed it. His manhandling of women—onstage as well as off—probably bears at least some responsibility for the macho posturing that has kept stand-up a predominantly male preserve for so many years. He was, moreover, an exhausting genius. If stand-up comedy from the borscht belt to the '70s could be described as a long march from joke telling to truth telling, Pryor was the marathon man. Comedy could hardly get any closer to the bone. But it could also not go much farther in that direction without turning into something that was no longer comedy. For a restless art form, Pryor was not the be-all and end-all. There were other roads to explore.

CHAPTER 4

Improv

I want an orderly nuclear holocaust.

—Robert Klein

Barely five years after its birth, Chicago's Second City theater company was already being acclaimed as the progenitor of a new style of comedy. Started in December 1959 by Paul Sills, a visionary director who saw improvisational theater as a force for democracy, self-realization, and the "liberation of the people," the company occupied a cramped, 120-seat theater in a converted Chinese laundry in Chicago's restored Old Town district. There, half a dozen performers (their ranks continually changing as new cast members came and went) would perform a nightly potpourri of sketches, most of which had been developed out of improvisations. The company, along with its spiritual predecessor in Chicago, the Compass Players, had produced such illustrious grads as Barbara Harris, Alan Arkin, Shelley Berman, Mike Nichols, and Elaine May. A few years later, alums from the Chicago company and a spin-off troupe in Toronto—among them John Belushi, Dan Aykroyd, Bill Murray, and Gilda Radner—would help launch *Saturday Night Live*. But in the spring of 1965, Second City was home to two future stand-up comedy stars who were butting heads.

David Steinberg had grown up in Winnipeg, Canada, the son of an Orthodox Jewish rabbi. He came to Chicago in 1960 to attend Yeshiva, but switched to the University of Chicago and studied English literature. He made two discoveries in Chicago that turned him on to comedy. One was seeing Lenny Bruce perform at the Gate of Horn. The other was Second City, which had drawn its founding members and intellectual spirit (along with, Steinberg thought, most of the cute girls) from the University of Chicago. "It was like seeing the Rolling Stones for the first time," Steinberg says. "So smart, so funny—I was ready to follow them like a kid follows the circus."

He and a friend put together an act of sketches and began performing in small clubs in the Chicago area. After two Second City members caught their act one night, Steinberg got offered a job with the company. He was a bit lost at first, as the newcomer in a well-oiled cast that also included Jack Burns (recently split from his former partner George Carlin) and Avery Schreiber. But within a couple of years he was the company's star attraction. An elfin performer with a bookish but mischievous air, he was best known for his mock Bible sermons, which he would improvise from Old Testament names called out by the audience.

Steinberg was king of Second City when Robert Klein joined the company in April 1965. They were about the same age (Klein had just turned twenty-three, Steinberg was a few months away from it), both Jewish, and both big fans of Lenny Bruce. But they had little else in common. An outgoing six-footer, Klein brought with him the hustle of the Bronx streets and the chutzpah of the borscht belt tummlers he had watched during his summers in the Catskills. People had warned him about Steinberg, who had an ego and, Klein heard, could make things tough on newcomers. But Steinberg invited Klein over to his apartment, a twenty-fifth-floor luxury pad he was subletting from singer Chad Mitchell, and told him not to worry; they'd get along fine.

They didn't. Klein felt he was being hazed from the start. He thought that Steinberg hogged the stage, stepped on his lines, and grabbed the best roles in improvisations. What really galled him was the way Steinberg tried to pass off as improvised the Bible sermons that, by now, had developed into set routines. "He had his shtick down," says Klein. "It bothered me. He was very good at self-promotion."

Fred Willard, who had joined the company at the same time as Klein, was used to Steinberg's antics. Before every sketch, for example, it was customary for each new set of actors taking the stage to quickly rearrange the props and scenery themselves. Once, for a scene they were to play together, Steinberg told Willard he needed some time to concentrate and asked if Willard would mind handling the setup chores himself. "I said sure," Willard recalls. "Then I did it for a few nights, and I found out he was just gonna have me do it forever." Another time, Willard came backstage and told Steinberg a joke he had just heard and was thinking of using to introduce a sketch. Steinberg thought it was so good he used it himself on his next trip onstage.

"He came back and said, 'I couldn't help it,'" says Willard. "But David was the kind of guy you just couldn't be mad at. He was so charming." It helped that Steinberg was also good at what he did. "If you got into an improv bit with David, you knew you could just relax," Willard says. "Bob Klein worked a little more at the improv stuff. I think he always had an angle he wanted to get in. As a result, I think Bob was a funnier stand-up. David was very funny, but you kind of had to go along with his stuff."

Steinberg and Klein left Second City at the same time—in the spring of 1966, after traveling to New York with the company for an off-Broadway engagement. Both set their sights on Broadway but got waylaid into stand-up comedy. And both adapted their Second City experience to their new solo careers—though in very different ways. Steinberg simply took some of his popular Second City bits and turned them into stand-up material. Klein used the techniques he had learned at Second City to create a more free-flowing, improvisational stand-up style. Slightly younger than either Carlin or Pryor, they were the first two major comedians of the late '60s who didn't have to remake their image or rethink their approach to connect with the emerging new audience. Steinberg's stand-up career petered out relatively quickly (he went on to become a successful director of movies and TV series like *Seinfeld* and *Curb Your Enthusiasm*), but he found himself, almost by accident, on the front lines of two of the era's major cultural-political battlegrounds. Klein, meanwhile, developed a comedic voice that was perfectly pitched to the attitudes, political views, and cultural obsessions of the baby boom audience, and he became very possibly the most imitated comedian of the '70s.

After leaving Second City, Steinberg's acting career got off to a fast start. He was cast in the original Broadway production of Jules Feiffer's *Little Murders*; replaced Paul Sand (another Second City graduate) in *The Mad Show*, a Broadway revue based on the satirical magazine; and starred as a Jewish man who hires himself out as a slave to a black couple in a short-lived Broadway play, directed by Sidney Poitier, called *Carry Me Back to Morningside Heights*. But he ultimately concluded that he wasn't cut out for acting. "I was a great audition person," he says. "I would improvise and it was great. But by Tuesday I couldn't duplicate it or repeat it. I had no acting chops."

So he reached back to the comic sermons he used to do at Second City and tried to build a stand-up act around them. Typically he would start by asking the audience to call out names from the Bible, then would retell the familiar Old Testament stories, adopting the rabbinic cadences he knew so well from his Orthodox Winnipeg childhood. "Today we're going to talk about Moses," he would begin (or Esther or Joshua, depending on what name was suggested), "who had a wonderful rapport with God . . . whom I'm sure you'll all remember from last week's sermon." Then he'd give the biblical lesson an impish, contemporary spin. King Solomon is granted one wish by God and asks to become all wise and all knowing. "And at that second," Steinberg would say, "he knew he should have asked for money." Lot's wife keeps nagging him as they flee Sodom and Gomorrah, saying they should have stayed. In Steinberg's version, Lot finally turns to his wife and says, "Dear, God told me to tell you to look back." Job's desperate attempt to connect with the Lord gets this absurdist twist:

"God!" Job cried.

God didn't answer.

He looked up again. "God!"

Nothing.

Finally, on the third try, he hollered, "Mike!"

And God answered.

How mysterious are the ways of the Lord.

Steinberg lived in the same apartment building as a young singer-songwriter named Carly Simon, and he suggested they do an act together: she would sing, and he would handle the comedy. After trying out at the Bitter End and getting a good response, they got booked at the Cellar Door in Washington, D.C., opening for the Modern Jazz Quartet. But Simon had an attack of stage fright just before the show and fled on the train back to New York, leaving Steinberg to try to do an act alone. He stretched his sermons as far as he could and scrounged up enough other material to fill out the set (including an old Second City bit called "How to Win a Friend," a parody of self-help records, for which Simon had recorded the voice). He got through one show all right, but the Modern Jazz Quartet was cooking that night, and most of the audience stayed around for their second show—which meant Steinberg had to do another set without repeating any material. "I had used up almost every sermon, so I just started to talk to the audience," he says. "And it was moderately successful. Enough that I felt, if I didn't have to do a second show to the same audience, I had something. So I developed an act under fire."

Still, he struggled. Back at the Bitter End in the summer of 1968, he opened for folksinger Tom Paxton, but the crowds were small and the laughs sparse. A Gray Line tour bus unloaded its patrons into the club one night, and when Steinberg asked the audience for Old Testament names, nobody would give him any. "Honey, leave the Old Testament alone!" a woman shouted. After that, Gray Line scratched the Bitter End off its itinerary. But just before his engagement there ended, the *New York Times* ran a rave review of his act. "At 26, Mr. Steinberg is the funniest new comic since— Woody Allen? Shelley Berman? Lenny Bruce? In that league anyway," wrote Dan Sullivan. "Like these men, Mr. Steinberg has a quick mind, a sharp tongue, a highly developed taste for fantasy, an equal zest for the absurdly real." The next night there were crowds lined up outside the club, and Paxton offered to open for Steinberg—afraid the audience might leave before he got on. Soon Steinberg was getting TV guest spots, and in the fall of 1968 he was booked for an appearance on *The Smothers Brothers Comedy Hour*.

Tommy and Dick Smothers, the popular comedy folksinging duo, were in the midst of trying to bring the '60s revolution to network TV. Tommy— the "dumb" half of the pair but the most politically committed—had become radicalized during the peace-and-love years, and when CBS gave the duo a variety show in January 1967 (opposite NBC's long-running hit *Bonanza*), he set out to make it the voice of the protest generation. "What was happening on the street was much more exciting than what was happening on TV," says Mason Williams, the show's head writer, a folk singer and poet from Oklahoma (and later the composer of "Classical Gas") who was into radical politics and avant-garde art. "There was nothing on TV for us or our friends. So we said, let's put on a show for us, rather than the sanitized and homogenized stuff on TV at the time."

The Smothers Brothers' show brought on rock groups like the Doors and Buffalo Springfield, who had never before been seen on network television. It tested network standards with jokes about sex and drugs. (In a sketch about Romeo and Juliet, someone asks Romeo, "Did you get that girl in trouble?" CBS ordered the line cut.) It took frequent potshots at President Johnson and the Vietnam War. In the fall of 1967, as antiwar protests in the country were heating up, the show invited on Pete Seeger, the once-blacklisted folksinger, to perform "Waist Deep in the Big Muddy," an old World War II song being recycled as a not-so-veiled critique of the Vietnam War. But CBS cut the song's last stanza, with its potent final line, "And the big fool says to push on." After widespread media criticism for its political censorship, CBS relented and allowed the show to invite Seeger back in February 1968 to perform the song uncut.

David Steinberg's sermons were hardly as incendiary as "Waist Deep in the Big Muddy." But even mild satire of religion in those years could ruffle feathers. When Steinberg made his first appearance on *The Smothers Brothers Comedy Hour* in October 1968, delivering a sermon on Moses, the network raised no objection. But after a deluge of angry viewer mail, the network told Tommy that Steinberg could return as a guest, but only if he did no more sermons. Tommy, who by this point was relishing his role as the protest movement's thorn in CBS's side, immediately called Steinberg and invited him back. "And have you got any more of that Bible stuff?" he asked. "Tommy was very confrontational," says Judy Steinberg, Tommy's assistant and girlfriend at the time (and later David Steinberg's wife). "He considered himself a spokesman for a generation. He felt it was his destiny to challenge the rules. In a lot of ways he was very irresponsible and irrational. He didn't realize the need to compromise. He wanted to rub their noses in the dirt all the time."

When Steinberg made his second *Smothers Brothers* appearance—in April 1969, in a show taped to air on Easter Sunday—relations between Tommy and the network were near the breaking point. Tommy expressed his defiance by introducing Steinberg with a reference to the flap over his earlier appearance. "Now, we don't want to offend anybody out there," he said. "But if you get offended—that's the way the cookie crumbles." Doing a sermon this time about Jonah, Steinberg talked about the debate among biblical experts over whether he could have been literally swallowed by a whale. Skeptical New Testament scholars, Steinberg said, "literally grab the Jews by the Old Testament"—indicating with a hand gesture the particular scroll he was referring to.

It was the hand gesture, as much as the line, that set off network alarms. CBS censors said the monologue would have to be cut. Tommy refused. Then CBS, claiming the brothers had breached their contract by failing to submit the episode in time for review, pulled the show two days before it was to air and announced that *The Smothers Brothers Comedy Hour* would not be back in the fall.

Tommy Smothers called the Steinberg incident a red herring, a cover for CBS's decision to dump the program because of its left-wing politics (a decision made easier by the fact that the show, once in the top 20, was dropping in the ratings). Steinberg thought it showed that religion, for much of mainstream America, was an even more sensitive subject than politics. "It was one thing to do politics. It was a whole other thing to go after God in a very Calvinist country. And I think it gave CBS a perfect excuse. Who's going to go against them for throwing [the Smothers' show] off the air for the evil sermons?" In any event, the Smothers Brothers' TV revolution was over. And Steinberg came away with a Purple Heart.

The brouhaha didn't hurt Steinberg's career, however. In his stand-up act Steinberg was branching out from his sermons, adding material about his Jewish family, Woody Allen–like accounts of his dating life, and adaptations of more bits from his Second City days, including one in which he played an unhinged psychiatrist who torments an unsuspecting patient ("Whatever you do, don't think about your mother's gigantic bosom!"). But he found himself back in the center of the era's political storms a few years later when he started talking about Watergate.

As the scandal over the break-in at the Democratic national headquarters in 1972, and the White House's efforts to cover up its involvement, began to unfold, the counterculture's worst fears about Richard Nixon were playing out on the network evening news. Steinberg was one of the first comedians to take on the subject. "I was very political at the time," he says. "I felt that Nixon was a crook." His Watergate material went over well in nightclubs. But on *The Tonight Show*, Johnny Carson told him to stay away from the subject; the country wasn't ready yet.

Steinberg, by then a frequent Carson guest (and one of the few younger comedians who socialized with Johnny off the show), claims the famously nonpartisan *Tonight Show* host shared his anti-Nixon views. "Johnny was very liberal," he says. "He had the same politics I did. In fact, he always said that he and I bonded because we both hated the same people." But he respected Carson's instinct for the mood of the country. "It's hard to remember how polarizing it was to talk about Nixon. What I didn't realize is that in stand-up, being ahead of the country is the same as being behind. All that matters is the right moment."

That moment appeared to come when Steinberg was a guest on *The Tonight Show* in July 1973, in the midst of the televised Watergate hearings. During their conversation, Carson coaxed Steinberg gingerly into the subject. Carson's verbal bobbing and weaving was almost comical (frequent hedges like "must say 'allegedly'" and "the people like it if you don't get cruel"), and Steinberg's gibes were mild stuff. He observed, for example, that Donald Segretti, who ran Nixon's "dirty tricks" operation, "was the only man in the whole group with true creative imagination, because it was his job to plant that Senator Humphrey was sexually promiscuous." What the *Tonight Show* audience didn't know, however, was that Steinberg himself had become an unwitting player in the Washington drama he was holding up for ridicule.

A year earlier, while getting ready for an appearance at the Oak Room in New York's Plaza Hotel, Steinberg got a knock at his hotel room door from two men who identified themselves as FBI agents. They had learned of a death threat against him, the men said, and they were there to protect him. Steinberg, despite some trepidation, went ahead with the show, which went off without incident. But over the next few months he seemed to be dogged by pro-Nixon hecklers—as well as by the FBI agents, who followed him around for protection.

Some of the heckling seemed peculiar to Steinberg. One drunk heckler in the audience at Washington's National Press Club (not a crowd noted for drunk hecklers) shouted a nearly obsolete anti-Semitic insult—calling him a "mockey bastard." Even odder, after the show Steinberg ran into the same heckler in the hotel elevator—now seemingly stone sober. Steinberg's friend Paddy Chayefsky, who was with him, slammed the bigger man against the wall, and Steinberg had to break them up.

A few months later, Steinberg saw the two FBI agents on TV—standing behind Donald Segretti, the Nixon dirty trickster, at the Watergate hearings. When Steinberg confronted them later on the phone, they admitted to being White House agents, who had been assigned to watch him because of his anti-Nixon material. "How could you be doing this to me?" Steinberg asked in dismay. "We gave you a clean slate," they reassured him. "I didn't have the presence of mind to tell them, you don't have the right to give me a clean slate," Steinberg says. "At the time I was just thankful."

After Nixon resigned and Watergate passed from the scene, so did Steinberg's stint at the vanguard of stand-up comedy. He remained a favorite of Carson's, with 130 guest appearances on *The Tonight Show*, but began to seem an increasingly mainstream figure. Almost alone among his major stand-up contemporaries, Steinberg was never asked to appear on *Saturday Night Live*. Steinberg thought it had to do with bad blood between him and Bernie Brillstein, the manager who had briefly represented Steinberg and who now numbered Lorne Michaels and several of the *Saturday Night Live* cast members among his clients. Yet despite his politics (and his Second City pedigree), Steinberg by this point was a poor fit for the show: his puckish and more refined style already seemed a generation removed from the more in-your-face satire of the Not Ready for Prime Time Players.

Being snubbed by *Saturday Night Live* accelerated his career downturn. "It was a profound setback," says Judy Steinberg, "a loss of confidence, snowballing depression." David Steinberg says: "I felt my stand-up career waned around the time of *Saturday Night Live*. Even the college audiences started to change. Whooping and hollering at things you were saying—wanting to be noticed more than listening to you." Steinberg moved out of performing and into directing—and watched as his former classmate from Second City made a more lasting impact on stand-up comedy in the '70s.

Robert Klein was born on February 8, 1942, and grew up in the Bronx, in a household where show business was an amateur passion. His father, a textile salesman, did impressions and told funny stories and was friends with the Yiddish-dialect comedian Myron Cohen. His mother played the piano by ear and would often accompany herself singing Broadway show tunes. As a kid, Robert gravitated to music as much as to comedy; he and some DeWitt Clinton High classmates formed a doo-wop group called the Teen Tones and appeared on *Ted Mack's Original Amateur Hour*. (They lost to a one-armed pianist.) He went to Alfred University in upstate New York, where he entertained frat brothers by imitating professors, and worked during the summers as a lifeguard and busboy at resorts in the Catskills. There he got his first taste of the borscht belt comics, once filling in as emcee for two weeks—borrowing a tuxedo from the band, doing Jimmy Durante impressions, and even delivering punch lines in Yiddish.

At Alfred he was a standout in the school's tiny drama department (he played Shylock in a production of *The Merchant of Venice*), and at the urging of his teachers, he went on to the Yale Drama School. There he took classes in movement, acting, and elocution, but he spent most of his time figuring out how to get laughs. For one class exercise in makeup, he put war paint on one side of his face, wore half a cowboy hat on the other, and swiveled back and forth to play both parts in a scene from an old western. But after a year he quit Yale and moved back home to the Bronx, auditioning for off-Broadway roles and supporting himself with a job as a junior high substitute teacher. Then he decided to try stand-up comedy.

It was 1964, and like Carlin and Pryor before him, Klein headed down to the folk clubs in Greenwich Village. For a green kid like Klein, the best chance to get onstage was on "hootenanny night," usually Monday or Tuesday, when the regular acts were off and amateurs could perform. Klein worked up some material based on his substitute-teaching job and tried it out on Monday hoot night at the Café Wha?. He did well enough after a few weeks to try out on hoot night at the more prestigious Bitter End and soon was bugging the owner, Fred Weintraub, for a regular paying gig. Then he bombed two nights in a row, had no idea why, and went back home to rethink his career plans.

When a friend from Yale, Jim Burrows, told him that Chicago's Second

City company was coming to New York to look for new cast members, Klein decided to audition. He did improvisations with another aspirant, Fred Willard, who had been working as part of a comedy team with Vic Greco. Klein and Willard both got offered jobs, and in the spring of 1965, Klein packed up and moved to Chicago.

Despite his problems with Steinberg, Klein made an instant impact. "He was very political, very opinionated," says Willard. "He used to do funny bits backstage. He would imitate James Dean, lean his head up against the door—'What is Christmas to me? I got no father! I got no mother!' He'd tell funny stories about guys he had met, working guys—'Hey, do you still have my wrench?' 'No, I t'rew it out in the middle of Webstah Avenue.'"

Onstage Klein—still calling himself Bob—did song improvisations and an impression of Lyndon Johnson, scratching his ears a foot out from his head. He teamed especially well with Willard. In one sketch, Klein played a general who has to break the news to Willard's gung ho colonel that his battalion won't be part of the first wave of a big attack. Willard objects, insisting that his unit should lead the attack. They argue back and forth with mock-military bravado ("We go back to the Point together." "That's not the point." "What is the point?"), but the general won't budge. Finally the colonel accepts his orders, salutes smartly, and leaves. Once out of the general's sight, he does a silent jump for joy.

It was the kind of comedy Klein was looking for—smart, grounded in recognizable human behavior, making a sharp social-political point. It depended on the performers' ability to put it across—characterization, timing, an ear for which syllables to hit hard for the laugh. "For performance, technique, and everything, there was nothing like Second City," says Klein. "It was a year in the most grueling training ground, in front of audiences, learning the nuances of getting a laugh. You work six nights a week, every night there's an improv session, Saturday night there's two and a half shows, so you hone your chops as an actor too. The timing became so razor sharp."

After a year at Second City, Klein traveled with the company to New York for an engagement at the Square East Theater in the Village. The show got mixed reviews, and the run ended after five weeks, but Klein decided to stay and look for acting work. Within a few months he landed a small role in *The Apple Tree*, a new musical directed by Mike Nichols and starring another Second City alum, Barbara Harris, along with Alan Alda and Larry Blyden. After the performances, Klein began dropping by a club near the theater district, which David Steinberg had told him about, and made another try at stand-up.

The Improvisation had been opened three years earlier by Budd Friedman, a pudgy Bronx native and Korean War veteran who went to work in advertising. When his dreams of becoming a Broadway producer weren't panning out, he rented a former Vietnamese restaurant on Forty-fourth Street and Ninth Avenue, stripped the walls down to the bare brick, and turned it into a club for the showbiz crowd. He and his wife, Silver, a Broadway chorus girl who was appearing in *How to Succeed in Business Without Really Trying*, invited all their theater friends to drop by after their shows were over, have a couple of drinks, and maybe get up onstage and entertain.

By the time Robert Klein started coming there in 1966, the Improv had become a popular hangout for comedians. Ruling the roost was a former aluminum siding salesman who had started out doing stand-up under the name Jack Roy, left the business to raise a family, and was making an unlikely comeback calling himself Rodney Dangerfield. When Dangerfield first walked into the club, after a well-reviewed engagement at the Living Room, Friedman says he "expected to see a guy right out of Princeton, and this middle-aged drunk showed up. He didn't want to get up [onstage]. I told him, I'll buy you a bottle of wine. He always told the story that I bought him for a bottle of wine." Dangerfield soon became the club's regular emcee.

Dangerfield was a larger-than-life character, a man of manic energy, dark depressions, and consuming appetites. Friedman recalls a Thanksgiving dinner at Jerry Stiller and Anne Meara's house when Dangerfield had too many martinis and fell asleep over the turkey. After dinner he woke up, went into the kitchen, and began attacking the carcass so ravenously that the caterer ran out to complain. Dangerfield drank lavishly, drove a car like a maniac, and smoked pot before most of the pot generation was born. But when it came to comedy, he was a disciplined pro. Weeks before he had a guest spot on *The Ed Sullivan Show* or *The Tonight Show*, he would gather new jokes—jotting them down on the shirt cardboard from his dry cleaner, testing them onstage night after night, crafting a surefire five minutes. And though he was a classic "necklace" comic—stringing disconnected one-liners together—he was hip to the new wave too. He especially liked Robert Klein.

"You were brilliant, man. And I'm a tough cocksucker," Dangerfield told the younger comic the first time he saw him. "He took me under his wing," says Klein. "He was my Yale Drama School for comedy." Klein and Dangerfield became close—pupil and teacher, son and surrogate father. Klein would even jokingly call him "Pop," until Dangerfield told him to knock it off. Klein learned from Dangerfield—how to handle the microphone, how to size up an audience and deal with hecklers. He hung out with Dangerfield, watched him work, smoked pot with him. In Cape Cod once,

Dangerfield insisted that he and Klein take out a sailboat, even though neither knew a thing about sailing. Out on the ocean, Dangerfield impulsively
jumped off the boat for a swim. By the time a frantic Klein maneuvered
the boat back to him, he had almost drowned.

Klein became a regular at the Improv bar, hanging out with the crowd of
young comedians, cabaret singers, waitresses with dreams, and gong-show
contestants looking for a stage. "I used to go to the club every single night,
park my car right on the block there," says Klein. "I began having friends
there, meeting people and other performers. I got laid about four trillion
times. I was happy to have lived through the sexual revolution. And at the
Improv I met many ardent female revolutionaries." Among the comedians
he met there was Richard Pryor, who was already getting guest spots on
The Merv Griffin Show. Klein did improvs with him and quizzed him
about his career. Pryor told Klein he thought they developed their comedy
onstage in very much the same way. Klein was impressed with the ingrati-
ating young comic in his white collegiate sweaters. One night, outside the
club, Klein saw Pryor fly into a rage and slap his girlfriend around—and
realized there were sides to Pryor he didn't know.

Klein developed fast at the Improv. Friedman was a big fan—and not
just because Klein got the cast of *The Apple Tree* to come into the club one
night to see him. "I loved his material, that edgy, intellectual approach,"
says Friedman. "He knew he was the club favorite." Klein talked about his
Bronx childhood, his '50s school days, old TV shows—memories that he
rendered in crisply evocative word pictures. His old public school teachers,
for example:

> They had these sort of older women who had gone to normal school in
> 1899, graduated in two years, took religion and first aid. They gave
> them each a bun in the back—a chignon—a large black dress, and Boy
> Scout shoes and sent them into schools to say, "No talking!"

He relived the trauma, for a child of the cold war, of civil-defense drills in
the 1950s, with air-raid sirens that went off every day at noon ("I used to
second-guess, what if the Russians *bombed* at twelve o'clock?") and the
dog tags distributed to students, rumored to be able to withstand the heat
of a nuclear explosion:

> Children, no talking! Take these tags home, they're to be used in the event
> that you're burnt beyond recognition in a nuclear holocaust. And no talk-
> ing *during* a nuclear holocaust! I want an *orderly* nuclear holocaust.

Klein was one of the first comedians to tap into the nostalgia of baby boomers, just then starting to get out of college. But he also played on one of the major themes of the '60s youth rebellion: a rejection of the benighted politics and moral authoritarianism of the '50s. And he did it in a style that captured the beat and energy of rock 'n' roll: fast, free-associating, jumping in and out of voices, narrating and acting at the same time. When he marveled at New Yorkers who fish in the Hudson River, he became the tough New York fish that might emerge from the water: "Get that hook outta my mouth, you idiot! Twenty years dodging tugboats, I'm gonna fall for that hook, you rube?" In a takeoff of the old *Our Gang* comedies, he nailed everything from the laboriously amateurish kid actors ("I don' wanna go to *school* today!") to the endlessly repeating loop of Hal Roach background music. He loved throwing in snatches of doo-wop or the blues, sometimes accompanying himself on the harmonica. ("He was a much better musician than he ever let on," says Bette Midler, another Improv regular in those years. "He could have gone either way.") His references were smart, even esoteric. Only Klein could build a routine out of encyclopedia entries for an obscure American president, James A. Garfield, and not come off as a snob:

It always says the same thing. You read his name, it says, "Shot by a disappointed office seeker." You get a child's milk container collection of the presidents, it says: "George Washington, father of his country . . . Abraham Lincoln, Emancipation Proclamation . . . Thomas Jefferson, purchased Louisiana . . . James Abram Garfield, shot by a disappointed office seeker." You look in the encyclopedia under "Garfield, James Abram," it says, "See 'Office Seeker, Disappointed.' "

Listening to Lenny Bruce on records (Klein never saw him perform), he had discovered that the comedian could be a social commentator as well. "I came out with a kind of arrogance. I wanted to be more than a cuff link guy," Klein says, referring to the old-time comics in their crisp formal wear. "I had an education. I was intelligent. I wanted to say something." His other comic hero was Jonathan Winters, who broke down the traditional monologue into a mélange of voices and free-association nuttiness. To them Klein added a new twist: the performance techniques he had learned from Paul Sills at Second City. Sills taught that the actor should not impose his ideas on a scene, but simply react to the here and now—to the other actors onstage at the moment. Doing stand-up comedy, Klein liked to think of the audience as the other actor; his routines evolved, night after night, according to the reaction he got from the crowd. Klein began taping all his performances on a Wollensak reel-to-reel recorder (as he had seen Joan Rivers do). He'd listen to them afterward, throwing out what didn't work and refining what did, shaping his material the way the Second City players had pounded sketches from rough improvisations into comedy jewels.

Rodney Dangerfield convinced Jack Rollins, the most respected comedy manager in the business, to come see Klein at the Improv. Rollins decided to take him on as a client after one viewing. "The first time I saw him I wanted to represent him," says Rollins. "The big thing to me was that he was observing reality, not just telling jokes. It was commentary on behavior, social commentary. He was introducing a fresh approach."

Getting Rollins to manage him was a big step for Klein. Rollins was already something of a legend, famous for discovering new talent and guiding careers. Years earlier, while working for theatrical producer Max Gordon, he had taken on a struggling cabaret singer named Harry Belafonte, retooled his act with old songs excavated from John Hammond's library of American folk music, and made him a star. He took Mike Nichols and Elaine May, a satirical duo from Chicago who no one thought had commercial potential, and turned them into one of the hottest acts in comedy. And he convinced a nervous young comedy writer named Woody Allen that he ought to try performing his own material, babysat him through stage fright so bad he would throw up before performances, and helped shape a unique comedy career. He was picky about clients (Dangerfield was among those he had turned down) but devoted to the few he had, a shrewd critic of material, and a sympathetic hand-holder. "OK, lad, you fouled out," he might say to a comic coming off a bad club appearance—then stay up with him all night to try to figure out why. "You had to find excuses to get to bed," says Dick Cavett, another of Rollins's discoveries. "No one knew when Jack slept."

In the shark-infested waters of New York showbiz, Rollins was an anomaly. He smoked big cigars and liked going to the track (only betting on the trotters, and rarely more than two dollars), but had a gentlemanly, sweet-natured bearing and a foggy, absentminded-professor air that the comics loved to imitate. He and Cavett once were shaken up in a cab accident, and Jack took quick action to get them to the hospital. Hearing about it later, Woody Allen quipped, "He must have been knocked cogent." Rollins was sometimes better at discovering talent than keeping it; he never forgave Belafonte for leaving him after the singer's therapist (as Rollins tells the story) advised him to switch managers—to the therapist's husband. But he was a man of clout and class; his firm, Rollins and Joffe, had plush, high-ceilinged offices on Fifty-seventh Street and displayed a hand-quilted sign reading, DON'T EMBARRASS THE OFFICE. "We all wanted to be Jack Rollins, to have that dignity," says Bernie Brillstein, who managed a later generation of comedy stars like Chevy Chase and Gilda Radner. "He stood above everyone. After him, it became a business."

Rollins's first advice for Klein, however, was to turn down work. On the same night that Rollins saw Klein at the Improv, scouts from *The Merv Griffin Show* were there too and offered the comedian five guest appearances on the spot. Though Griffin's show had been an important launching pad for both Carlin and Pryor, Rollins advised Klein to say no; he thought his new client's TV debut should make a bigger splash. And a few weeks later, he had one lined up: a commitment for three guest appearances on *The Dean Martin Show*, one of the top-rated variety shows on TV.

Klein put together his best material ("Never mind the intellectual shit," Dangerfield told him; "it's fuckin' America here") and flew out with Rollins to Los Angeles. Arriving at the Beverly Hills Hotel, however, they were told that Martin's producer, Greg Garrison, wanted to see a run-through of Klein's routines in his office first. Performing in front of Garrison and three other staffers, Klein felt lost; jokes that had killed at the Improv were greeted with dead silence. When he was through, Garrison simply rapped on the table with his palms—a lame substitute for applause—and asked to see Rollins alone. When he returned, Rollins had to break the news that Garrison didn't think Klein was ready. His TV debut was canceled.

Klein was crushed. Rollins consoled him with a drink at the Polo Lounge. But it was only a temporary setback. After picking up some gigs at nightclubs like Mr. Kelly's and the hungry i, Klein landed a spot on Johnny Carson's *Tonight Show* in January 1968.

It was the start of the most tumultuous year of the '60s protest era. Yet on television, the '60s were just beginning to happen. Carlin still had short hair; the Smothers Brothers' big battles against the CBS censors were yet to come; the three top-rated series on network TV were *The Andy Griffith Show*, *The Lucy Show*, and *Gomer Pyle, U.S.M.C.* A comedian with even Klein's moderately shaggy hair and new-generation attitude was enough of a shock to the system that Rollins struck an unusual deal with *The Tonight Show* producers: Klein was brought onto the guest couch to talk with Johnny *before* his stand-up act, so the audience could "get to know him." Klein thought the sit-down session was a bust, but his routine about his substitute-teaching days killed. Soon Klein was appearing on Carson's show nearly once a month, learning how to make his material work for an audience much broader than the crowd that filled the tables at the Improv. "If I was going to have a career on *The Tonight Show*," he realized, "I couldn't be talking past people."

Klein's stand-up was hip and pointed—but a slicker, soft-rock alternative to the harder-edged comedy of Carlin and Pryor. He mastered the art of sneaking social criticism into funny, beautifully crafted parodies and personal stories. He lampooned bad commercials, not just for their silliness, but also for their misplaced values: the sexist Geritol ads ("My wife—I think I'll keep her"), self-righteous oil companies touting their concern for the environment, insecticide commercials in which cute bugs party away until the fascist Raid bottle shows up: "It's a typical American kill mentality: to personalize them, make them humanlike, make me love them—and then annihilate them." Klein's story of saving a kid from drowning at the summer resort where he was a lifeguard turned into a metaphysical exploration: the boy's parents tipped him five dollars. Mused Klein: "How'd they come up with the figure?" [*Father, calculating:*] "I don't know, how long have we *had* the boy?" His account of the kid in a school assembly who accidentally dropped the American flag became a critique of our reverence for patriotic symbols. "They imbue the flag with a special power beyond itself . . . Children fantasize George Washington's gonna pop out—[*furious founding father:*] "Hey, you drop me? After all I suffered at Valley Forge, you little Jewboy?"

By 1970 Klein was big enough to host a summer-replacement series on CBS, *Comedy Tonight*—a *Laugh-In*-style hour with an ensemble cast featuring Peter Boyle and Madeline Kahn—and later that year he opened for Barbra Streisand at the Las Vegas Hilton. In Vegas, however, Klein realized—as Pryor and Carlin had, though somewhat more dramatically— that much of the mainstream audience still wasn't ready for him. "I had a natural disinclination toward Vegas," says Klein. "I had a lot of trouble in that engagement. My shows were inconsistent. And I was not that experienced that I could fight my way out of it." One night a drunk in the crowd threw a straw at him and he stormed off the stage, cutting short his routine and enraging Streisand's manager because the star had to go on early. (Streisand later defended him.) Dangerfield came to one of his shows and brought along Jack Benny. When Klein used the word *shit*, Benny turned to Dangerfield and said, "The kid works dirty." When Dangerfield repeated the comment to Klein later, Klein was mortified.

Yet Klein was also having trouble breaking through with the college crowd. Compared with Carlin's long hair and drug references, Klein seemed a little too safe and showbizzy. He worked hard to change that impression, auditioning for college bookers and sending out hundreds of promotional pieces ("Robert Klein will make you laugh—and sometimes think"), but got little response. Then, after Carlin's *FM & AM* album was a surprise hit in 1972, Klein shelled out $7,500 of his own money to record a performance at the Bitter End. That earned him a record deal on the new Brut label, started by the fragrance company Fabergé. Klein's first album, *Child of the '50s*, was released in April 1973.

It wasn't as big of a hit as Carlin's, but it gave Klein's career the boost it needed. Over the next couple of years he was one of the hottest acts in stand-up. He played Carnegie Hall (with all the tickets priced at a low three dollars to ensure a sellout), and the college bookings started to come. He followed *Child of the '50s* with two more albums, *Mind over Matter* (1974) and *New Teeth* (1975). When HBO launched its influential *On Location* series of comedy concerts, Klein was the comedian it turned to first—taping his performance at Haverford College in early December and airing it on New Year's Eve 1975. He returned to old haunts like the Bitter End in triumph— a big, beetle-browed, high-voltage performer who looked like your favorite college T.A., and, when he was on a roll, probably delivered more quality laughs per minute than any comedian working. Steve Martin, who was still struggling to find his footing as a stand-up comedian, saw Klein around this time at a smoky club in Philadelphia that was so packed he had to stand in the back. "He was just hot," says Martin. "I was nowhere near that level of intelligence, tightness."

For the next generation of stand-up wannabes, who saw him on TV and heard his records, Klein was the crucial inspiration—someone they could both relate to and learn from. Jay Leno was doing comedy at Boston strip clubs when he first saw Klein on TV. "He was the first comedian that spoke to me," says Leno. "A middle-class kid whose father yelled the way my father yelled, who didn't have a hook—the black guy or the Jewish guy. He was just a funny guy." Jerry Seinfeld, who studied comics on *The Ed Sullivan Show* from his childhood living room in Massapequa, New York, saw something new in Klein: "I loved Jackie Mason and Alan King, but they were like my parents' friends. And he was a guy that reminded me of *my* friends. I understood that kind of funny. The references were contemporary and intelligent. He wasn't afraid of going over the audience's head." Says Paul Reiser, another Long Island kid soon to be working the New York clubs: "Even George Carlin was not quite as accessible. Klein was a guy who made it seem like we could do it."

It was not just Klein's subject matter but also his style that they began to imitate. Carlin transferred his routines from the page to the stage fully formed, improvising little. Pryor developed his material in performance like Klein, but preferred sustained scenes, character pieces, and autobiographical monologues. Klein picked up the pace and multiplied the voices—a style closer, really, to Bruce's stream-of-consciousness riffing but with more shape and coherence. A visit to an all-night deli, for instance, became a one-minute slice of New York street life, with Klein playing all the parts, starting with the hostile West Indian sandwich maker:

> "You want lettuce, mon? Oh, you want pickle *too*, huh, mon? Oh, you want *two* pieces of bread . . ." Just a mean guy, hates his work. Funny company there, four in the morning. A lot of people scratching their necks—[*Stoned-out junkie:*] "Oooh, give me four thousand Hershey bars and a pack of Camels." Allergic apparently, scratching his arm. They like sweets a lot, the junkies. [*All-business junkie:*] "Gimme three Yoo-hoos, twelve Pepsis, a pound of sugar, and a pack of Camels." [*Another junkie:*] "Gimme seventeen Devil Dogs, three Hostess Twinkies, fourteen tons of brown sugar, and a pack of Camels . . ."

Klein packed his monologues with impressions, jokes, snippets of scenes, characters, song. Sometimes he'd elide words and phrases, leaping ahead as if he couldn't wait for the laugh. Or he'd stretch out a thought, landing hard on key words and pushing the hyperbole to drive home the joke. He loved the absurdist exaggeration, the incongruous juxtaposition. Lots of comics did parodies of commercials; Klein's were the sharpest. His takeoff of greatest-hits record collections, for instance:

> Now you can get every record ever recorded! Yes, in this one-time-only, mixed-bag special, every record ever recorded! From the same people who brought you *Hits of '51, '52, Hungarian Love Songs, Songs That Begin with the Letter "P"*—every record ever recorded. We mean literally that: we drive a truck to your house and deliver *every single record ever recorded!* You get classical—*Ich habe genung*, Cantata 82, by Bach. [*Mournful vocal:*] "*Ich habe genung . . .*" Johnny Cash "I Walk the Line." Lithuanian language records—[*teacher reciting:*] "*Sessu*, yes. *Sessu*, yes. *Sessu*, yes . . ."

Or his re-creation of those guilt-inducing late-night public-service ads:

> [*Silky voiced announcer with British accent:*] "One-hundred twenty-six unfortunate Americans suffer from Jurgen's myasthenia, a dreaded disease in which the nose mysteriously slides off. There is no known cure for Jurgen's myasthenia. But there is hope . . ." [*Klein, exasperated:*] Aw, Jeez, hope! Are you kidding me, hope? They don't even have the

laboratory set up for this one yet! [*Businesslike doctor:*] "I think put the Bunsen burners in here . . ."

These were gems of comedy writing and performance, stripped to the bone and sealed with the killer detail—the pack of Camels, the Bunsen burner. Klein went after the Watergate scandal with the same kind of impassioned, hyperbolic, acted-out style. He lampooned former presidential secretary Rose Mary Woods, who claimed she accidentally erased the key portion of Nixon's Oval Office tapes ("We are from a circus family, Your Honor"), and the infamous John Stennis compromise, a proposal that the seventy-two-year-old senator from Mississippi be the only person allowed to hear the tapes. "What a brilliant maneuver in history that was. Why couldn't the tapes record that? When President Nixon said to Alexander Haig, 'Al, get me a deaf senator. I'll do the rest.'" Vice President Spiro Agnew's resignation in the wake of bribery charges brought out Klein's finest outrage:

He was the law and order cat—"There's too much permissiveness!" Permissiveness—oh, my lord! All I know, if I get caught robbing an A&P, I want—"The Agnew punishment, please. I think I'll opt for that . . . According to my calculations, you owe *me* sixty days."

Topical late-night monologuists from Jay Leno to Jon Stewart have been using Klein's satiric template ever since.

Even at his peak, however, Klein never got the acclaim of Pryor or had the counterculture credibility of Carlin. "Klein's comedy isn't radical. He's safe," pronounced *Rolling Stone* in an otherwise complimentary 1973 profile. Even among the people who helped build his career, there was a feeling that something was missing. "For about two years there was no one better," says Buddy Morra, the Rollins and Joffe manager who took over Klein's career when Jack Rollins went into semiretirement. But he remembers Rollins's rueful assessment when walking out of a Klein concert in the mid-'70s: "Effective, but not winning."

Klein, meanwhile, seemed caught between his craving for acceptance by the young, hip crowd and unhappiness at his lack of mainstream stardom. He landed a few movie roles in the early '70s, in films like *The Landlord* and *The Owl and the Pussycat*, but his Hollywood career never went anywhere. He was offered the part Wayne Rogers eventually played in the TV version of *MASH* in 1973, but with his stand-up career just gaining heat, he turned it down. He had high hopes for a 1977 sketch-comedy pilot for

CBS, *Klein Time*, but the network's meddling irked him (censors nixed a sketch in which he showed a film of paramecia reproducing, to the strains of Bread's "[I'd Like to] Make It with You"), and he was brokenhearted when the show wasn't picked up. He refused to move to Los Angeles, where most of the TV and movie work was, preferring to remain in New York with his wife, opera singer Brenda Boozer, whom he married in 1973. He had some success on Broadway—he was nominated for a Tony Award for his costarring role (with Lucie Arnaz) in the 1979 Neil Simon–Marvin Hamlisch musical *They're Playing Our Song*. But by the start of the '80s, his stand-up career had stagnated.

Klein's career frustrations grew, and he put some of the blame on his managers. The days when Jack Rollins would hold his hand in the Polo Lounge were long past. The Rollins and Joffe agency had turned into a formidable machine. Charlie Joffe, Rollins's partner, had opened an of-fice in Los Angeles and was concentrating on movies. New members of the firm were bringing in hot new clients like Billy Crystal and Robin Williams—who seemed to Klein to be getting most of the attention.

The team at Rollins and Joffe had their own complaints about Klein. Some thought he was coasting, not coming up with enough new material. He could be demanding and petulant. "He was not easy to live with," Morra says. "He could be his own worst enemy." Larry Brezner, who managed Robin Williams, recounts a phone call in which Klein lamented missing out on the costarring role in *MASH*. When Brezner pointed out that Klein himself turned it down, he says, Klein shot back: "You should have made me take it." (Klein insists he had no second thoughts about the *MASH* decision. He had more regrets about turning down another offer a few years later: the starring role in *Night Court*, which made Harry An-derson a star.)

Klein also thought Rollins and Joffe had something to do with his cool relations with the TV show that might have helped rejuvenate his comedy career in the late '70s, *Saturday Night Live*. Klein was one of the show's first guest hosts (the second stand-up comedian to front the show, after Carlin). But he was clearly not one of producer Lorne Michaels's favorites—which Klein blamed at least partly on an incident from the very first show, one that had nothing to do with him.

Among the scheduled guests on that debut show was Billy Crystal, a twenty-six-year-old comedian from Long Island who had, until a few months earlier, been working as part of a comedy trio. Jack Rollins and Buddy Morra liked the group but thought Crystal was the real talent, and when he got a solo gig to entertain at a fraternity house at NYU, they trekked downtown in a cold rain to see him. Within days, Crystal was split from the group and being managed by Rollins and Joffe. ("I felt like I had cheated on my two friends," says Crystal. "But we had been together four or five years, and we weren't going anyplace.") In short order he got a potentially career-making gig: a stand-up spot on the first episode of NBC's much-anticipated new comedy show.

During the chaotic first week of rehearsals, however, with the show running hopelessly long, Michaels told Crystal his five-and-a-half-minute spot had to be cut to two minutes. Morra, Billy's rep at the show, refused, saying it would gut his routine—an elaborate African-safari bit. The dispute got heated. Morra thought Michaels was reneging on promises that had been made to Crystal, who had passed up a Bill Cosby special to do the show. Michaels resented that Morra seemed to be trying to produce the show over his shoulder—suggesting that Andy Kaufman, who had another spot on the show, be cut instead. At an impasse, just a few hours before the live broadcast, Morra took his client and walked out.

Crystal was in shock. For years he would tell the story of his lonely train ride back to Long Island, crestfallen, to face his disappointed family. But Klein thought the incident had another unintended victim: Robert Klein. He was convinced the bad blood between Michaels and his managers hurt his own standing on *Saturday Night Live*. To be sure, Lorne Michaels was no fan of the Rollins-Joffe machine; he thought they were too controlling and high-handed, often making decisions for their clients without even consulting them. Still, his reservations about Klein went well beyond his management team. Though he recognized Klein was a better sketch performer than Carlin (and did invite Klein back to host once more, in the show's third season), Michaels thought he had too much of a whiff of old showbiz. "Lorne didn't want him," says Morra. "He thought he wasn't 'vulnerable.'"

The tensions between Klein and his managers came to a head in 1981 when Klein was doing a special weekend gig at the Improvisation in Los Angeles, which Budd Friedman had opened in 1975. After one of his shows, as friends and celebrities gathered in Friedman's upstairs office to congratulate him, Charlie Joffe walked in. "Kleinsie, you were brilliant tonight," he said, as Klein tells the story. "But you make me furious. You were on *The Tonight Show* last night and you used old material."

Klein blew up. On the show, Carson had asked if Klein remembered his very first *Tonight Show* routine, and Klein had repeated part of his old substitute-teacher bit. Joffe had been little involved in Klein's career and had a well-known drug problem at the time; Klein questioned whether he had even seen the whole segment. "You make *me* furious, Charlie," Klein shouted, as a hush fell over the room. "You come in here, you can't even stand up. You haven't done anything for my career in a dozen years. And you come in here with your advice!" What was worse, says Klein, was that his wife, Brenda, chimed in and backed Joffe—though in private she had been urging him to break with his managers. "She said, 'Charlie is right; you should listen to his advice.' It was a complete knife in the back."

Klein parted ways with Rollins and Joffe shortly after that. Klein says it ended amicably. "I was saving myself fifteen percent of my salary, and a lot of aggravation. Because I used to resent them. They're busy making a fortune with these other guys who came in after me. And I didn't want to get into a sibling thing—what about me?—but that's what it amounted to." His rocky marriage lasted a little longer. He and Brenda had a son in 1983, reconciled for a few years, then started divorce proceedings in 1987—a two-year battle that Klein called "pure torment," giving him ulcers and affecting his work. On one *Tonight Show* appearance during that time, he appeared so bitter over his marital problems that the producers scratched him from the guest list for more than a year.

Klein never stopped doing stand-up—returning to *The Tonight Show*, doing regular HBO specials, popping up in an occasional sitcom or Broadway role—but there was a sense of disappointment among those around him about a career that never quite fulfilled its promise. "He stayed the same and the country got used to it," says Joffe, "and that was it." Rollins, Klein's old mentor, was more charitable: "He never got that big break, that out-of-left-field stroke of luck," he says. "He's one of the most underrated comedians I've ever seen. Among young comics, he was the trendsetter—more than the public knows."

Klein himself had regrets: that he never could fill concert halls as consistently as Carlin; that he didn't make a real mark in movies; that he missed out on the big TV series that might have boosted his profile, and his paychecks. In later years he became something of an éminence grise for the younger generation of comics, many of whom surpassed his fame. For a short but crucial period in the '70s though, Klein was arguably the most influential comedian in America. He made stand-up comedy hip and relevant and accessible for that vast group of younger comics who weren't ready to storm the barricades like Carlin and who didn't have the autobiographical raw material of Pryor. He devised a smart and supple form of expression that was capable of tackling everything from the most controversial issues to the most disposable trivia. For a new cadre of comedians who began to haunt the New York comedy club where he had got his start, Klein's comedy became the house style.

CHAPTER 5

Clubbing

I left my shrink too soon; I had to take an incomplete.

—Richard Lewis

The Improvisation was just a long block away from the bright lights of Broadway. But with a butcher shop just around the corner on Ninth Avenue and a lumber yard next door, it hardly seemed the setting for Budd Friedman's show business dreams. When you walked in the door, on the right was a small bar and on the left a showroom not quite deserving of the name, with a bare brick wall behind the vest-pocket stage. In the passageway between the bar and the showroom was a tiny restroom—so grungy, Robert Klein liked to say, "you put paper on the door when you went *in*."

Only seventy-four people could fit at the cramped wooden tables, and for the first year and a half Friedman didn't even have a liquor license. But the club became a magnet for young talent. Liza Minnelli, still a teenager, would come in and sing, sometimes with her mother, Judy Garland, and later on with her first husband, Peter Allen, accompanying her at the piano. Bette Midler, who was playing one of Tevye's daughters in *Fiddler on the Roof*, would sing old Mae West numbers or goof on ditties like "She'll Be Comin' 'Round the Mountain," doing it over and over again in different styles, from Latin to country. Dustin Hoffman sometimes played the piano. Danny Aiello was the doorman, bouncer, and occasional backup singer. Friedman himself, sporting a goatee and occasionally affecting a monocle, would ham it up as emcee—calling himself "your charming, bearded host."

But it wasn't long before stand-up comics took over the place. The Pied Piper, as Friedman recalls it, was a comedian named Dave Astor, who had a brief moment in the early '60s as one of the hot young stand-ups on the New York nightclub scene. Astor, who did New Frontier–era wisecracks about the First Family ("Caroline Kennedy, absolutely brilliant child . . . of course, her father is never, ever gonna let her plan another invasion"), beat poetry, and the nuclear arms race, was appearing at the Blue Angel, the hip midtown club where Nichols and May had got their start, when he began dropping by the Improv.

"He was very well respected by the other comedians," says Friedman. "They would all come to see him at the Blue Angel, and he'd bring them over to the Improv. He loved the place." More comedians began to drop in: old-schoolers like Jackie Vernon, the sad-sack one-liner guy, who would sit at a table with his writers until Friedman could coax him on-stage; newcomers like Dick Cavett, a writer for *The Tonight Show* trying out a stand-up act, with jokes so highbrow they sometimes went over Friedman's head. (He went to a party, Cavett quipped, that was so expensive the caviar was flown in all the way from Beluga.) There was David Frye, a choleric impressionist becoming well known for his LBJ and Nixon impressions, and Lily Tomlin, making an uneasy stab at stand-up in between her cabaret gigs across town, and especially Robert Klein, who started working there in 1966 and continued to use the club as home base, even as he broke through to national TV stardom.

It was a new kind of club, a "showcase" for new talent: no headliners, no billing—and for many years, no pay. Friedman wasn't much of a businessman, but he stumbled on a business model of symbiotic ingeniousness. He got his talent to perform for free. In exchange, they got a workshop where they could hone their acts, try out new material, and get seen by the agents and managers and bookers who were coming in with growing frequency. Friedman would audition the comics himself and put together the nightly lineups on the fly. The Darwinian rules of the place were pretty clear. The proven laugh-getters got the prime spots, between ten and midnight. The newcomers would be relegated to the wee hours, when the crowds were sparse and they could bomb with relative impunity. And any of them could get bumped if a visiting dignitary, like Bill Cosby or Milton Berle, happened to drop in and could be enticed onstage.

Because they had to wait around for Friedman's nod, the comics spent a lot of time hanging out at the bar. It became both holding pen and social center for the comedians—a place to critique each other's material, grumble about time slots, and maybe pick up a waitress or comedy groupie for the night. Friedman liked to call himself the "benevolent dictator" of the place—though not everyone was so sure about the benevolent part. He was tight with a buck, had a temper, and patrolled the club like a stern school principal, continually ordering customers and the comedians to "get out of the aisle."

"He was a hard-core boss," says Danny Aiello, a former union leader at Greyhound who had lost his job after a wildcat strike and got hired by Friedman for $190 a week off the books to work as doorman. "He didn't take any shit from anybody. There was an arrogance about him. But he was very protective of his people onstage." Aiello was there the night Bette Midler got into a shouting match with an unruly woman in the audience, who then threw a glass of wine in Midler's face. After Midler fled the stage, Budd kicked out the customer, grabbed the microphone, and told the crowd to help him get the singer to come back. She returned in tears, apologized, and went on with the show. "I think it was a put-on," says Aiello. "But at that moment I said to myself, this woman is going to be big."

As the keeper of the nightly lineup, Friedman was loved or hated by the comics roughly according to how well he treated them. One young comedian with a beef against Friedman was David Brenner, a former news producer from Philadelphia who moved to New York and began doing stand-up in the Village in the late '60s. He fumed that Friedman would put him on only late at night or when the club was dead—and that he charged twenty-five cents for a Coke at the bar but upped it to seventy-five cents if you took it into the showroom. "He was Shylock," says Brenner. "He never stopped being a bastard."

Ed Bluestone, a dyspeptic former *National Lampoon* writer, struggled with his performing and often griped about being relegated to the late-night no-man's-land. "If you had ten minutes that didn't work too well, you'd have to sit there and wait, and he'd put you on last, when there were, like, two tables that were falling asleep," says Bluestone. "Sometimes you'd get angry and rationalize that it's not your fault. But he was a pretty fair guy. I would say, like most people in show business, his interest in you was in exact proportion to how he could use you at the moment." Friedman was "the only game in town, and he didn't have to kiss anybody's ass," says Bob Shaw, a University of Rhode Island grad who was an Improv regular in the mid-'70s. "If you did something he didn't like—you did Folk City in the Village and didn't make your time by ten minutes—he'd berate you and put you on last for two weeks. But when you heard him laugh, this guy who really knew comedy, who had seen everyone—oh my God, it was from heaven."

Friedman admits he could be "a son of a bitch in those days," something he blames on the pressures of trying to keep his hand-to-mouth operation from going under. "I was uptight. It was nerve-racking. I never knew if I was going to be there the next day financially. I had never run a business before, especially a restaurant business, and I was growing into it." He tried more lucrative angles—for a while managing some of the talent he discovered, like Midler, whom he helped get many of her early TV guest appearances, and a brash young comic from Boston named Jay Leno. But he gave it up, Friedman says, because he couldn't stand the "babysitting." He had been running the Improv for ten years before he felt financially secure enough even to take a vacation.

"He was an original," says Robert Klein. "A very strong-willed man. He could lose his temper. He wasn't afraid of throwing somebody out of the club. But he was a guy from the Bronx who had a great idea. He wanted to be Rick from *Casablanca*." Emily Levine, one of the few women on the Improv scene in those early years—a member of the New York Stickball Team, an improv group that performed at the club in 1969 and '70—recalls him as "an indulgent but strict father. He had his little principles: 'You can never blame the audience. It's a poor workman who blames his tools.' I give him a lot of credit. He created something that had not been in existence before, and he really made it work."

"I found his passion for stand-up to be almost boundless," says Richard Lewis, one of Friedman's favorites in the early '70s. "His approval meant everything. He had the right to choose who he liked. For every one of me, there were scores he wouldn't let on and who hated him. There was a touch of arrogance about him that kept this aesthetic distance. He was such an important person for everyone that he had to have that arrogance because the flipside of it was he would have been crushed by a mob of hungry comedians."

Lewis was one of the hungriest of the comics who formed the core of the post–Robert Klein class of Improv regulars in the early '70s—a group that also included Steve Landesberg, Jimmie Walker, Ed Bluestone, Freddie Prinze, Andy Kaufman, and Elayne Boosler. They were a small, close-knit group, and they saw themselves as pioneers. "There were only fifteen or twenty of us recognized as being top of the line, getting regular spots at the Improv and the better showcases," says Lewis. "We watched each other's acts; we helped each other; we supported one another. It was a magical time for my generation, from '71 on, because we were all in some kind of new experiment. We were trying to break through the mold of the old Catskills-type of comedians. And yet we weren't big enough to be recognized as celebrities. So we were in a rarefied state."

They were early baby boomers who had grown up watching the classic comedians from TV's golden age—Red Skelton, Sid Caesar, Jack Benny, Jackie Gleason—as well as the new-wave stand-ups like Bob Newhart and Shelley Berman and Woody Allen. Then, as college kids in the late '60s, they saw Carlin, Pryor, and Klein begin to do comedy that seemed more relevant and socially engaged, stand-up that was influenced by Lenny Bruce but reflected the attitudes and experiences of a new generation.

Bruce's social-political passion, however, was fast receding. The '60s youth revolution had run its course, the Vietnam War was winding down, and these new comedians were less intent on changing the world than in figuring out how to get along in it. They joked about riding the subway and going grocery shopping; growing up in the suburbs and getting into trouble in school; watching bad TV shows and poking fun at stupid commercials; asking girls out on dates and trying not to embarrass yourself during sex. Because they were working stiffs themselves—living in cheap studio apartments, taking part-time jobs to make ends meet—they brought a grounded, accessible, workaday reality to their comedy. They were the Me Generation comics. And the Me Generation embraced them.

Richard Lewis's path was typical. Raised in New Jersey, the son of a caterer, he worshipped rock 'n' roll gods like Jimi Hendrix and John Lennon before a professor at Ohio State, where he was majoring in marketing, turned him on to Lenny Bruce. Determined to get into comedy, Lewis headed back to New York after graduation and tried to get a job writing jokes for Robert Klein. When Klein informed the youngster that he wrote all his own material, Lewis instead began churning out gags for Catskills jokesters like Morty Gunty. Then, frustrated that his best lines were the ones getting thrown back, he decided to try performing himself—spurred on also by the death of his father, whose fatal heart attack following a series of business reverses left Lewis, he says, with a "sudden blackness that propelled me onstage."

He would drive in from Hasbrouck Heights and hang out at the Improv bar, where he got friendly with David Brenner. Despite Budd Friedman's snubbing of him, Brenner was already having some success on television. After a *Tonight Show* producer saw his act at the Bitter End and pronounced it "vomit material," Brenner cleaned up his material and dedicated himself to getting on Carson's show. In early January 1971, two weeks after auditioning for the show, he got a call from a *Tonight* booker asking if he could be ready to go on the following night. Brenner replied with the old line from movie westerns: "I was born ready." He quickly became a Carson favorite.

Brenner gave Lewis some advice: before taking a crack at the Improv, he should get experience in some of the more low-rent Village dives first.

So Lewis went downtown to the Champagne Gallery, a scruffy joint he had seen in the Joe Bologna–Renee Taylor movie *Made for Each Other*. It was a suitably obscure proving ground for a neurotic kid from New Jersey who had no idea if he could make people laugh. "There was a good chance that one out of every two acts were lunatics," Lewis recalls. "A guy would walk on with a seal—it was almost Felliniesque. So it wasn't like there was a lot of pressure." Then in June of 1971, he tried out on open-mike night at the Improv. "I blew the roof off," says Lewis. "Budd Friedman walked on the stage, put his arm around me, and said, 'We found our new rookie of the year.'"

Lewis didn't give himself much time to savor his big moment. When Friedman asked if he wanted to stick around for the regular show and do another set, Lewis said yes—then waited around until two A.M., bombed in front of the few drunks left in the audience, and ended the night in despair. "Rather than go out and celebrate with my girlfriend at Mamma Leone's, I just got carried away. Instead of driving home absolutely euphoric, I came back wearing that feeling of, I bombed. Then I realized what was ahead of me. For the showcase, I was tops. For the real show, I was in the coal mines."

He spent years in those mines, working at Friedman's club at night and supporting himself with three jobs during the day. Finally, he told Brenner that he wished he could chuck them all and be a full-time comedian. Brenner asked Lewis what it would take. A grand, Lewis replied. Brenner wrote a check for a thousand dollars on the spot. "Here, you're a full-time comedian," he said. Lewis never forgot it. (Brenner apparently did. He says he never carried a checkbook around in those days—but he might have given Lewis the cash.)

Lewis was one of the first stand-ups to show the influence of Robert Klein: the same autobiographical material, the same stream-of-consciousness style and herky-jerky rhythms, the same knack for ironic hyperbole. But in contrast to Klein's brash New York self-confidence, Lewis was a fidgeting bundle of nerves onstage, acting out a depressive psychodrama with every muscle of his body. Lewis would pace the stage in a half crouch, a mess of nervous gestures and verbal tics (frequent swipes at his mop of dark, unruly hair; his favorite embellishment, the phrase "quite frankly," which usually meant just the opposite).

He talked about his overprotected childhood—being forced by his mom to wear a yellow rain slicker to school, so conspicuous that "child molesters could see me through a dense fog"—and his overanalyzed adulthood: "I left my shrink too soon; I had to take an incomplete." He recounted his dates "from hell" (a phrase Lewis claims he originated) and his inadequacies at sex. "I can't express myself sexually," he lamented. "Once I tried to yodel. Three game wardens knocked at my door." Breakups are hard for everyone; for Lewis, they were almost biblical. A simple invitation to dinner, too soon after one split, and Lewis was a helpless puddle of regret: "Ah! Sharon always ate too!"

If Lewis was the dark prince of the Improv comedians in the early '70s, Jay Leno was his sunny opposite. Born in 1951, two years younger than Lewis, Leno grew up in Andover, Massachusetts, outside Boston, the son of an insurance man who ran motivational classes in which he'd inspire his salesmen with the Sinatra song "High Hopes." Leno struggled through high school and enrolled at the Bentley School of Accounting and Finance—then realized he had no aptitude for either accounting or finance and switched to the communications school at Emerson College. There he and a roommate, Gene Braunstein, teamed up on a comedy act (they dubbed it Gene and Jay's Unique and Original Comedy) and played college coffeehouses around the Boston area before Leno decided to strike out on his own. "It was a wonderful time to be a comic," says Leno, "because everybody else wanted to be a folk singer: 'Stop your war machine, Mr. President!' As comics, the audience couldn't wait to see us."

Leno memorized George Carlin's class-clown routines and would recite them verbatim at the start of his act, just to get up a head of steam before segueing into his own material. But like Lewis, he was mostly channeling Robert Klein—foraging through the shared experiences of his baby boomer audience and teasing out their absurdity with ironic exaggeration. He got his first laugh with a joke about the new permissiveness of college dorms: "You can have girls in your room, you can have liquor in your room, you can have drugs in your room. The only thing you aren't allowed to have is a hot plate. [*Shouting through the door:*] 'I smell soup in there!' " He joked about the restrooms in gas stations and eating at McDonald's and dinner-table conversation with a father who had lived through the Depression and wouldn't let you forget it. (Jay: "Pass the salt." Dad: "We never had salt when we were kids! We didn't have underwear or potatoes! Your mother and I hunted wild dogs for food . . .") "I'm from the United States," Leno used to say by way of introduction. "Any United States people here?" He was Joe Sixpack with a punch line.

Leno pursued his stand-up career with the same dogged, can-do optimism of his dad's motivational lessons. In Boston he picked up work at Kiwanis clubs, retirement homes, hospitals, even prisons. He would walk into bars, plunk down a fifty-dollar bill, and tell the owner he wanted to do a set of stand-up; if he bombed, the proprietor could keep the money. (Most gave him back the cash no matter how he did.) He worked as the opening act in strip clubs, then at a jazz club called Lennie's on the Turnpike, where he opened for acts like Linda Ronstadt and Kris Kristofferson.

He got a day job prepping automobiles for a fancy foreign car dealership in Boston (Robert Klein bought a Mercedes there, and Leno later figured out he must have prepped it). He made frequent trips to the Rolls Royce headquarters in New Jersey, and when he did, he'd take a detour into New York to do a set in the Village or try to get on at the Improv. Budd Friedman remembers his first encounter with the eager youngster: "He said, 'Mr. Friedman, my name is Jay Leno. This is the third night in a row I've driven down from Boston. I don't get on. When can I get on?' I said, 'You drive down from Boston and back in the same night?' 'Yeah.' 'You're on next.' "

Leno became one of Friedman's favorites. He continued to shuttle back and forth between Boston and New York—spending the night in his car at Dykes Lumber Yard, next door to the club, if he was too tired to drive back. Later on, he'd stay with comedian friends like Mike Preminger and would loan out his apartment in return when comics came to Boston for gigs. "The deal was, I had an apartment in Boston and any comic, whether I knew them or not, could stay at my place for free. I'd get these calls—'Hi, I'm Billy Crystal . . .' And when I went to New York, there was always someplace I could crash, sort of this underground network."

There was something appealing, almost inspiring, about Leno's dogged, Horatio Alger–style enthusiasm. He went on TV auditions wearing his only suit, the one he had bought for the Bentley School of Accounting and Finance; when he tried out for Jack Paar's variety show, they laughed at him. "They said, 'Is that your suit?' It was so heartbreaking. I remember crying all the way home because I failed the audition." His strategy was simply to work harder, and stick to it longer, than anyone else. "You'd spend your whole day sitting on the curb, waiting and waiting," he wrote of lining up for auditions in his memoir, *Leading with My Chin*. "Inevitably, somebody in front of you would say, 'This sucks!' and walk away. I always enjoyed that. All of a sudden, I had moved up! Without my doing a thing, my standing in show business had just improved!"

The Improv was, by this time, no longer the only place where young comics were standing in line. For nearly a decade, Friedman's club had the stand-up market in New York largely to itself. Comics could still get some work at a few clubs in the Village, or go out to Pips, a club in Sheepshead Bay, Brooklyn, that regularly booked comedians. But if you were a beginning stand-up who wanted to work on your craft every night, the choice was pretty much the Improv or your bathroom mirror. At the end of 1972, however, a new club opened on the Upper East Side that duplicated Friedman's formula almost precisely. Located in the heart of the singles'-bar district, Catch a Rising Star was the place that turned the showcase comedy club from an industry curiosity into a mass-audience phenomenon. At its height, it would rival Studio 54 and Elaine's as a celebrity-studded icon of the drugs-and-disco decade. More important, it would supercharge the stand-up comedy explosion of the 1970s.

Rick Newman had grown up in the Bronx, like Friedman, and had run a popular singles' bar downtown before he took over a defunct saloon on First Avenue between Seventy-seventh and Seventy-eighth streets and looked around for a gimmick for it. His first notion was a western-themed antiques emporium and restaurant, where patrons could buy antiques while ordering their strip steaks. Then he got a better idea: a club that would showcase new talent, both singers and comedians. Driving home one night he heard Perry Como singing "Catch a Falling Star" on the car radio, gave the name a twist, and opened Catch a Rising Star a week before Christmas in 1972.

From the start, Newman was savvier about promoting his club than Friedman had ever been. He put ads in the showbiz trade papers, inviting agents and producers to come in and check out his "pre-screened" new talent. He courted press coverage by turning the club's opening into a fiftieth-birthday party for former middleweight champ Rocky Graziano and corralling a few B-list celebrities to show up, like boxer Jake LaMotta and comic Jackie Vernon. He hired waiters and bartenders who could also sing and do comedy, so he'd have some acts to fall back on if the hoped-for flood of new talent failed to materialize. To discourage the singles' crowd that he feared might mistake the club for a less glitzy version of Maxwell's Plum, he put up (but didn't enforce) a sign warning, COUPLES ONLY.

Like the Improv, Catch a Rising Star started out with a mix of singers and comedians, but the comics soon dominated. Newman hired Bill Mahru—a University of Wisconsin grad newly arrived in New York, who was a fan of Second City, Abbie Hoffman, and counterculture street theater—as his first emcee. Mahru put together an improvisational group for the club that did skits, songs, and parodies in between the regular acts and doubled as waiters and waitresses. "It didn't work; nobody was getting served," says Mahru (who later moved to L.A., formed an experimental rock band, and changed his name to Conan Berkeley).

For the first year, the club struggled. When business was slow, the performers would often start out the evening by sitting at the tables, just to give the illusion of a crowd. A turning point came when David Brenner walked in one night and let Newman coax him onstage. Brenner—by now a *Tonight Show* regular who paraded around in mink coats, usually with a buxom model on his arm—became a frequent patron of the club, helping to generate buzz. One afternoon Brenner sat in while Newman was auditioning new talent—laughing as Newman suffered through the parade of bad singers and amateurish comedians—and told him it was such a hoot that he ought to move the auditions to his slowest night of the week and charge for them. Thus was born Catch's "open-mike" Monday, which ultimately became its second busiest night, after Saturday.

"It was a gong show before there was a *Gong Show*," says Newman. "I had a few people who were so bad I would book them on purpose. One girl, Nancy T. LeVallee, was the worst singer you ever heard. In real life she was a ten-cents-a-dance girl. Used to wear bad outfits—a cowgirl's outfit, with cowgirl hat, two guns, short skirts, the welts of her stockings sticking out from the bottom of her skirt. She couldn't sing a lick, but she became a star."

Catch and the Improv were the twin towers of the New York stand-up scene in the 1970s. While their formats were almost identical—an emcee introducing the nightly lineup of comedians (and an occasional singer), each doing a fifteen- or twenty-minute set—they had distinct personalities. The Improv, on the edge of seedy Times Square, had a funky, Village-jazz-club feel, with a crowd dominated by industry insiders and comedy aficionados. Catch was a spiffier place, with a more diverse clientele, and put a little more emphasis on music. A three-piece combo was onstage on weekends, to accompany singers and play the comics on and off. Rocker Pat Benatar—who was discovered at a Catch open-mike night, when she was still doing standards like "Bye Bye Blackbird"—became a regular, a symbol of the spiritual link between rock and stand-up that Catch a Rising Star seemed to epitomize in the '70s. "We were attracted to each other," says Benatar. "Everyone was pushing the envelope on both sides."

As a place to hang out, a lot of the comics preferred the bar at the Improv because it was separated from the showroom; unlike at Newman's club, where you passed through the bar on the way to the tables. But the broad, shallow showroom at Catch—decorated with faux bookcases, old-fashioned show posters, red-and-white checkered tablecloths, and large, gilt-framed mirrors at the back, so the comics could see themselves as they performed—seemed more like a big-time nightclub. "The Improv was grittier, no-frills, more sandlotish," says Alan Zweibel, who did stand-up at both clubs before becoming a writer for *Saturday Night Live*. "Catch was more Upper East Side, more of a living room. Some people got a sense that the Improv was a better place to start out at. You felt more comfortable failing at the Improv. Catch was more of a gig."

The clubs reflected the contrasting personalities of the two men who ran them. Newman, with his disco-era curly hair and mustache, was a charismatic and gregarious impresario, both a patron and a pal to the comics. "He was the most congenial guy I ever met," says Buddy Mantia, who performed with the Untouchables, a comedy trio that was a hot act at Catch in the mid-'70s. "Everyone loved him. He was the perfect front man." Friedman was crustier and more intimidating. "Budd was the kind of guy who came out of the '50s, old-school comedy," says Richard Lewis. "He was like a street guy. Rick Newman looked like he could have been the host of *The Love Boat*. He had the same love of comedy, but he didn't have the rough edge that Budd had. He seemed to have more fun at being an entrepreneur. He socialized more. Budd was more like an authority figure. You could hang out with Rick."

Newman paid the comics the same as Friedman—zilch—but he treated them better. He gave them a few dollars for cab fare to get them to and from their next gig. (The ones who were hardest up just pocketed the money and took the subway.) He looked the other way when the comics sneaked out of the club with silverware and toilet paper for their barren studio apartments. He let his regulars order food from the menu—burgers for the journeymen, steak and shrimp scampi from the other side of the menu for the top acts. "He never made any money because he fed us all," says Benatar, who was managed by Newman for several years. "I don't think anybody ever paid for a drink at the bar." The most coveted perk at Catch, however, was an invitation to Newman's basement office, the inner sanctum where the cool comics would hang out, pass around the drugs, and enjoy the knowledge that they had made it to the hip epicenter of the New York comedy world.

Through the 1970s, the comics went back and forth between the two clubs, and if one of the two ran short of performers late at night, Newman or Friedman might get on the phone to see if the other had any spare comedians hanging around the bar. Which didn't mean there wasn't an edge of friendly rivalry. Friedman regarded his club as the true original and Newman as a shrewd upstart. "Rick was very smart," says Friedman. "He was able to live off of what I created. And he could afford to be a little nicer. He had to be." Newman, for his part, felt it was his club that really launched the stand-up boom of the '70s. "Yes, Budd was around a few years earlier," he says. "But when Catch caught on, that's when the stand-up explosion started to happen." By the mid-'70s, the lines to get into Catch a Rising Star on Friday and Saturday nights stretched around the block. On any given night you might find Mick Jagger or Robert De Niro or a couple of *Saturday Night Live* cast members hanging out at the bar or at one of the tables. "You walked into that club," says Jerry Seinfeld, who failed his first audition at Catch in 1976, "and it smelled like show business."

For the younger comics like Seinfeld who came up in the late '70s, Catch was the big prize, the cool fraternity on campus. "We were like kids looking in the window of the candy shop," says Larry Miller, who turned from music to comedy after graduating from Amherst in 1975. "When Rick Newman walked into Catch, every head turned. He was a starmaker. I remember one night, around ten o'clock on a Wednesday, we're standing at the bar and Rick is on the phone to the Improv. He's looking right at us and saying, 'There's no comics here. Send me anyone you got!' No one is that oblivious." It took a few months for Miller to grab Newman's attention; one night the Catch owner invited him downstairs into his office, told him he'd been hearing good things about him, and said he wanted to put him on more. Miller left with some Catch a Rising Star notepads. That was big.

Many of the early Improv regulars—like Lewis and Bluestone and Andy Kaufman, the glassy-eyed kid from Great Neck with the childlike performance pieces and a killer Elvis impression—became fixtures at Catch as well. Freddie Prinze, the Puerto Rican prodigy who had auditioned at the Improv on the same night as Jay Leno (and would soon make a smash debut on *The Tonight Show* before getting cast in *Chico and the Man*), came in with Pryor-like material that featured language so rough Newman had to urge him several times to tone it down. (X-rated language was still rare at Catch and the Improv in the early '70s. Just a couple of years later—after Pryor's breakthrough albums, Carlin's "seven dirty words," and the rise of cable TV—that changed fast.) Gabe Kaplan, another popular Catch act in the early days, did routines about his Brooklyn school days, and an impression of Howard Cosell broadcasting the crucifixion of Christ, before heading to Hollywood for his own TV sitcom.

But Catch developed its own stars as well, and none was bigger than its longtime emcee, resident rock star, and emblem of cool, Richard Belzer. With his lean frame, pockmarked face, and ever-present shades, Belzer was a dominating, vaguely dangerous figure on the Catch stage in the mid- and late '70s. He had grown up in a poor neighborhood in Bridgeport,

Connecticut, gotten thrown out of two colleges, and wangled a psychiatric discharge from the Army before breaking into comedy in the satirical video-theater show *The Groove Tube*. When he began coming into Catch, Newman was impressed with his ad-libbing ability and New York edge and made him the club's regular emcee. The two were close (Newman managed him for several years), and Belzer became a kind of player-manager at the club, helping Newman pick the acts and "passing" scores of new comics—giving them the OK to become regulars—at Catch's open-mike nights.

Belzer had a relatively small repertoire of prepared material. A good impressionist, he strutted around the stage doing Mick Jagger as a "rooster on acid" and did an aging Dylan singing "Like a Rolling Stone" as a Jewish grandpa. But his specialty was impromptu banter with the audience: in-your-face, X-rated ad-libs that could strike fear into the heart of anybody who made the mistake of getting up to go to the restroom (which meant a long walk through the showroom) while the Belz was at the mike. Every comic at Catch knew the feeling of being ready to bound onstage to a Belzer introduction, only to be left hanging as the emcee went off on a tangent over some big-haired blonde in a giant fur ("Hey, did you have to blow Sergeant Preston of the Yukon for that coat?"). "He was incredibly, wonderfully, deliciously vicious," says Billy Crystal, who would drive in from Long Island, where he lived with his wife and young daughter, to get spots at Catch in the mid-'70s. "He always gave you a great intro. He knew the art of resettling the room, after somebody had either killed or bombed." Adrianne Tolsch, who began doing stand-up at the club in the late '70s and became its first female emcee, was one of many younger comics who regarded Belzer as a mentor: "He was Halley's comet," she says. "When he was onstage, he knew what was going on everywhere in the room. There was nobody like him."

The rap against Belzer was that he was lazy—generating little new material and relying instead on his ad-lib skills. And his clout around the club could be intimidating. Jimmy Brogan, a lanky, Jimmy Stewart–like stand-up who built an act out of genial ad-lib banter with the audience, once ran afoul of Belzer's girlfriend, who complained that Brogan was "doing Belzer" (they were as much alike as Will Rogers and Don Rickles); the result, Brogan says, was an edict that, whenever the two were in the club on the same night, Belzer always had to go on first. Paul Reiser, who worked there in the late '70s, saw Belzer's excesses as a symptom of the dark side of Catch in those years. "There were a lot of big egos, a lot of self-indulgent behavior," he says. "There were nights people would feel very entitled—I'm a big shot and fuck you. A lot of near fistfights. Belzer was one of the guys who was very indulged. He was given the run of the house, whether high or drunk."

And in a club well known for its fast crowd and heavy drug scene, Belzer was one of the big indulgers. "I never once saw him do a set sober," says Bill Maher, a Cornell University grad who was passed by Belzer at Catch in 1979 and soon began filling in for him as emcee (and selling him pot). "I remember, one night after John Lennon died, he went on so long that Buddy Mantia and I had to carry him offstage. He still had the mike in his hand—horizontal, still talking." Belzer, like Carlin and many other comics at the time, saw only the creative upside of a little chemical enhancement onstage. "Cocaine makes you talk," Belzer liked to say. "Comedians talk. Cocaine gives you more chances you'll say something funny." He cleaned himself up a few years later, but at the time, he says, "Drugs made us more daring, less inhibited. It was a kind of fuel at that stage of the business."

Some of Belzer's edge may have come from his career frustrations, as he watched other Catch performers go on to stardom while he remained the best-known club comic in New York who never made it on television. In 1975 he befriended a young TV producer named Lorne Michaels who was hanging out at Catch looking for talent for *Saturday Night Live*, the new late-night NBC show that was being touted as a showcase for hip, alternative comedy on network TV. Belzer introduced Michaels to future *SNL* cast members like John Belushi and Gilda Radner and hoped to be part of the cast as well, but was crushed when Michaels—reportedly wary of his drug use—passed over him. (Belzer did audience warm-ups for the show's first season, appeared in a few sketches, and years later made a couple of stand-up appearances on the show.) For years he had trouble cracking *The Tonight Show* as well. "He was not someone who was a safe booking," says Peter Lassally, Carson's longtime producer. Belzer let his bitterness show in a *Rolling Stone* profile in 1981. "I'm the kind of guy who tells the truth, and that's why I'm fuckin' broke," he griped. "I'm up there trying to be an artist, and what some of these other guys are doing is tracing. But they're making millions and I have to hide from my landlord."

But Belzer, a big Lenny Bruce fan, seemed to enjoy his renegade rep. When agents or talent scouts came into Catch, far from toning down his act, Belzer was just as likely to say "fuck it" and really let loose. Even when he tried behaving himself, things didn't work out. Once in L.A., when *The Tonight Show*'s comedy booker Jim McCawley came to see him at the Comedy Store, Belzer did an act so squeaky-clean that Richard Pryor berated him afterward: "Who the fuck was that? I didn't recognize you!" And still he didn't get the gig. (Belzer finally got booked on *The Tonight Show* in the early '80s. Carson treated him well, he says—even coming backstage beforehand to meet him and joke about Belzer's reputation for X-rated material.) Years later, he reinvented himself as a dramatic actor on the TV cop shows *Homicide* and *Law and Order*. But in the club days, Belzer admits, "I could have been my own worst enemy."

The dangerous vibe at Catch a Rising Star in those years didn't emanate only from Belzer. The tables were often populated with tough-looking, well-dressed patrons whom the comics widely assumed were Mob connected. "There were a number of Italian gentlemen who seemed to be together," recalls Tolsch. "There were certain tables you didn't respond to." Some comics learned that the hard way. Jimmy Brogan, the sweet-souled ad-lib artist, was emceeing one night when a white-haired man at one of the tables got up for a bathroom break. "Ladies and gentlemen: Lorne Greene," Brogan cracked. Later, the man cornered Brogan during a break.

"You think you're funny, kid?"

"Yeah, I think I'm a little funny."

"Well, you're not funny. I'll break your legs unless you say you're not funny."

"I was scared to death," Brogan recalls. "I apologized like a madman. Then I had to emcee the rest of the show with this guy sitting there. And you know what? He was right—I wasn't funny the rest of the night."

Joe Piscopo didn't get off so easy. An aspiring actor from Passaic, New Jersey, Piscopo preferred working at the Improv (a closer drive through the Lincoln Tunnel), doing impressions of King Kong and Frank Sinatra. But he was doing a Sunday-night spot at Catch a Rising Star when he started razzing a group of well-dressed customers in the back. "What are you, a hit man for the Mob?" Piscopo cracked to one of them—a bantamweight tough guy well known to Catch regulars, who suspected he was just that.

The man later confronted Piscopo at the bar. "He says, 'I don't appreciate you talking like that,'" Piscopo recalls. "Then the manager says the words you should never say: 'Why don't you guys take this outside?'" They got as far as the coatroom, where a couple of other goons grabbed Piscopo from behind while the first thug gave him three hard slaps to the face. Comics at the bar claimed they could hear the crunch of Piscopo's nose being broken. "I remember John DeBellis yelling, 'Run, Joe, run!'" says Piscopo. "I think the other comics were just looking at me and thinking, maybe I can get Joe's spots. I broke away and ran like freakin' hell down First Avenue."

He wound up in the hospital, with a chipped tooth and black eye to go with his fractured nose. One of his first visitors was Chris Albrecht, then the manager of the Improv. (Albrecht later got into television and wound up running HBO.) Furious that one of his regulars—and the third baseman on the Improv's softball team, no less—had been roughed up in a rival club, Albrecht called up Rick Newman, who had been away the night of the incident. "I was very upset with Rick," says Albrecht. "I told him that he needed to be sending a message that this was not acceptable." Piscopo, for his part, stuck to the Improv after that. And took up bodybuilding.

Incidents like that led some Catch regulars to assume the club had ties to the Mob. Kelly Rodgers, an emcee in the late '70s, claims he used to see a well-dressed restaurant owner from up the street come in every week and take money away in a brown paper bag. Newman dismisses the Mob rumors as nonsense. "We definitely had wiseguys who came in, but not any more than any hot club in New York at the time," he says. "It upset and bothered me as well. Maybe because of my Bronx street smarts, they befriended me. And I was nice to them. But when you have a hot place, they come." As for Rodgers's supposed bagman, Newman says he was actually a friend from the Bronx who ran the restaurant next door and liked to come in every Monday to watch open-mike night.

Catch a Rising Star was, to be sure, one of the hottest clubs in New York in the mid-'70s, and before long it began to attract imitators. In 1975, two bar owners from the Bronx, Richie Tienken and John McGowan, came into Catch to see one of their friends, a bartender at the club, do a set of stand-up. They waited for hours, and when he still hadn't got on by one A.M., the frustrated comic went up to Newman, pleading that his friends were there especially to see him and that Newman was ticking off some good paying customers. "Don't tell me about customers," Newman replied. "I've got plenty of customers."

"That's a nice business to be in," Tienken said to himself when he heard that. A few months later he and McGowan, along with an entertainment lawyer named Bob Wachs, opened their own comedy club, the Comic Strip, on Second Avenue just a few blocks away from Catch. Though showbiz neophytes, they shrewdly went after younger comics who were having trouble cracking Catch's tight playlist, and they developed their own stars, among them Jerry Seinfeld, Paul Reiser, Larry Miller, Carol Leifer—and a couple of years later, a brash high school kid from Roosevelt, Long Island, named Eddie Murphy.

The Comic Strip, with its more clean-cut, suburban ambience, and roster of less established comics, never had the cachet of Catch or the Improv.

Indeed, its owners didn't seem to know how to play the part. When celebrities walked into Catch a Rising Star, Newman would clear out a prime table for them, usually booting out seated customers with a promise of a free night back at the club. One night at the Comic Strip (in a story the comics repeated in horror), Chevy Chase showed up unannounced and was turned away, with apologies, because the club was full.

Yet the Comic Strip was an important new outlet for the growing band of stand-up wannabes who were laying siege to the New York clubs in the late '70s. Barely a decade after Carlin and Pryor had to scrounge for gigs in the folk clubs of Greenwich Village, the city now had three showcase clubs offering all comedy, all the time. The career path became as formalized as a medical internship. At Catch, newcomers would line up outside on Monday morning, waiting for a club employee to emerge and dole out numbers. The first in line got the lowest numbers, and thus the earliest time slots. Those who failed the Monday night audition could come back a few weeks later and try again. The ones who passed were allowed to come in every night and hang out at the bar—hoping to get on before all the customers went home.

The established comics could squeeze in six shows a night on a typical weekend—an early and a late show at each of the three clubs. Jimmy Brogan managed it so often that comics referred to the double hat trick as "doing a Brogan." "The whole night you'd be in cabs, yelling at the driver, 'Go through the park!'" says Brogan. "By the sixth set, at three forty-five in the morning, you'd be calling back [referring to] stuff that didn't even happen in that show." Even for the comics who weren't fortified with booze or coke, the evenings could go by in a haze. "Sometimes onstage, you'd forget," says Reiser. "You'd be doing a bit and it would feel familiar. And you'd say, Is it familiar because I did it an hour ago at the other club? Or did I just say this a minute ago? That used to just make my knees buckle." Emcees could earn fifty or seventy-five dollars a night, but for most of the comics—at least until the end of the '70s, when a strike at L.A.'s Comedy Store forced the club owners to start paying a token amount—the salary was still essentially nothing but cab fare and maybe some food at the bar.

There were other perks. The sex was free and plentiful. Stand-up comics, with their onstage swagger and macho one-liners, were as hot as rock stars and had the groupies to prove it. "The women were all over you," says Buddy Mantia. "They came out of the woodwork. Very aggressive. They'd come up and talk, send drinks over, let you know they were available." It could be frighteningly easy. "Sometimes you'd spot somebody in the audience," says Conan Berkeley (a.k.a. Bill Mahru), "you'd get a vibe, more than normal eye contact. She'd be saying, come and get me after the show. It was very clear, totally unspoken. You'd walk off the stage and go to her apartment, never have to say a word. We called it 'getting laid from the stage.'" For twentysomething guys just a few years removed from their high-school-nerd days, it was heady stuff. Says Berkeley: "Every Jewish comedian said, 'So this is what it's like to be a rock star.'"

But it wasn't just the sex that imbued those years with romantic nostalgia for so many of the comics. It was the boys' club camaraderie (and it was, for most of the '70s, overwhelmingly boys) of a band of night-crawling young comedians on the make. After the clubs closed for the night, they would gather at the Green Kitchen, a Greek diner down the block from Catch a Rising Star, where the shop talk was a cross between the Algonquin Round Table and *Broadway Danny Rose*. "It was like going to a great cocktail party every night," says Seinfeld. "You knew everyone. You'd hang out and bullshit with these incredibly witty, intelligent people. Everyone had the same struggles. We were a community, and that made it great." "The conversation wasn't about girls, family," says Reiser. "It was all about comedy. 'Did you hear so-and-so's line?' It was very communal and supportive. It was the fun of staying out late, hanging with the guys, eating cheeseburgers, going home and watching two hours of TV and waking up whenever you felt like it, because you didn't have to go to work until eleven at night."

The drawback to this communal spirit was a certain sameness to the comedy. The comics who hung out together and critiqued each other's material inevitably came to sound a lot alike. The house style at the New York clubs in the late '70s—the ironic wisecracks about girlfriends, drugs, television, sex, rubes from out of town—settled into a style and rhythm that became as predictable as that of the old borscht belt gagsters. "The showcase clubs had ceased for some years to be great venues of experimentation," Bill Maher wrote in his thinly fictionalized novel *True Story*, based on his years in the New York comedy clubs. "The Club [his stand-in for Catch a Rising Star] in 1979 was not the Village Gate in 1963; in the audience there were no poetic types hoping to be challenged by Lenny Bruce. It had a lot of tourists and bachelor parties from Brooklyn and New Jersey hoping to hear dick jokes. The more the non-cognoscenti took over the club scene, the more the comedians tailored their acts along crowd-pleasing lines to survive. And the more the comedians did that, the more the people in berets stayed away."

There were a few eccentric exceptions, of course: Andy Kaufman's deadpan put-ons, for example, or the raucous physical comedy of "Crazy Lenny" Schultz, a burly, bug-eyed high school gym teacher who brought on pornographic props, screamed at the top of his lungs, and usually left the stage such a mess that no one could follow him. And there was Larry David, a frizzy-haired University of Maryland graduate who did skewed, cerebral one-liners that could clear a room too. ("One thing I admired about Hitler: he didn't take any shit from magicians.") "When he went on, all the comics in the bar would rush in to see him," says Albrecht, "and all the people in the audience would rush to the exits." David was so hypersensitive onstage that he'd walk off at any sign of inattention or hostility from the crowd. A comic scheduled to follow him on the bill had to stay alert at the bar: a clunk of the microphone on the floor meant David had finished early. One night at Catch (in a story told so often that every comic in New York seems to have been there), David came out, silently scanned the audience, muttered, "I don't think so," and walked off without saying another word. David says the story is not just urban comedy legend. "I just didn't like what I saw," he says. "I was very temperamental onstage. If things didn't go well, I took it personally."

By the end of the '70s, however, the heyday of the New York clubs was fading fast. Most of the top stand-ups who launched their careers at the Improv and Catch a Rising Star in the early part of the decade—Lewis, Leno, Boosler, Kaufman, David, Seinfeld, even Belzer—had moved out West. So had Budd Friedman, who opened a branch of the Improv in West Hollywood in 1975, leaving his New York club in the hands of Albrecht. A former comic himself (he had partnered with Bob Zmuda, later Andy Kaufman's collaborator and writer), Albrecht was well liked by the comedians and he helped nurture new talent like Keenen Ivory Wayans and Robert Wuhl. But when Friedman got a divorce in 1978, custody of the New York club was awarded to his ex-wife, Silver—and that wasn't good news either for Albrecht or for a lot of the comics.

Silver had helped Budd run the club in the scrappy early years—tending the cash register, helping judge the talent, shooing customers out of the aisles. Danny Aiello thought of her as "the intellectual of the group; she would give advice to the comedians and they'd heed it." Some of the comics liked her. "She was very supportive in helping me," says Piscopo. But she was a volatile personality who rubbed many of them the wrong way. Marvin Braverman, who started at the Improv in the late '60s and became part of the Untouchables comedy trio, got into a fight with her when his friend Rob Reiner came to the club and Silver seated him near the back, behind a post. After Braverman told her to go fuck herself, he says,

Silver had him and his group banned from the club. "Budd could be prickly, but you knew when it was coming," says John DeBellis, an Improv regular in the late '70s. "With Silver, you never knew when it was coming, and you never knew why. She had her own ideas of what was funny. She pushed a lot of us away."

Albrecht remembers walking into the club's kitchen not long after Silver had taken over. She had fired the chef, George, who was brandishing a knife because she wouldn't pay him what he thought he was owed. "I'm gonna get my money, or I'm gonna die tonight!" George was screaming. "Silver was hard to get along with," says Albrecht. "She was a very different energy than we had gotten used to." He left the club in 1980 to become an agent for ICM, and many of the comics began drifting away as well. The Improv struggled along for another decade before declaring bankruptcy in 1993.

Catch a Rising Star, meanwhile, was going through its own changes. In 1982 Newman brought in a partner, Richard Fields, who tried to instill more financial discipline and expand the franchise. The two clashed almost from the start. Fields closed the kitchen, hired a talent manager, and pushed out some of Newman's cronies who worked as bartender/managers. "We had a different opinion of how the club should run," says Newman. "He didn't care about the comics." Fields also ticked off Newman by demanding that his name be taken down from the marquee (from the start it had been called Rick Newman's Catch a Rising Star) or else that Fields's name be added. Within a couple of years, Newman had sold his share of the club and left.

Most of the comics who were close to Newman couldn't stand Fields. "He hired a talent coordinator who had *meetings*," says Kelly Rodgers, an emcee in those years. "Who are the A acts and who are the B acts? He didn't want the B acts hanging out anymore. But you needed those B acts. Sometimes those B acts become A acts." Pat Benatar—who became a client of Fields when he went into partnership with Newman, her manager—had a falling out and sued him. Says Mark Krantz, who managed the club during the transition years: "He didn't have the front-of-the-house chops that Rick had. It became a business." And not a very good one. After taking the company public and opening nine clubs around the country, Fields eventually shuttered them all—including Catch's original First Avenue location, which closed in 1993.

The center of the comedy world, however, had long since shifted away from New York. Even before the New York comics started migrating to Los Angeles, a fresh wind was blowing from the West, in the form of two breakthrough stand-ups from Southern California. They were comedians whom no one could have imagined surviving in the rough-and-tumble New York club world. They didn't do jokes about social issues or their girlfriends or the funny things that happened when they went to the grocery store. They weren't even very comfortable telling jokes in front of a live audience. Yet they changed stand-up comedy for good.

CHAPTER 6

Put-on

I don't experience basic human emotions. It's not my thing.

—Albert Brooks

Even at Beverly Hills High School, where showbiz talent was hardly in short supply, Albert Einstein stood out. A big-boned, curly-haired kid, sturdy enough to play lineman on the school football team, he was given his punch line of a name by his father, Harry Einstein, a radio comic best known for his Greek-dialect character Parkyakarkus. Lots of budding comedians are class clowns in school, but Albert was a comedy prodigy. In geometry class, he livened up a friend's presentation by doing impersonations of all the theorems. When he hosted the high school talent show, he brought down the house even during rehearsals. "He had the rhythms of a professional comedian in place at fifteen years old," says Larry Bishop, a friend who formed a comedy team with him called Larry and Al. Or Al and Larry, depending on which one you ask.

One day they polished up their best material and went over to their friend Rob Reiner's house to try it out for his father, Carl. As Bishop recalls it, they did three routines. In one, Albert played Noah Webster, the dictionary man; the joke is that he's constantly at a loss for words, fumbling to look up even the simplest ones. In the second bit, Albert was an effeminate pro football player. In the third, Albert played Harry Houdini, being interviewed by Bishop. When the famous escape artist tried to make his entrance from the patio, however, he couldn't even negotiate the screen door. As he struggled with the handle—and finally had to race around to the front door to get in the house—Carl Reiner broke into hysterics, gales of laughter so violent that some of those present began to get worried.

"He couldn't stop laughing," says Bishop. "There were tears dripping down. We kept bringing in more tissues. In my life, I've never seen any-body laugh that hard." Not long after that, Carl Reiner was a guest on *The Tonight Show*. When Johnny Carson asked him to name the funniest people he had ever seen, at the top of his list was his son's sixteen-year-old high school friend Albert Einstein.

So began the legend of Albert Brooks (he changed his name a few years later, when he turned pro), the man many of his comedy colleagues re-garded as the era's greatest genius. By the age of twenty-one he was taking the nonsense bits he was doing for friends directly onto network TV. Off camera, he was famous for his bursts of improvisational brilliance. Parties stopped as show business guests, used to seeing talent up close, became a slack-jawed audience for his extemporaneous floor shows. Journalists sim-ply had to turn on the tape recorder and their profiles became autopilot comedy gems. "The funniest white man in America," Paul Slansky fa-mously dubbed him in a *Playboy* profile. Not everyone thought the racial hedge was necessary.

Brooks was also a world-class neurotic, who suffered through a stand-up career that began and ended so quickly that many people barely re-member it. He had a famous breakdown onstage in Boston, after which he all but gave up live performing. He started and backed out of projects and could drive producers crazy. Friends and colleagues knew that in order to bask in his brilliance, they also had to put up with his obsessiveness, his ego, his knack for worrying things to death. "Most comedians worry about being funny," says Dennis Klein, a comedy writer who was friends with him for years. "Albert is the only one who doesn't worry about that. He worries about everything else."

As a stand-up comic, Brooks represented an almost complete break with what had come before. Most of the comedians of Lenny Bruce's gen-eration and just after came from New York, or other urban centers in the East or Midwest. Brooks grew up in Los Angeles, a child of show busi-ness. Other comedians spent years working their way up in clubs before they became TV stars. Brooks began doing national TV before he ever set foot on a club stage as a professional. Bruce and his acolytes set out to make comedy more self-revealing and socially relevant. Brooks's comedy didn't seem to be about anything but show business itself—or more to the point, making fun of show business. "I don't experience basic human emotions," he said on his album *A Star Is Bought*. "It's not my thing." He was joking. Maybe.

His comedy might have looked like a retreat from the social conscious-ness that Bruce, Carlin, Pryor, and Klein had brought to stand-up. But

Brooks was an artistic radical just the same. Whereas Bruce and the rest were modernists, breaking down the traditional joke-joke monologue and inventing a new, more free-form kind of stand-up comedy, Brooks was a postmodernist, resurrecting the old style and encasing it in irony and self-parody. He didn't use stand-up to expose society's injustices or stick a thumb in the eye of the censors, but he was indebted to Lenny Bruce nonetheless. Bruce bared his soul, put the focus on the stand-up comedian himself. Brooks built an entire aesthetic out of deconstructing that strange, angst-ridden creature. It was Pirandellian comedy, doubling back on itself, satirizing the very notion of being an entertainer—comedy *about* comedy.

Brooks was born on July 22, 1947, in Beverly Hills, the youngest of three boys in a show business family. His father was a comic who appeared in movies and on Eddie Cantor's weekly radio show; his mother a former actress. "Comedy was almost a religion in the house. You were supposed to make people laugh," says Cliff Einstein, the older of Albert's two brothers, who went into advertising. (His next older brother, Bob Einstein, became a writer and comedian, best known for his character Super Dave Osborne.) Despite his buffoonish radio character with his Greek-accented malapropisms, Harry Einstein was a refined Bostonian. "He wasn't goofy and clowny," says Cliff Einstein. "Very dry, very smart. He would tell great stories, but he would never over-tell them, never shove himself at you." He also enjoyed cutting up in public. In a restaurant he might shout something funny at a waiter, just as the waiter was going back into the kitchen, to see if he'd drop his tray. Or he'd announce to the whole restaurant that little Albert wouldn't eat his vegetables.

In 1958, when Albert was eleven, his father appeared on the dais at a Friars Club tribute to Lucille Ball and Desi Arnaz. Albert worked on his routine with him the night before. By all accounts it got a big response. After Harry Einstein finished and went back to his seat, he slumped over and died from a heart attack. "The interesting thing is that he *finished*," Albert would say later. "That's what makes you believe in something."

Without a father, growing up with two somewhat distant brothers who were several years older, Albert tended to withdraw. Despite the family's comedy pedigree, he found little support when he announced that he wanted to go into show business. "Nobody was going, 'Great. Oh, good news,'" he says. "When I became friends with Rob [Reiner] early on—my dad had died, I spent a lot of time with Carl, and he did feel sometimes like a dad to me—I would say something at the dinner table about Carl, and one of my brothers would say, 'Don't fuckin' name-drop.' I felt I could count on my brothers for a lot of things. They were there for me in the crises of life. Cliff became more like a dad. I used to do things with Bob—I remember Bobby protecting me from bullies at school. The only thing was that show business was not to be discussed. That wasn't part of the condition of being brothers. So I didn't openly discuss my show business aspirations. I just found as a little kid it was easier to clam up about what I wanted to do."

In high school, his circle of friends included Reiner, Larry Bishop (the son of comedian Joey), and Richard Dreyfuss. When they hung out together, it was often hard to tell where Albert left off and the comedy routine began. "He drove a Volkswagen and he'd pick me up and we'd go places," says Bishop. "One time we went to a driving range to hit golf balls. He started a conversation: Who do I think is sexier to women—me or him? We had a long conversation about why the other one wasn't sexy. It gets real honest and heated. Finally Albert has an idea. We'll get a third opinion. And he comes up with the guy who gets the bucket of balls for you—this is the guy we're going to ask. Then we got in an argument over who was going to ask him, since that might affect his answer. We never did it. I just remember I had to walk home that night."

He appeared in plays in high school, and went to Carnegie Tech to study acting. There he took mime and dance classes and played Holden Caulfield in a student-written adaptation of *Catcher in the Rye*. But when his favorite teacher left after two years, he quit school and came back to L.A. to look for acting work. He auditioned for and thought he had won a role in the film version of *Goodbye, Columbus*. But he didn't hear back for months and read in *Variety* that the movie was already shooting without him. "They didn't even have the decency to call and say you don't have the part," he says.

But he had a comedy bit he did for friends called "Danny and Dave," the world's worst ventriloquist act: the ventriloquist moves his mouth more than the dummy, inadvertently drops his wooden partner on the floor, and does a crackpot variation on the old *Ed Sullivan Show* stunt in which the ventriloquist drinks a glass of water while the dummy sings—only this time it's the ventriloquist who sings, while he pours water down the dummy's gullet. "It was one of those things that could make anybody laugh," says Brooks. (Years later he would try to make people in India laugh with it, in his movie *Looking for Comedy in the Muslim World*.) Herb Nanas, a young agent at William Morris who had heard about him from another Morris agent, George Shapiro—who was Rob Reiner's cousin—spent an afternoon with Brooks and immediately got on the phone with Steve Allen's producers. "I just met the funniest kid I've ever seen in my life," he told them. When he brought Albert in for an audition, Nanas claims one of the producers laughed so hard he fell over backward in his chair. Brooks made his TV debut on *The Steve Allen Show* the next day.

It was the fall of 1968. By the following summer the cherubic young comic with the Brillo-pad hair was booked for six guest spots on *Dean Martin Presents the Golddiggers*, Martin's summer-replacement series, and starting to get calls from all the top talk and variety shows. When he had used up all his bits, he created new ones on the fly. Many he barely had time to try out in advance but simply rehearsed them in front of the bathroom mirror and showed them to a friend or two before taking them on television. He did most of them just once. Many aren't even preserved on videotape and live only in the memory of a cult of Brooks fans that grew with each new bit of lunacy.

For the most part they were lampoons of bad showbiz acts. Brooks played an animal trainer, for example, whose elephant has gotten sick at the last minute and has to be replaced by a frog; he gamely tries to do his routine with the stand-in, apologizing when the tricks (roll over; grab a peanut) don't come off. He did a parody of the old vaudeville stunt in which a man tries to keep a dozen plates spinning simultaneously on top of poles. Instead of plates, Brooks brought a half-dozen people onstage and tried to keep them all laughing at the same time; whenever the yuks started to die down, he scurried around trying to rev them up again with a new joke. In another bit, Brooks dressed up in leotard, slippers, and Marcel Marceau whiteface to play the world's worst mime. He starts out by telling a bit of his life story ("My mother was quite domineering. I was afraid to speak . . .") and becomes so caught up in the monologue that soon he's puffing on a cigar and delivering Vegas zingers ("Take my wife—*si vous plait*!"). When he finally performs his mime, he provides a running commentary to explain what he's doing ("climbing ze stairs"), before finally belting out "Make Someone Happy" for the schmaltzy, Jolson-style big finish.

It was inspired nonsense, Brooks's demolition of the entire history of cheesy showbiz. He kept finding new variations on the theme. On Johnny Cash's variety show, he played a terrible mentalist—with Cash as the stodgy straight man—trying to divine the serial numbers on dollar bills and missing every one. At the first American Music Awards, he appeared as a children's songwriter who performs a Vegas-style tribute to his own greatest hits, simplistic ditties like "Eat Your Beans" and "Brush Your Teeth." In the early '70s there was a brief vogue for fast-cut film montages set to music; in one of them, thousands of works of art flash by in under three minutes, to the accompaniment of Mason Williams's "Classical Gas." Brooks announced he had made his own two-and-a-half-minute film on the history of the animal kingdom, but unfortunately, the film had been lost in the mail, so he had to try to re-create it live. To a recording of "Classical Gas," he began flipping madly through the pages of a Time-Life book on the animal kingdom; then, after exhausting the pages, he raced backstage to bring out props—a live dog, a beach ball (in lieu of a seal), even a can of sardines.

Probably his most popular bit was one he called "Rewriting the National Anthem." The premise: someday the unsingable song will have to be rewritten, and the only fair way to do it is to hold open auditions in Washington, D.C., where ordinary Americans can get onstage and try out their new versions. Brooks, accompanying himself on the piano, plays the parade of amateur songwriters, running through a gamut of song stylings and showbiz clichés. One fellow simply pastes bouncy new lyrics on the tune "26 Miles" ("Three thousand miles from coast to coast / Every citizen has reason to boast . . ."). A black militant gets off one angry line—"You jail all your black!"—before he is sent on his way. A slick Vegas entertainer filibusters with syrupy nightclub patter ("Originally I'm from a much quieter place, a place up north out west, a place I call . . . Portland"), before delivering his Bacharach-style pop anthem: "Got a Country! / I spell it—A-M . . . E-R . . . I-C . . . AAAAAY."

Some dubbed it post-funny, or anti-comedy: the joke was how bad the jokes were. Comedians before him, like Carlin and Klein, had poked fun at the slick and foolish and insincere in show business. But Brooks carried it a step further: he was making fun of how show business had infected all of us, creating a world of amateurs and wannabes so desperate for applause that they could barrel through any kind of inanity. It could have been patronizing, but it wasn't. Even as he satirized the audience, he was flattering it: you had to be savvy enough to understand what his put-ons were putting on. Brooks helped usher in the modern comedy era, when everybody became a showbiz insider.

The real showbiz insiders were among his biggest fans. One was Johnny Carson, who invited Brooks on *The Tonight Show* often and seemed genuinely tickled by him. "He really liked me. He said, 'Do anything you want; surprise me,'" says Brooks. "I did Johnny Carson shows where nobody was laughing, but he was laughing. To me that's all that mattered." He came on one time and simply annotated the ingredient list on a container of Cool Whip. (The top ingredient, it turns out, is water. "Let me tell you something, folks," said Brooks. "When water is your headliner, you got a weak show.") Relaxed and animated in plaid shirts and jeans, he chatted easily about his day—getting stuck in a car wash, say, or being kept awake at night by the dogs next door. Still, his favorite subject was Albert Brooks, the stand-up comedian. On one show he told Carson that he was having trouble making ends meet and announced a going-out-of-business sale—offering cut-rate Albert Brooks routines, delivered in person in your own home, "at a fraction of their original cost." Another time he brought out a chart that he proceeded to fill with arrows and circles, diagramming a generic joke—a send-up of the kind of the formulaic comedy that he was in the process of dismantling.

Most memorably (on a night when Carson was sick and Joey Bishop, his high school friend's dad, was filling in), he sat down in an easy chair and announced solemnly that he had "run out of material." "Last Thanksgiving while you people were celebrating, I was down to my last bit," Brooks confided. Sure, he said, he could do stupid things for a laugh, like drop his pants, paint a silly face on his chest, or smash an egg on his head. And then, of course, he dropped his pants, stripped off his shirt to reveal a funny face, and smashed an egg on his head. After working himself into a frenzy—covering himself with whipped cream and seltzer and topping it off with a pie in the face—he cried out, "This isn't the real me!" Then, pulling out an eight-by-ten glossy from his shorts, he exclaimed, "*This* is the real me!" and exited dramatically, Jimmy Durante–style, through a trail of spotlights at the rear of the stage.

Brooks had not heard much Lenny Bruce (growing up he was a bigger fan of Bob Newhart, Jonathan Winters, and Bill Cosby), but this was the logical extension of Bruce's "Comic at the Palladium" bit: Brooks's final kiss-off to the old in-your-face comedy of vaudeville and Vegas, which he had been lampooning ever since his high school Houdini bit. "At that time," says Brooks, "when you told someone you were a comedian—and I fought this all during my stand-up years—the next question would always be, 'When do you play Vegas?' Partly what I was doing was trying to rip down that part of the comedy world. Because it all was Shecky, the cigar, the nightclub. I was trying to rebel against that. And there was a lot to rebel against."

Yet this wasn't just satire of old showbiz. It was character comedy of a high order, Brooks's creation of himself as his great stage persona—the insecure, narcissistic, desperate-to-be-loved entertainer. His model was Jack Benny and the other classic comics who used to play themselves (or at least some simulacrum of themselves) on their radio and TV shows. "I loved Jack Benny," he says. "I loved that whole idea that he was doing a show playing a comedian with his name in it. What I thought was so amazing was that the audience knew his persona so well that he didn't do anything. All he had to do was react. Most comedians have to create the confusion. All he had to do was look at it. And that was such a profound, clear comedy character. They all did that—Bob Hope, Fibber McGee—and then it went away. And I wanted to do that again."

Only after he had been on television for a couple of years did Brooks begin performing live in clubs and concerts halls. At first he was so green that he would simply string a few of his TV bits together with perfunctory segues: "And now, would you welcome—Danny and Dave!" Eventually he loosened up, adding material tailored to the cities he visited and talking about life on the road. Like many stand-ups of his generation, he got work as an opening act for touring stars like Neil Diamond and Sly and the Family Stone, fighting raucous crowds in giant venues where, as he put it, "the comedian is not only insignificant; in many cases the audience hates you for delaying their drug experience." Inevitably, he turned *that* into comedy material, recounting a nightmarish gig opening for Richie Havens in San Antonio, Texas. As the crowd chants, "*Richie, Richie, Richie*," Brooks has to introduce himself as the unexpected opening act. "Your name Richie?" asks a stagehand, just before Brooks is to go onstage. Brooks says no. "They're gonna *kill* you." And they nearly do, prompting Brooks to resort to the big gun:

> It's a word. It works in that part of the country every single time. It's a miracle word. The word is *shit*. I don't understand it, but six thousand people—"*Richie, Richie, Richie, Richie*"—"Shit!" "*Whoooooooeeeee!*" Hats come on the stage. People run out, begin to build a statue in the park—"He's a hero, he's a hero, he's a hero!" Parades are scheduled. How does that work? Do they talk about that after the show? [*Redneck at the bar:*] "What'd you think of the comedian?" [*Other redneck:*] "Lemme tell you one thing. When he said 'shit,' I almost DIED!"

That routine is a highlight of Brooks's first album, *Comedy Minus One*, released in 1973. The title track is another deconstructionist stunt, an interactive comedy routine in which Brooks plays one part in an old comedy bit, "The Garage Mechanic," while you, the listener, follow a script and play the other part. Most of the album, however, provides one of few samplings of Brooks's underrated skills as a concert performer—a blend of concept comedy and galvanic stage energy that few performers of any era could match.

After five years of doing stand-up, however, Brooks was frustrated. He still wanted to be an actor, and stand-up didn't seem to be getting him any closer to movie roles. "When I started out, everybody was saying forget about the acting; do the stand-up bits on television and the acting will come from that. I was getting further into a career that I wasn't comfortable with." He didn't like traveling—and this road seemed to be heading in the wrong direction. "You know, a lot of guys in clubs were trying to get to television. I was coming the other way. When I opened for Neil Diamond, I remember the introduction: 'You've seen him on *Merv Griffin*, you've seen him on *Dean Martin* . . .' And I'm standing backstage going, 'I've got a lot of credits! What am I doing here?'"

He refused at first to go on tour to promote *Comedy Minus One*. Then, he changed his mind and suffered through a belated tour to cities where, in many cases, his record was no longer in the stores. In Boston, in early 1974, a radio interviewer said to him, "Jonathan Winters went insane doing this. Do you think you will?" That weekend he almost did.

Brooks was playing Paul's Mall, a cramped, low-ceilinged jazz and rock club where stand-up comedians occasionally headlined. When Brooks showed up for the first night of his weeklong engagement, he found a surreal scene: the audience was filled with people in clown suits, part of a promotion for his opening act, singer Leo Sayer. He had a panic attack. "I had to come out to that. After [Sayer] got his ovation, it was like, wait a minute. I got shit on as an opening act, and now I'm the headliner. How did this happen? And I just sort of reached the end of my rope."

He barely managed to get through his two shows on Friday night. Then he told Nanas, his manager ever since that first *Steve Allen Show*, that he was through and wanted to cut short his engagement. Nanas stayed up all night trying to talk him out of it. But in the morning Nanas had to call the club's owner. "I said, 'We got a problem. We've got to cancel.' He said, 'Are you insane? There are lines around the block. They'll burn my club down!'" The two of them negotiated all day with Brooks and talked him into doing one final show on Saturday night.

The owner packed the place with as many people with tickets for the night's two scheduled shows as he could; Nanas thought the fire marshals would arrest everybody if they came in. Then, when Brooks went onstage, Nanas watched in horror as he did fifteen minutes of his act and went straight to his closing bit. "I was in a complete state of panic," says Nanas. "I'm thinking, if he walks off the stage now, they'll kill him." Brooks managed to double back and do his full show. Later he described it as the "most painful hour I've ever endured in my life." Says Nanas: "He did that show by rote. I don't think he even knew he was onstage. I knew he was done. He was never going to do stand-up again."

The story was that stage fright ended his performing career. Brooks saw it as something more complicated. For years he had been reeling off TV appearances with almost preternatural calm. Backstage at *The Ed Sullivan Show*, he could be casually talking to a friend just minutes before his spot, get summoned onstage, and calmly return after he was done to finish the conversation. "I never, ever got nervous, and it was really unnatural," he says. "What happened was that I had to catch up with all those emotions. It's like an invisible thing tapped me on the shoulder and went, 'Here's everything you never thought of before. Think about it.' And then it was like I was examining everything: Who are these people, and where am I going, and what am I doing? I hit a brick wall."

It was the end of his live-performing career. After his Boston meltdown, Brooks returned to L.A., went into therapy, and took six months off. Then he went to work on a new album, more comfortable in the security of a studio and collaborating with Harry Shearer, a member of the L.A. radio comedy group the Credibility Gap. *A Star Is Bought*, Brooks's second and last comedy album, was released in early 1975. It is one of the finest comedy records of the decade, and Brooks's most sustained and ingenious satire of show business yet.

A Star Is Bought is a concept album about (what else?) making a comedy album. Since records need to get promoted on as many radio stations as possible, Brooks announces in the opening track, he has created cuts geared at every kind of radio format. For Top 40 stations, he apes one of those novelty records from the '50s in which snippets of pop hits are edited together with a silly "outer space" theme. Brooks's twist is that, to avoid paying royalties, he has made up his own hit songs, which he's edited into unrecognizable chunks. For talk stations, he supplies his own prepackaged call-in appearance—guest Albert Brooks answering questions from call-in listeners, all voiced by Brooks. For country stations, he delivers a patriotic talk-song, a lament for lost American values that rises to a fever pitch of indignation as the music swells. Brooks's satiric writing was never sharper:

Where has it all led? To hamburgers, french fries, and a malted? To go, my country? Why can't we eat it here? There was a time when Mother's Day was a whole week in July. What happened, gals? America can put a man on the moon, but we still forget our trash day . . . Today we have golden arches, but our feet still hurt. We play "The Star-Spangled

Banner" at ballgames, but still one team always loses. We check into hotels, but hotels won't take our checks. Well they won't take mine! Angry? You bet I'm angry!

In the album's pièce de résistance, Brooks unearths an old episode of *The Albert Brooks Show*, his supposedly lost radio show from 1943 ("my prenatal work")—an imitation so dead-on you can practically smell the Lucky Strike cigarettes. Brooks plays a '40s radio star named Albert Brooks, in an episode (in the self-referential mode of the shows of that era) about trying to find the script for this week's episode. Along the way he trots out the usual gallery of radio-show sidekicks—the wisecracking secretary, the stuttering assistant, his jovial lawyer with a catchphrase ("*Oh, nothing!*") that draws knee-jerk applause from the audience. There's a musical interlude to showcase the house band (this week a drum solo), and even a war-bond commercial worked seamlessly into the show.

It was Brooks's great, loving send-up of the old radio comics of his dad's era. Brooks and Shearer even tried to get Jack Benny himself to make a guest appearance on the record. (As a child actor, Shearer had actually appeared on Benny's TV show.) But when they met with the aging comic, just days before he died of stomach cancer, the confused Benny thought they wanted him to do a radio show. "I've done movies, I've done television—I don't need to do radio!" he exploded. Brooks and Shearer were mortified. "We said, 'You're like a God to us!' " says Brooks. "But we couldn't say enough. He just wasn't in the mood that day, four days before he died, to hear about radio."

By the mid-'70s, Brooks was no longer performing live and rarely on television. But his reputation only grew as one of the comedy world's great untapped resources. Friends told stories of his spontaneous bits at parties the way an earlier generation would recount lines from Dorothy Parker or Groucho. Ad-libbed routines poured out of him—material other comics could have built careers around, but which evaporated in the air, never to be repeated. "I never met anyone who was as good extemporaneously," says Rob Reiner. "If Albert was in the house—and sometimes there would be people like Robin Williams and Chevy Chase and other really funny people—once he started, everybody stopped. Nobody could compete with Albert." Billy Crystal was a newcomer in Hollywood when he went to Reiner's thirtieth-birthday party and watched as a roomful of guests tried to top each other with gag gifts. Carl Reiner gave his son a live goat. Brooks's offering was a book on the history of games, which he pretended to read aloud from. "The games were astounding," says Crystal.

"One of them was the Major League Baseball game: get twenty of your friends to contribute forty million dollars a year to buy up Dominican and black players. There was a Kennedy assassination game. It was genius. It went on and on. We all just looked at each other saying, 'I'm seeing something pretty extraordinary.' At the end of it, he didn't know what to do. So he got up and left. He had finished this amazing riff. And there was nothing else for him to do but go."

The well-timed exit was a Brooks specialty. Rob Reiner was at a party with him a few years earlier when Brooks gave another knockout performance and capped it off by leaving. A half hour later, Reiner got a call from him. Brooks had left his car keys in the apartment but felt it would spoil everything to come back. "He had been walking around outside," says Reiner, "trying to figure out what to do because he couldn't get into his car." Reiner had to sneak outside and slip him the keys.

One of Brooks's biggest fans at the time was Lorne Michaels, who was in the early stages of developing *Saturday Night Live*. Michaels thought Brooks had just the kind of avant-garde comic sensibility he was looking for and asked him to host the show. But Brooks was still leery of performing—especially on a show that planned to air live on Saturday night in New York City. "It was too much pressure," he says. "To me, *The Tonight Show* was as much pressure as I needed—it's a live show, but you get to do it at five thirty. You don't have to wait the whole week, until eleven thirty at night to do it, to see if everyone can make a mistake. And when you see what happened to a lot of those [cast members]—there's a reason for that. It's too much pressure."

Brooks turned down the job of regular host (he suggested Michaels use rotating guest hosts instead) but had another idea. Brooks had gotten a taste for filmmaking a couple of years earlier, when he made a short for PBS's *Great American Dream Machine*, based on an article he had written for *Esquire*: an infomercial for the Albert Brooks Famous School for Comedians, with Brooks, as the school's dean, giving a tour of the campus, where students learn things like pie-throwing techniques and the Danny Thomas spit take. Brooks proposed that he do some short films for the show instead, and Michaels commissioned six of them.

The films were sporadically funny elaborations of the sort of parodies Brooks had been doing in his stand-up act and on records. One was a take-off of network promos for new fall TV shows, among them a sniggering sit-com about a horny guy living with two women. (*Then* it was a joke; a year later, when *Three's Company* debuted on ABC, the real thing.) Another was a newsmagazine parody called *The Impossible Truth*, featuring stories like

George Carlin in 1966
and 1976, before and
after his counterculture
transformation: "I
was living out this
mainstream dream,"
he says, "not realizing
that I was an outlaw."
(LEFT, COURTESY OF
GEORGE CARLIN; BELOW, BY
GREG PAPAZIAN)

Richard Pryor, the rubber-faced kid from Peoria, Illinois, was an Ed Sullivan favorite in the '60s. "He did not like playing the game of conformity," says Sandy Gallin, his former agent. "But he was bright enough to know that this was gonna help him advance his career."
(CBS PHOTO ARCHIVE/GETTY IMAGES)

Robert Klein onstage in the early '70s, when his high-energy, improv-based style was influencing nearly every young stand-up in New York.

Billy Crystal and Robin Williams, both of them TV stars by this time, at the tenth anniversary of Catch a Rising Star in New York. Watching in the background is the man who helped supercharge the '70s stand-up explosion, Catch's owner Rick Newman. (COURTESY OF RICK NEWMAN)

After a meltdown in Boston, Albert Brooks abandoned live stand-up, and by 1975 was working entirely in the studio—on his album *A Star Is Bought*, and then a series of short films for NBC's new comedy show *Saturday Night Live*. (JULIAN WASSER/TIME & LIFE PICTURES/GETTY IMAGES)

When he first wandered into the New York Improv, Andy Kaufman adopted his "foreign man" guise and told Budd Friedman (at far right) that he was from an "island in the Caspian Sea." In 1982, after a decade of subversive stand-up, Kaufman helped Friedman launch *An Evening at the Improv*. (COURTESY OF BUDD FRIEDMAN)

Steve Martin began doing *The Tonight Show* in late 1972, experimented with his look, and got relegated to appearing with guest hosts for a while. But by 1974, Martin had adopted his trademark white suit and full-fledged "ramblin' guy" persona. (MICHAEL OCHS ARCHIVES/GETTY IMAGES)

Mitzi Shore, the controversial owner of L.A.'s Comedy Store, making up the all-important nightly lineup in 1978. Argus Hamilton, a former frat boy from Oklahoma, was one of the comics closest to her.
(ABOVE, COURTESY OF MITZI SHORE; LEFT, COURTESY OF ARGUS HAMILTON)

Regulars at the Belly Room, Mitzi Shore's affirmative-action effort for women comics, in 1979. That's Mitzi fourth from the right; Lotus Weinstock, Lenny Bruce's last girlfriend, lying on the bar; Maureen Murphy, with blonde hair, third from the left in the middle row; Emily Levine at the center rear; and Sandra Bernhard at the far right. (MARK SENNET/*PEOPLE* MAGAZINE)

Out of the ashes of '70s comedy came the two stand-ups who would embody the new, milder mainstream. Jay Leno, the hardest-working man in the stand-up biz, is seen here at Catch a Rising Star in the early '70s. He would go on to replace Johnny Carson, the old arbiter of stand-up. (COURTESY OF RICK NEWMAN)

Jerry Seinfeld at the bar of the Comic Strip, the club where he became an emcee, scarcely a year after failing his first audition at Catch a Rising Star. "Catch was the cool place," he recalls. "The Comic Strip was lame." Fittingly, Seinfeld would build a huge career by riffing on the uncool details of everyday life. (COURTESY OF THE COMIC STRIP)

the signing of a treaty in which Israel and the state of Georgia agree to trade places on the map. "I hope that New Orleans will be easier to deal with than Cairo," jokes the Israeli prime minister. "And *we're* looking forward to heat without humidity," says the Georgia governor. In his thirteen-minute magnum opus, Brooks played himself, a stand-up comedian who sets out to fulfill a lifelong dream: performing heart surgery. After an older couple, big fans, agree to let him do the husband's bypass, Brooks has to bring a Visible Man model into the operating room to guide him, forgets to deliver the anesthetic before starting to cut, and gets huffy when a real surgeon in the O.R. with him tries to offer advice: "Watch out, you'll cut the aorta!" "*I'm not gonna cut the aorta!*" It was Brooks's most acid commentary yet on our obsession with celebrity—and on himself, the stand-up comedian as diva, neurotic, and big baby.

But Brooks's stint making shorts for *Saturday Night Live* wasn't happy. He and Michaels had arguments about the length of his films: nearly all came in longer than the five-minute limit Michaels had set. Michaels ran the thirteen-minute heart-surgery film uncut only out of deference to Brooks's friend Rob Reiner, who was hosting the show that week. Michaels thought Brooks, working in California, was too high-maintenance; he got tired of the constant phone calls and the complaining. "Producing Albert in those days was the very definition of a thankless job," says Michaels. "He was over budget. And working 'round the clock. And whatever we were paying him was a pittance. And of course he'd use that as a club to beat me up with—'I'm working 'round the clock. How can you deny me those minutes?' And I'm going, 'Albert, I didn't ask you to work 'round the clock!'"

Harry Shearer, who worked on the films with Brooks, claims Michaels simply resented the one piece of the show's talent who was outside his New York orbit and thus his direct control. "Albert was working at a level so much higher than most of that show at that time, any producer would say thank you," Shearer says. "You get thirteen minutes of Albert, you should be grateful." Yet as the show's ensemble cast and live format began to jell, it became clear to everyone that Brooks's films didn't fit in. After his six-film contract was satisfied, Michaels dropped him.

"As soon as the New York show got its foot in the door, then I felt it was like jettisoning a rocket," says Brooks. "As soon as the concept took hold, [to have] someone in California working independently wasn't a good idea anymore." Still, Brooks—whose style seemed to influence much of the show's comedy—felt miffed that his role in its startup was never fully recognized or appreciated. "I think the sensibility of that show—making fun of show business, the satires of commercials, and that stuff—was sort of the act I was doing. I was happy to do the films, and it was a great experience for me. I just felt that in that first year, when people were praising everybody, I wasn't really a part of that. There was no inclusion."

Figuring out exactly where to include Albert Brooks was a major Hollywood puzzle for much of the '70s. After the end of his stand-up days, his career was a litany of sabotaged projects, missed opportunities, and narrow escapes. In 1976 Brooks was offered the lead in an ABC sitcom called *Our Man in Rataan*, about a reporter working in a godforsaken outpost in North Africa. After pestering friends like Shearer and Klein with his doubts about whether to do the show, he finally said yes. Then, at a meeting with the writers, producer Aaron Spelling, and ABC executives, the network's new programming chief, Michael Eisner, asked Brooks, "What do you see for this character in three years?" He thought about it for a second; answered, "Suicide"; and walked out.

Brooks had another last-minute change of heart in 1981, when he was asked to fill in for Johnny Carson for a night as guest host of *The Tonight Show*. He said yes, but a few days before the show, after realizing that he would have to coo over animals with Joan Embery of the San Diego Zoo, he abruptly changed his mind. "It was something I had really, really wanted to do a few years earlier," says Brooks. "But at the time, I was way past it. I think I said yes just so I could call my mother and say, 'I'm gonna host *The Tonight Show.*'" Nanas, his long-suffering manager, once again had to clean up the mess. "I told them he was passing a kidney stone. I said to Albert, you better go to Cedars Sinai, because I'm not making this call without you in the hospital." A then little-known comic, Garry Shandling, replaced Brooks as host at the last minute.

Brooks wasn't entirely to blame for all the aborted projects. In 1973, when he was still doing stand-up, he was offered his own summer series on CBS. But at a dinner honoring Carol Burnett, with CBS chairman William Paley in the audience, he performed his routine about saying "shit" at rock concerts. Offended by Brooks's language, Paley said he didn't want that foulmouthed young man on his network, and the series was scrapped.

Brooks's conflicts over his career and the compromises he had to make for his art became familiar themes. "Albert is smarter than anyone," says Dennis Klein. "He's always ahead of you. He's bored in most situations except exploring the inside of his mind, and he's fastidious about protecting his boundaries. He craves isolation and is willing to endure intimacy as a pathway to it." (A notorious commitment-phobe, he had a string of girlfriends, among them singer Linda Ronstadt and actress Kathryn Harrold, before finally marrying, at age fifty, artist and graphic designer Kimberly

Shlain.) For some friends and colleagues, the compulsiveness and ego eventually wore them down. "When you're a friend of Albert's, you're basically on twenty-four-hour duty," says Shearer, his frequent collaborator in the '70s, who broke off on his own when he finally got tired of the calls at three in the morning when Brooks wanted to talk about video equipment.

The obsessiveness could sometimes pay off. When one of the films he had sent to *Saturday Night Live* got lost in the mail, Brooks managed to track down the package long-distance, locating the particular clerk at the Grand Central Station post office who had handled it. There was something charming about the compulsiveness of a comedian who, when his debut on Dean Martin's summer show in 1969 looked like it might coincide with the first moon landing, called NASA in Houston and got an official on the phone to help him determine whether the landing would preempt his show. But something as simple as a lunch date could be high drama. "When he was hungry, he would get on the phone and really henpeck you into joining him for a meal, to the point where you wanted to strangle him," says Richard Lewis, one of the relatively few stand-up comedians Brooks became friends with. Brooks once called Lewis to go out for bagels, just as a swarm of bees was attacking Lewis's house. "I said, 'Albert, I gotta call the exterminator. I think I'm gonna be killed.' He said, 'Come on.' He had, like, tunnel vision on getting deli. I said, 'Albert, I can't.' And just before I hung up, he said, 'Look, throw some honey on your neighbor's roof and meet me at the deli in forty minutes.'"

His move into filmmaking was typically fraught. Brooks had broken into movies in 1976 with a role in *Taxi Driver*, directed by Martin Scorsese. But the *Saturday Night Live* films had whetted his appetite for directing. David Geffen, who had produced his second album, brought him to Warner Bros., where Brooks worked on a script about a self-help guru (modeled on est founder Werner Erhard) who tries to teach people how to control their dreams. After finishing a draft, he abandoned it. Then he turned to an idea inspired by the PBS documentary *An American Family*, about a filmmaker who moves in with a family in Phoenix to record a year in their lives. But by the time he had finished a script (collaborating with Shearer and Monica Johnson, a former *Laverne and Shirley* producer who shared an office with him on the Warner lot), Geffen was gone from Warner and the new studio chief, Ted Ashley, wanted nothing to do with him.

Brooks spent a year looking for financing to make the film. Finally the owner of the Chicago Bulls basketball team put up $500,000, with the proviso that if Brooks went over budget, he had to make up the difference himself. Brooks managed the feat, and *Real Life*, his first feature, was released in 1979. It was a quintessentially Brooks-ian portrait of the artist as a young narcissist: he plays a filmmaker so obsessed with his cinema verité project that he doesn't realize the family he's filming is disintegrating in front of his eyes. With his backers pulling out and the movie unfinished, the filmmaker makes a last desperate attempt to save it with a dramatic ending, setting the family's house on fire. He quickly dismisses his momentary qualms about tampering with the "reality" he's supposed to be recording: "What are they gonna do—put me in movie jail?" *Real Life* barely made a blip at the box office, but it launched Brooks on a directing career that reached its peak in his next film, *Modern Romance*— an unsparing, brutally hilarious look at an obsessive love affair—and then tapered off with a string of often very funny but progressively more conventional comedies.

He never went back to stand-up, save for a few spur-of-the-moment visits to comedy clubs when he was in the mood. Brooks, typically, chooses to barely remember them. "It was unpleasant," he says of one night he went onstage at the Improv in Los Angeles in the '80s. "Unattentive crowd, late at night. I don't know why I did it." But for his friends, and others lucky enough to have seen him, such appearances were like sightings of a rare, nearly extinct egret. "We'd be driving around and he had an idea and he would run in and nail it," says Monica Johnson, his writing partner on several of his films. "An hour or more off the top of his head. The audience knew they were in on something special."

Bill Scheft, a New York stand-up in the early '80s, was emceeing at Catch a Rising Star on one of those special nights. Brooks came into the club, sat at a table with Paul Simon and Carrie Fisher, and startled Scheft by saying he wanted to do a turn onstage.

Awestruck, the younger comic asked how he would like to be introduced.

"Just tell them you like me," said Brooks, as he walked off to the other side of the bar.

Then, realizing the humility was a perfect setup, he wheeled around and came running back at top speed: "And that I'm the funniest man in the world."

CHAPTER 7

Some Fun

I'm Steve Martin and I'll be out here in a minute.

—Steve Martin

Albert Brooks was hardly the only comic making fun of bad showbiz in the '60s and '70s. The hard-sell entertainers of Vegas and the borscht belt era were ripe for parody, and the baby boomers who had grown up watching them on TV were primed for it. John Byner, a blond, bantamweight comic and impressionist who was a staple on the TV-guest circuit in the mid-'60s, did a character (suggested to him by Steve Allen) called Lenny Jackie, a knock-'em-dead Vegas comic who would burst from behind the curtain and almost literally slide into the audience's lap, before assaulting them with bad one-liners punctuated by rim shots. Art Metrano, a husky, curly-haired comedy writer and actor, became a popular TV-variety-show guest in the early '70s with a tongue-in-cheek act in which he did bad magic tricks (making a finger jump from one hand to the other) while accompanying himself with the theme song "Fine and Dandy"—*da da DA-DA, da DA da DA DA!*

The man who may have done the most to turn the entertainer himself into the butt of jokes, however, was Johnny Carson. For all of *The Tonight Show* king's skills as a host, comic, and straight man, his greatest innovation—what set him apart from predecessors like Steve Allen—was his perfection of the "saver." The snappy comeback meant to "save" a joke that bombs ("What is this, an audience or a jury?") had been part of the nightclub comic's arsenal for years. But Carson made it an integral part of his *Tonight Show* comedy. When a joke would draw a disappointing titter or dead silence from the studio audience, Carson would always react: a sarcastic or self-deprecating wisecrack, a panicked double take, or maybe just a pained Jack Benny look of exasperation. After two or three stinkers in a row, the band might strike up "Tea for Two" and Carson would slip into a vaudeville-style soft-shoe routine—the dying comedian's last desperate plea for love. Whatever the topic of Carson's monologue, the subtext was always his own predicament: a grown man onstage, trying (imagine it!) to make people laugh.

Steve Martin took Carson's subtext and put it front and center in his comedy. But where Carson went for empathy—I'm dying up here, folks!—Martin cast himself as the buffoon. He played the supreme show-biz jerk: sporting a phosphorescent white suit, voice dripping with fake sincerity, limbs flailing in spasmodic fits of "happy feet," brazenly cheer-leading for himself—"We're havin' some fun now!" It was, of course, an-other put-on—all irony, all the time. And it was one of the most wildly successful acts in comedy history.

Brooks and Martin were the yin and yang of 1970s put-on comedy. Both of them took a sharp turn away from the social relevance that Bruce and Carlin and Pryor had brought to stand-up, and both made show busi-ness itself the target of their satire. But they came at it from very different places. Brooks was a Jewish kid who grew up in the insider world of Hol-lywood. Martin was a WASP product of the suburbs, who learned to en-tertain in no less a bastion of wholesome Americana than Disneyland. Brooks's deadpan concept bits could go on for minutes without a laugh, before the satire kicked in. Martin's over-the-top antics got the audience laughing from the moment he walked onstage. Brooks was funny when the TV cameras were on, and reputedly even funnier when they were off. Martin, the "wild and crazy guy" onstage, was a notoriously reserved and serious guy after the curtain came down. Brooks's stand-up comedy had a fervent but relatively limited following. Martin, at his peak, may have been the most popular stand-up comedian of all time—selling out arenas, releasing number-one albums, drawing rock-star-like hordes of adoring fans.

Martin stood apart from most of the stand-up crowd in the 1970s. He never worked in the showcase clubs of New York or L.A. and was not close with other stand-up comics of his generation (though he was a poker partner of Carson's in later years). Some of those fellow comics found him frosty and aloof. Robert Klein remembers his encounter with Martin at a charity event where both were appearing: when Klein was cracking jokes backstage before the show, Martin pulled him up short, asking coolly, "Are you always on?" After he took off the white suit and put away the balloon animals, Steve Martin never seemed to be on. Like Brooks, he was ambivalent about live performing and he gave it up entirely in 1981 to pursue a movie career. "I rarely look at it," Martin says of his early stand-up. "When they present clips to me for shows, I don't know what was funny. I respect people like Carlin, who went on and rose from the ashes of their original burst of fame. But I didn't like the life."

He was born in Waco, Texas, on August 14, 1945, the younger of two children of Glenn and Mary Lee Martin, who moved the family to Los Angeles when Steve was five. His father had done some acting, and even toured with the USO, but went on to make his living in real estate. Theirs was a straitlaced, Baptist, *Father Knows Best*–sort of household. In his memoir, *Born Standing Up*, Martin describes his father as moody and distant and says that after a particularly severe beating, they "hardly spoke" for much of his childhood. John McEuen, a high school friend (and later a founding member of the Nitty Gritty Dirt Band), compared the Martins to "the Stepford family." Says McEuen: "You'd go over there and it was, 'Would you like some cookies?'" Another school friend, Morris Walker, recalls: "When we were kids, and I would arrive at Steve's house to catch the bus, the Martins always had the same breakfast waiting for Steve. They would bow their heads and say the same blessing. They would each have a single piece of white toast, two strips of crisp bacon, and two eggs. It was always precisely the same."

In high school Steve dressed well, drove a white '57 Chevy that looked like it just came off the showroom, and spent his lunch hours playing chess. He and Walker were class pranksters: putting "closed" signs on all the school restrooms or walking down the hallway carrying an invisible pane of glass, then dropping it with appropriate sound effects. They got elected to the school cheerleading squad and made up nonsense cheers that no one else could understand. In their most elaborate stunt, they snuck a canvas full of bird droppings into the Los Angeles County Museum of Art and hung it in an empty spot in a new exhibit of modern art. (Walker lovingly recounts all this in a memoir, *Steve Martin: The Magic Years*, but his most telling anecdote comes from a few years later. After seeing *Roxanne*, Martin's 1987 comedy based on *Cyrano de Bergerac*, Walker says he wrote Martin to remind him about the spoofs they used to do of *Cyrano* in school. Martin wrote back to say their improvisations had not influenced the movie, that he'd rewritten the film script more than forty times, and that Walker "had no claims on the writing of the screenplay." After getting a hurt reply from Walker, Martin apologized and said he was under a lot of pressure.)

The Martins lived in a tract home in Garden Grove, California, just a couple of miles down the road from Disneyland, and the newly opened theme park became Steve's home away from home. He started selling park guidebooks on weekends at age ten, moved up to twirling ropes in Frontierland, and at fifteen got a job in Merlin's Magic Shop. There, peddling gags like rubber vomit and disappearing ink, he learned how to do magic tricks and keep a crowd entertained. "I would say about one third of his early material came from that magic shop," says McEuen, who worked there with him. "It was a new audience every fifteen minutes. You'd develop your close-up timing. You'd do the same bunch of tricks for them. Then you'd start your patter—'Would you like a bag with that? We're out of sacks.' Or when the cash register would ring—'We have a winner!' "

During his breaks, Steve would wander over to the Golden Horseshoe Revue to watch Wally Boag, an old burlesque man who did a fast-paced act of songs, comedy, and shtick like balloon animals. Steve learned juggling from another Disneyland entertainer, and McEuen taught him the banjo. By the time he graduated from high school, Steve had a bag full of stage skills, which he parlayed into a job at Knott's Berry Farm, acting in melodramas and doing a comedy-and-magic act at the Bird Cage Theater. But when a girl there encouraged him to go back to school, Steve enrolled at California State University, Long Beach, to study philosophy. For two years he grappled with Kant and Wittgenstein, then transferred to UCLA and switched to theater. "As I studied the history of philosophy, the quest for ultimate truth became less important to me, and by the time I got to Wittgenstein, it seemed pointless," he told *Time* magazine. "Then I realized that in the arts, you don't have to discover meaning; you create it."

And, he got more laughs than Wittgenstein. He began performing at small clubs in the L.A. area, among them the Ice House, the folk club in Pasadena, where he could make $125 a week as the comedian sandwiched in between two singers. "He was very clean-cut. Always wore a suit," recalls Bob Stane, who opened the club in 1960 and ran it until 1978. "One of his first jokes I remember was about his clothing—he talked about Italian suits that had pants that start at the belt buckle and taper down to the cuff, where they disappear in an infinite point." That was the sophisticated stuff; mostly he was doing artfully dumbed-down nonsense based on his Disneyland and Knott's Berry Farm antics. There was the "nose on microphone" trick, for example, in which Martin would slowly and dramatically place the microphone on his nose, and then take a bow. Or the "napkin trick," in which he'd hold up a napkin in front of his face and stick his tongue through it. Big flourish—big nothing.

A frequent visitor to the Ice House in those days was Mason Williams, the folk singer and songwriter who was writing for *The Smothers Brothers Comedy Hour*. Williams would watch the Ice House shows with a friend who operated the club's light booth. "We looked at the comics more intently than anyone in the audience," says Williams. "I'd watch their mechanics, delivery, timing, the way they relate to the audience, the way they set up jokes." He was impressed with Martin, first because he was a surprisingly good banjo player, and second because of his original approach. "He was laughing at himself," says Williams, "saying this is a dumb thing to do. I thought he had something special."

In the spring of 1968, near the end of *The Smothers Brothers* second season, Tommy Smothers decided to hire ten new writers for his show's summer-replacement series, hosted by Glen Campbell, as a kind of farm team for the regular-season show. Williams brought Tommy down to the Ice House to see Martin's act. Afterward Smothers said he wanted to hire him, but he didn't have enough money left in the budget; Smothers was already paying for a couple of the new writers' salaries himself. Williams offered to chip in three hundred dollars a week from his own paycheck to get Martin on board. Martin only found out about it later.

Martin was brought in on a trial basis, and they didn't even have an office for him at first, so he sat in the hallway. But he did well enough to get kept on as a staff writer when the Smothers' show returned for its third season.

In the fall of 1968, the most turbulent year of the protest decade, *The Smothers Brothers Comedy Hour* was causing a ruckus as network TV's self-styled voice of the counterculture. Critical jabs at the Vietnam War were frequent; the Harry Belafonte song "Don't Stop the Carnival" was intercut with scenes of rioting at the Democratic national convention in Chicago (and cut from the show by the CBS censors); and during the fall presidential campaign, *The Smothers Brothers Comedy Hour* ran its own joke candidate, Pat Paulsen, who took deadpan swipes at the politics of both parties. Williams, the show's head writer by this point, was leading the political charge; Rob Reiner, another young writer who had been hired along with Martin, was one of the firebrands. Martin was "kind of a fish out of water," says Reiner. "We were doing all this socially relevant stuff, and he was going to the Ice House and putting arrows through his head." But he had "terrific ideas," says Bob Einstein—Albert Brooks's older brother and a more seasoned writer for the show, who was teamed with Martin. Williams remembers Einstein as being "kind of a bully" who tended to push for his own material and "lorded it over Martin." "He was a better writer than I was," recalls Martin, who says he and Einstein became good friends. "I was very virginal, just learning the whole process. But I had enough going for me that I could survive."

Martin also teamed with Reiner frequently. They wrote a sketch satirizing '50s rock 'n' roll; a bit that never aired about a Hollywood premiere for a film called *Renegade Nuns on Wheels*; and what Reiner figures was "the first fart joke on network television." (Paulsen, as the head of a novelty company being interviewed, sits down in a chair and a noise erupts. Someone is playing the old whoopee cushion gag on him, he says. When he looks under his seat, however, nothing is there.) In another of their bits, Reiner and Martin had Tommy Smothers sing "Woman Woman," the old Gary Puckett song, to his girlfriend; as he sang the line "Have you got cheatin' on your mind?" she would be making out with his brother Dick in front of him. "Every time Tommy got to the line 'Have you got cheatin' on your mind?' " says Reiner, "he'd turn away while they were making out. I said, 'Tommy, it's not funny that way; you've got to be looking straight at her.' He said, 'But how could I sing that?' I said, 'That's the joke.' Then he did it his way on the air, and it didn't get any laughs. And he said, 'See, I told you it wasn't funny.' "

Tommy Smothers liked letting writers perform their own material, and on one show in early 1969, Steve Martin got a stand-up spot. His hair still dark, with a modish cut, he walked out and introduced himself to America for the first time: "I'm Steve Martin and I'll be out here in a minute." That simple twist on autopilot TV introductions seemed to announce a fresh, self-mocking comic sensibility. He went on to do his "napkin trick" and a few other bits from his Ice House act. For a twenty-three-year-old comedy writer just a couple of years removed from Knott's Berry Farm, it was a heady moment.

But it was only a moment. Later that spring, the Smothers Brothers' show was canceled, and Martin was out of work. He continued to develop his stand-up act in clubs and on daytime shows like *Steve Allen* and *Merv Griffin*, while supporting himself with writing jobs. He worked on *The Andy Williams Show* and a Ray Stevens summer series, then got a $1,500-a-week staff job on *The Sonny and Cher Comedy Hour*. Chris Bearde, the producer who hired him, remembers Martin coming up with "the most extreme stuff" on the show, like a sketch in which Martin rolled tumbleweeds out on the stage for a rendition of "Tumbling Tumbleweeds"—and then, when the tumbleweed supply ran out, tumbled himself across the stage. But he was unhappy at not getting more time in front of the camera, and in 1972 quit to devote himself full-time to his stand-up act.

It wasn't easy. In a period when Vietnam was still dividing the nation, the Watergate scandal was just beginning to unfold, and Carlin and Klein were using stand-up to express the social and political dissent of the young generation, Martin's silliness just seemed out of it. "People didn't know what to make of him," says Bearde. "We'd go to see him at the Troubadour, and sometimes it would just be me and two writers and four other people in the audience. He'd ask me afterward, 'Do you think I should keep doing this?' I'd say, 'It's up to you, Steve.'" George Shapiro, the William Morris agent who would later manage comics like Andy Kaufman and Jerry Seinfeld, joined Martin's agent to see the comedian at the Horn, a small club in Santa Monica where singers like Vikki Carr and Jack Jones were the usual fare. "I want to give you some advice," Martin's agent told his client afterward. "You should be a writer. Forget the comedy."

He played folk joints and Playboy clubs, did college gigs that paid less than it cost him to travel there. He opened in Vegas for stars like Ann-Margret and Helen Reddy. He toured with the Nitty Gritty Dirt Band, his friend John McEuen's group (John's brother Bill, who managed the Dirt Band, became Martin's manager), where he had to face crowds chanting, "Dirt Band! Dirt Band!" He'd practice crowd control in front of the mirror backstage before the show—"Good evening, you fucking assholes"— then clench his teeth and try to make them pay attention. "Sometimes he was wonderful," says McEuen. "Sometimes he died a miserable death."

Martin was never comfortable with the wild and crazy scene around him. He had anxiety attacks (on top of the migraine headaches that had kept him out of the Army). He wasn't a drug user—he tried pot for a while but didn't like it and quit—nor a party guy. "Steve was absolutely dead straight," says Bearde, who roomed with him in 1972 and '73. "I'd have these crazy parties and Steve would be up in his side of the house and wouldn't come down." In 1973 Martin moved to Santa Fe with a girlfriend named Iris, grew a beard and long hair, and started wearing purple hippie beads onstage. After a year of that, he shaved and cut his hair and went back to suits—eventually settling on form-fitting white ones because he thought they'd make him stand out more onstage.

You could see his evolution in *The Tonight Show* appearances that Martin began to make in late 1972. At the beginning he wore a formal tux, later switched to collegiate sweaters, then back to suits. A beard showed up in late '73. The white suit made its first appearance in '74. His material evolved as well. His routines at the beginning were heavy on his old Disneyland shtick. He'd come out with a novelty-shop arrow through his head, play the banjo, and make balloon animals ("Venereal disease!" he'd announce after twisting one into an unrecognizable shape). With a flourish he'd introduce "The Incredible Shrinking Man!" Then he'd tell the audience to close their eyes for a few seconds and he'd simply raise the mike a couple of feet. Or he'd take out a deck of cards and say he was going to make "the king of hearts come down and dance." Then he'd fan out the deck, find the king, and simply bounce it along his arm—*doo de-doo de-doo.*

The bits gradually became more elaborate, the twists on showbiz clichés more sophisticated. There was the "comedy routine for dogs," which Martin opened with a disclaimer: "If you're a human being, you won't get the joke. But if you have a dog, call him over." Then he brought on an audience of four pooches, who sat in a row as he performed for them: "Bowser and Fido were walking down the street . . ." He even took out a dog whistle and played a "doggie jam" that nobody could hear. One by one, the bored dogs trotted offstage.

Another routine took off from the showbiz cliché that great actors can make an audience cry simply by reading the phone book. "If I'm any good," Martin said, "I should be able to read the phone book and make people laugh." And so—natch—he opened up a white pages and began reading names at random, cracking himself up at each one ("I got a million of 'em!"). When the laughs didn't come, he began trotting out desperate burlesque gimmicks—false nose and glasses, bunny ears, splattering an egg over his head—to try to save the bit. "Well, don't look at me," he said at last, stalking off with his phone book. "I didn't write this stuff!"

Johnny Carson didn't much care for that last bit, and after it Martin was demoted to appearing with guest hosts for a while. But in September 1974 he was back on the show with Carson, exhibiting a new level of maturity and confidence. He was the supercool "ramblin' guy," his prematurely silver hair giving him a plastic, almost otherworldly air, like a well-groomed alien from a '50s sci-fi film. "How many people are here tonight?" he opened brightly, another of his goofs on meaningless nightclub banter. He strummed on his banjo, informing the audience proudly that one of his songs was going to be recorded by Crosby, Stills, and Nash. "I'm a personal friend of one of the guys in the group," he confided. "I know Crosby Stills." He compressed an entire Vegas act into a few seconds of manic, fast-forwarded gobbledygook, only a stray word or snatch of song ("gambling joke" . . . "*I gotta be me!*") decipherable through the blur. When he was done, Sammy Davis Jr., another guest on the show, came over and hugged him. Carson, doubled over with laughter, called it "five or six minutes of the funniest things I've ever seen here."

There was method in these madcap bits, a philosophy major's theorizing behind the zaniness. "What I was rebelling against in my head was the comics of the fifties, the one-liner guys," says Martin. "I decided that to deny the audience the punch line was the secret of modern comedy. I sort of analyzed the one-liner, which was the style before I started working—OK, here's the punch line, how funny do you think it is? And I thought, well, if there were no punch lines, it would create its own tension, and eventually the audience would start laughing and they won't know why. And that's a better kind of laugh."

Martin had grown up listening to Lenny Bruce and Nichols and May, and had been influenced by everyone from Stan Laurel to Jack Benny. He was a fan of both Carlin and Klein too, though he had little in common with them. He greatly admired Pryor and had seen him perform twice; at the Troubadour in L.A., what shocked him most was that Pryor showed up two and a half hours late for his set—something the precise and punctual Martin could never fathom—and still got a standing ovation. (A few years later, when they were both doing concerts in Chicago, Martin asked to meet Pryor. According to Pryor's manager David Franklin, Martin came to Pryor's suite and shook his hand, but was so awed that he couldn't look him in the face.)

But Martin was sensing a shift in the cultural climate. For a time he had a few Nixon jokes in his act, but soon dropped them. "I felt the winds of change," he says. "As far as I'm concerned, there's two very important decisions in my life professionally. One was, when I was in college, working at Bird Cage Theater and different clubs around, I don't know why it hit me one day, but walking across campus I said, oh, if I'm going to be original, I'm going to have to write everything myself. And I didn't know how to do that at all. And so I came up with a plan, which was to observe myself when I laughed, and figure out what it was that made me laugh, and try to put it into material. And the second biggest artistic and commercial decision I made was to drop the politics, to go very solipsistic. I just wanted to break from the depth of that political infestation in comedy. It was very pervasive. It was just making me another one of the group."

By late 1974, when he was twenty-nine, Martin was still struggling to get traction as a stand-up act. He gave himself just one more year to make it. He talked to David Brenner, the most successful comedian he knew, and asked what he should do. Brenner gave him some practical advice. When he headlined in clubs, Brenner said, he took the "door" (the cover charges) and the owner took the bar; Brenner would then hire a college student to count all the patrons, to make sure he didn't get cheated. The lesson for Martin: he needed to stop being an opening act and hold out for headline spots—even if it meant going to smaller clubs. "My opening act was going nowhere," he says. "There's a kind of psychological aspect to opening: even if you killed and you're better than the headliner, they only remember the headliner."

The first place that booked him as a headliner was a little club in Miami's Coconut Grove early in 1975. The *Miami Herald* gave him a rave review, and that gave him confidence. Then he held out for a headline gig at the Boarding House, the hip San Francisco music club where he had previously been an opening act. David Allen, the club's owner, took a chance on him, and Martin sold out a two-week engagement there in August. He saw it as a breakthrough.

"I think my material didn't change so much as its delivery," says Martin. "And the delivery was just that total confidence." He was leaving behind the early prop gags—the magic tricks, the balloon animals—and developing a more sophisticated kind of metacomedy, a comedy act in ironic quotation marks. There was still plenty of class-clown goofiness. "Here's something you don't see every day," he'd say—then leap up and down like a demented four-year-old. Or he'd erupt in wild seizures of "happy feet," dancing in double time as if controlled by an alien force. But he was expanding his satire to include the whole distorted, narcissistic worldview of the showbiz star.

"I'm so mad at my mother," he griped. "She's a hundred and two years old. She called me up the other day—she wanted to borrow ten dollars for some *food*. I said, Hey, I *work for a living*!" During concerts, he would ask the lighting people for a "blue spot" (he'd instruct them beforehand to ignore any orders he might shout out from the stage), then do a slow-burn star tantrum when the lights didn't change:

I am onstage. And it's my ass out here, you know what I mean? And I come out, and I'm giving, and I'm giving, and I keep on giving, and I give some more. And I make a simple request. I say, hey, can I possibly have a blue spot? But I guess the lighting crew feels they know a little bit more about show business than I do! Although I've been in this business a few years, and I think I know what works best! [*Really hot now*] I'm sorry, but I am *angry*! I come out here, and I can't get a little *cooperation* from the *backstage crew*?! *Excuuuuuse me*!

That last expression, dripping with self-righteous entitlement, became a national catchphrase, the encapsulation of Martin's portrait of the celebrity as asshole. Martin saw a broader resonance to such bits, however, than simple showbiz parody. "A lot of the routines are the distorted thinking that a person who has anxiety has to come up with in order to make an event logical," he told *Rolling Stone*. "It's sort of a West Coast thing. Like the East Coast thing is the neurotic, self-deprecating, never-can-get-ahead attitude. And the West Coast is like, 'Hey, I'm really makin' it.' Only I'm not. I mean it's obvious I'm not making it, and it's obvious to *me* I'm not making it, but I say, 'Hey, I'm makin' it.' I'm kidding myself."

Martin went further, playing with the whole power relationship between performer and audience. When he appeared in big halls, he'd offer sympathy for the folks at the top of the balcony, reassuring them that they'd be able to see everything. Then, for his first bit, he would introduce "the magic dime trick." When someone up front would leave to go to the bathroom, Martin would enlist the rest of the crowd in a practical joke: when the poor sap came back, Martin instructed them to laugh at everything he said even *before* the punch lines. Three thousand people playing a prank on one suspecting schlub. It was brilliant lunacy.

He broke down the performer-audience barrier in more experimental ways as well. After finishing a performance at Vanderbilt University in Nashville, he took his bows, said good night—and found there was nowhere else to exit but through the audience. When the crowd lingered, Martin led them outside, saw an empty swimming pool next door, and on an impulse, told everyone to climb inside, forming a human sea while he "swam" across their bodies. After that, he would improvise other audience-participation stunts after his shows were finished. He took one audience to McDonald's and ordered three hundred hamburgers—then changed it to a single order of french fries. He told another crowd to hide behind some bushes while he hailed a cab—then, when one stopped, had everyone jump out and ask for a ride too. A few years later Andy Kaufman would hire buses to take his Carnegie Hall audience out for milk and cookies after the show; Martin was inventing similar street-theater stunts years earlier in the hinterlands, largely unnoticed.

Within a year of his August 1975 Boarding House gig, Martin's career had exploded. He filled in for Carson as guest host of *The Tonight Show* and played giant halls like L.A.'s Dorothy Chandler Pavilion. But he got his biggest boost from the groundbreaking TV show that had been considerably less welcoming to some other stand-up innovators of the '70s, *Saturday Night Live*.

Lorne Michaels had little interest in Steve Martin at first. After auditioning him for Lily Tomlin's special back in 1973, Michaels felt his material was too "writerly." When Bernie Brillstein, who managed Michaels and several of the *Saturday Night Live* cast members, urged him to take another look at Martin, Michaels dismissed him as a retro West Coast phenomenon, hardly part of the comedy vanguard his show was trying to lead. "I wasn't tracking him," Michaels says. "I wasn't aware of what he was doing. I was so vigilant about everything that seemed old-school to us."

But when Martin's career began to take off, Michaels booked him as a guest host in October 1976. Martin didn't especially stand out in the so-so sketches (playing Ted Baxter in a takeoff of *The Mary Tyler Moore Show*, for instance), but his stand-up scored. "It's great to be here," he announced in his opening monologue. Then, moving a bit to the side: "No, it's great to be *here*." The sheer class-clown simplicity of the gag seemed to cut through all the layers of *National Lampoon* hipness and star ego that were enveloping the show. "He was a breath of fresh air in a very stale room at that point," says Michaels. "We were burned-out. He was sunshine. We were very much about being taken seriously. And Steve was braver than that. He didn't care."

His breakthrough appearance, however, didn't come until the following September, when Martin hosted *Saturday Night Live*'s third-season opener. Two sketches became Martin signatures. In one, he donned black-framed glasses to play a sleazy defense attorney who mercilessly grills a rape victim (Gilda Radner), bringing her to tears on the witness stand. After the case is dismissed and the courtroom has emptied, he swaggers up to Radner and asks for a date. She breaks down all over again, lashes out at him for his shameless ethics, and leaves in tears. Alone in the courtroom, the chastened lawyer soberly reflects on her words. "Gee, maybe she's right," he says. "Maybe I got off the track somewhere along the line in the pursuit of a buck. Maybe I lost sight of my ideals . . ." Then, after a short pause, snapping out of it: "*Naaaah!*"

In the other sketch, Martin and Dan Aykroyd played two hopelessly unswinging singles from Czechoslovakia, coming on clumsily to a couple of women in an apartment-house rec room. They dubbed themselves "two wild and crazy guys," and the appellation became Martin's calling card, as he returned to reprise the character several times. *Saturday Night Live* did for Martin what it couldn't do for the other leading stand-ups of the decade: it enhanced and ripened his comedy persona, rather than diminishing it. The show grew because of him, and he grew because of the show.

Over the next two years, Martin was as hot as any stand-up comedian in history. He released three best-selling record albums: *Let's Get Small* (1977), *Wild and Crazy Guy* (1978)—which reached number one on the *Billboard* pop chart—and *Comedy Is Not Pretty!* (1979). He recorded a hit single—

"King Tut," a number he created for *Saturday Night Live* to satirize the mania over the Tutankhamen exhibit—and published a best-selling book of his comic essays, *Cruel Shoes*. The crowds at his concerts treated him like a rock idol, wearing balloon animals and arrows through their heads and calling out for favorite bits. Journalists did stylistic backflips to try to mimic Martin's wild-and-crazy style, and hailed him as comedy's savior. "He breaks down barriers," said David Felton in *Rolling Stone*. "He allows us to see the comedian in all of us. In his own way, Steve Martin is a light, a source, an inspiration and a leader."

His so-dumb-it's-smart comedy was as far away as possible from the committed social satire Carlin and Pryor and Klein had been doing for much of the previous decade. But Martin had gauged the times perfectly. By 1976, the Vietnam War was just a memory, and the "long national nightmare" of Watergate was over. Kids were listening to disco, not Dylan; Hollywood's new-wave directors were turning out escapist blockbusters like *Jaws* and *Star Wars*, not counterculture parables like *Bonnie and Clyde* and *Easy Rider*. "The darkness of the era was lifting, and Steve Martin was helping," as Martin's old friend John McEuen saw it. "You could be silly again."

Martin's comedy was facetious and fun; any hint of intrusion by the real world was instantly undercut with irony. He told a story of running into Jackie Onassis in a Tucson Laundromat and inviting her out to lunch—only to discover that the most sophisticated woman in the world ate like a pig, shoveled food into her mouth without utensils, and slapped fried eggs on her breasts to try to crack up the waiter. (Martin's reaction: "What a letdown.") Comedians like Pryor and Richard Lewis poured out all their angst about women; Martin set up the angst, then pulled out the rug. He related the sad story of the death of his girlfriend. "I guess I kinda blame myself for her death," he said, then recounted their last night together, when she had too much to drink at a party and he wouldn't drive her home:

> She ran out to the car, and I followed her out. And I guess I didn't real-
> ize how much she had been drinking. She asked me to drive her home,
> and I refused. We argued a little bit further, and she asked me once
> again. "Would you please drive me home?" I didn't want to. [*Beat*] So I
> shot her.

Stardom gave him even richer opportunities for self-parody. "I bought some pretty good stuff," he said of his newfound wealth. "Got me a three-

hundred-dollar pair of socks. A fur sink. An electric dog polisher . . . And
of course I bought some dumb stuff too." He boasted about another new
possession, a group of hostages ("really nice people; they're tied in a
sack"), and said he was preparing three demands: "A hundred thousand
dollars in cash. A getaway car. And I want the letter *M* stricken from the
English language." And then, as always, the extra twist, undercutting even
his own put-on: "See, you have to make one outrageous demand, so if you
get caught, you can claim insanity . . . *Heh-heh-heh.* 'Getaway car'!" And
when he got even bigger, the star ego soared into outer space, literally. "My
goal now," he said, "I want to be the all-being master of time, space, and
dimension. Then I want to go to Europe."

The fortress of irony around his comedy was matched by his WASP reserve offstage. He had enough famous girlfriends (Linda Ronstadt and
Bernadette Peters among them) to get him occasionally in the gossip
columns, but he was notoriously private, guarded, wary of crowds, fastidious in his personal habits. ("To spend time with him," Tommy Smothers
once said, "is like being alone.") And he was the most serious of funny-
men: well read, a collector of art and student of music, almost (cue the
blue spot) an intellectual. "He knows what's going on in the world," said
Lorne Michaels. "And he doesn't have the thing some comedians have,
which is a yearning to be taken seriously. I think because he's more comfortable with his intellectual side."

In his peak years of 1978 and '79, Martin played outdoor amphithe-
aters and twenty-thousand-seat coliseums, sometimes two shows a night.
He was outdrawing even the top rock groups of the era. His opening acts,
frustrated at having to perform for thousands of Martin fans with arrows
through their heads, sometimes left the stage in tears. The intensity of his
fans often bothered Martin as well; people in the crowd would yell out his
punch lines, throwing off his timing. (Martin needed structure in his act;
he hated to ad-lib.) "It was a very serious job to him, and it became very
stressful," says Maple Byrne, his road manager during those years. "He
had created a monster. It had gotten past the point of where you could do
what you were there to do well." Lorne Michaels thought Martin's manager was partly to blame, trying to squeeze too much out of him. "Bill
McEuen kept him working, [telling him,] 'If you stop, you'll lose everything,'" says Michaels. "I remember one Tuesday night, late, he called
me. This was like 1979. I said, 'Where are you?' He said, 'Terre Haute, Indiana.' I said, 'What are you doing?' He said, 'Tertiary markets.'"

"It burned me out," Martin acknowledges. "But in order to keep your
chops up, you gotta keep doing it, and if you take six months off, you go,

where was I?" But the stress was getting to him, and he began to feel his act had peaked creatively. "The responsibility becomes so great. I just recall thinking, it's not a show; it's another animal, and it's about being a success. I would be a little bit depressed. Something was getting to me. I kept thinking comedy was in the delivery, and the delivery was being controlled by the mass hysteria in a way. And I realized later—what I should have seen—was that this is not a comedy show; this is an event. And if I regarded it as an event, I might have come out of it happier."

Martin looked enviously at the relatively stable world of movies. He took a single nonsense line from his stand-up—"I was born a poor black child"—and built it into a screenplay, about the imbecilic adopted son of poor black sharecroppers who tries to make his way in the world. *The Jerk*, directed by Carl Reiner, and released in December 1979, made a surprising forty-three million dollars at the box office and opened the door to his film career. "I knew that while I was hot, I had better switch to something," Martin says. "I had no intention of turning over my act and getting a new act. I knew it was over when it was over. And I thought, now's the time. I'm hot enough to make a deal. You're on a train and it's going one way and another train passes and it's going another way, you gotta leap onto that other train when your paths are crossing." Martin fulfilled the last of his road engagements and released one more less-successful album, *The Steve Martin Brothers*, in 1981. Then he quit stand-up for good.

Martin went on to a more successful and eclectic post-stand-up career than nearly any of his contemporaries: as an actor (*All of Me*, *Father of the Bride*), screenwriter (*Roxanne*, *L.A. Story*), novelist, essayist, playwright, *Tonight Show* host, and raconteur. Nothing, however, had the impact of his work as a stand-up. At the crudest level, he inspired a new band of comedians who tried to top each other with dumb physical antics—sometimes missing the irony. "Ten years ago, if you were the funniest guy in your high school shop class, chances are you would go on to be the funniest guy working at the hardware store or the insurance agency," noted David Letterman in 1980. "Now people see Steve Martin and they say, 'Gee, I can get up and act like a fool.' " But Martin made the world safe for Letterman too, and for all his progeny—from Craig Kilborn to Jon Stewart—who adapted Martin's pose of irony, and helped make it the enveloping comedic voice of the new millennium.

Martin and Brooks together inaugurated the age of irony, though with such different comic approaches that they seemed to divide the comedy world. Of the two, Lorne Michaels found Martin the more instinctive and liberating talent. "There was a lot of math in Albert," he says. "Steve had worked at Disneyland. You learn about audiences and being in front of audiences and holding their attention, which is a giant part of show business. He lets the audience work with him. He doesn't think of them as the enemy or something to be feared." Others saw Brooks as the greater artist and Martin as simply a brilliant entertainer. "At the time, I thought Steve was doing a lowbrow version of what Albert Brooks was doing," says Harry Shearer, Brooks's old writing partner. "Steve's defense is that he was just putting on funny hats and an arrow through his head to be ironic. But in the end—he was putting on funny hats and an arrow through his head."

There was another big difference. While both created great comic characters, Brooks's had more bite and resonance, because they had a connection to the real-life neurotic behind them. Martin's buffoonish, self-deluding "ramblin' guy" was never more than a comic construct. The real Steve Martin stayed well behind the curtain. Which may be one reason his wildly inventive but insular comedy didn't spawn any real imitators, or comics who were remotely like him. Steve Martin led stand-up into a beautiful cul-de-sac.

Which still left us with the laughs, which Martin delivered in greater abundance than virtually any other comic of his era. And his demonstration that experimental comedy was not inconsistent with entertaining huge numbers of people. And that comet of a career, which turned one stand-up comedian, for a little while at least, into the all-being master of time, space, and dimension. Until he went to Europe.

CHAPTER 8

Chasing Carson

If your dog is constipated—why screw up a good thing?

—David Letterman

Johnny Carson rarely went out to nightclubs; in fact, he hadn't been sighted much at all in New York since he moved his *Tonight Show* to Burbank in 1972. So when TV's late-night king walked into Catch a Rising Star one night in February 1977—unannounced, all by himself—the atmosphere could hardly have been more electric. Rick Newman, Catch's owner, had gotten advance word that Carson might drop by. But the club was full when Johnny walked in, and Newman had to evict some patrons at a center table near the back so Carson could have a prime seat to watch the show.

Jerry Seinfeld remembers the night well; he was waiting to go on next when Carson walked in. But someone grabbed him at the last minute and told him that he'd have to wait. The first act that Johnny Carson would get to see at Catch a Rising Star was the club's hottest comic at the moment, David Sayh.

A slim, mustachioed New Yorker with a slick routine of observational stand-up, Sayh delivered twenty minutes of his A material and got a big response. Sure enough, a couple of weeks later, he got a call from *The Tonight Show*. On April 27, 1977, David Sayh got to live out every stand-up's dream: being plucked from the chorus line to make his national TV debut on *The Tonight Show*. Carson had introduced plenty of first-timers on his show, but he took special pride in this one, his own discovery. "A couple of months ago I stopped by a place called Catch a Rising Star," he told the audience. "I saw this young man, and he had some very funny things to say. So I asked him to come out and be on the show tonight."

Sayh walked out and did six minutes of his best Catch material. He talked about public-service commercials on TV, giant crayon boxes in grade school, New York kids taking standardized aptitude tests. ("Use *ominous* in a sentence." "Hey, ominous gang.") The applause was still ringing after Sayh had taken his bows and left the stage, and a *Tonight Show* staffer had to retrieve him from the green room for a curtain call. Carson walked over and shook Sayh's hand personally. A few days later there were banners welcoming him back at Catch a Rising Star. No longer rising, this star had reached the heights.

But not for long. When Carson invited him back a few weeks later, Sayh had to dig down into his second layer of material, and his routine didn't make quite the same splash. Asked back for a third time a couple of months after that, he had to follow Richard Pryor and Rich Little, and he struggled for laughs. He had a few more *Tonight Show* spots and went on to a modest stand-up career, but the glow of his triumphant TV debut had passed.

For Seinfeld and the stand-up crowd back in New York, Sayh's *Tonight Show* experience offered some lessons. First—though you didn't need David Sayh to tell you this—Carson's show was the most important TV showcase for any young stand-up looking to launch a career. Second, once you got that *Tonight Show* break, you'd better be ready—with enough material to last more than one appearance. Third, the sheer rarity of Sayh's Carson encounter stressed what nearly all the New York comics were coming to realize: If you wanted to get on *The Tonight Show*—which is to say, make it in this business—you couldn't depend on Johnny Carson's once-in-a-lifetime visit to Catch a Rising Star. You had to be in Los Angeles, where you could be seen not just by Carson's bookers but by all the agents and producers and network executives who were the gateway to TV and movie roles. And so stand-up comedy's westward march began.

Though he influenced the path of comedy for decades, Carson had never been a stand-up comic himself. After growing up in Nebraska, he worked in local radio and TV, wrote for Red Skelton's TV show, and made his national reputation as the smooth, wisecracking host of a comedy-game show, *Who Do You Trust?*, before being tapped as Jack Paar's successor on *The Tonight Show* in 1962. But his obvious knowledge of comedy (Jack Benny, Groucho Marx, and Jonathan Winters were just a few of the masters you could hear in his delivery), his cultivation of the opening monologue as the centerpiece of the show, and his dominant ratings for his entire thirty-year run, made him uniquely positioned to be a tastemaker. Particularly after the demise in 1971 of *The Ed Sullivan Show*—the premier TV showcase for comedians in the 1950s and '60s—Carson's show was unchallenged as the make-or-break venue for a stand-up comedian on the way up.

The Tonight Show was still ninety minutes long in the 1970s, and virtually every night at least one stand-up was on the guest list. Many were Vegas veterans from Carson's generation, like Buddy Hackett and Don Rickles, but Carson took special pleasure in introducing newcomers as well. He would give them a warm buildup, often laugh out loud at their jokes, and give a supportive nod or a few words of encouragement afterward, even when it sounded like a strain: "Funny piece of material," or "You've got a strange head working there," or his old standby for the wacky routines he didn't quite get, "Crazy time!" The most coveted affirmation from Carson, however, was an invitation to come over to the guest couch for a few more minutes of chat. The show's producers would alert Carson in advance to the comics they were especially high on, the ones they felt might deserve the kingmaker's blessing. But in the end, it was Carson's call, and that made it all the more meaningful.

"It was so Olympic to step out on that stage," says Seinfeld, who in May 1981 made his *Tonight Show* debut—which he put off for months while he gathered enough material to avoid the David Sayh trap. "It was like someone coming up to you, tapping you on the shoulder, and saying, 'Would you like to play Major League ball? The only spot we have is in the World Series.' *The Tonight Show* was glittering, glamour. It was hope."

That first time out on Carson's stage became an almost mythic rite of passage for young stand-ups, the tales retold like war stories. "There's no describing the pressure," says Tom Dreesen, a Chicago-born comic who made the first of his thirty-plus *Tonight Show* appearances in December 1976. "Not only are all the agents and managers and nightclub owners watching. But your mom has everybody in your own neighborhood watching, so you can't even go back home if your shit goes into the toilet. They walk you back behind the curtain. Doc Severinsen is playing music during the commercial. You're talking to God—please, oh my God, I can't remember my first line. Now you're out of commercial and your heart stops. And then Johnny Carson says the most profound thing. He says, 'We're back now, and I'm glad you're in such a good mood tonight, because my next guest is making his first appearance on *The Tonight Show*.' *I'm glad you're in such a good mood tonight*. You'd hear that for every comedian the first time. And he only did it the first time.

"Then they open up that curtain, and at that moment you feel something nudging your Adam's apple, and it's your asshole trying to get out.

Of course, you're not going to get sick, because you haven't eaten in two days anyhow, so there's nothing inside. You walk out into what seems like an operating room, with bright lights, and you can't see the audience. And there's a T on the floor that you've got to hit—that's your mark. And the audience is applauding. And then you do that first joke."

A successful *Tonight Show* debut could ignite a career. The morning after his Carson spot, Dreesen got a call from CBS offering him a one-year development deal—which meant a struggling young comic "didn't have to worry about rent, groceries, shoes for the kids," Dreesen says. "I could work on my craft. And I never stopped working since." David Brenner, who was plugging along in the Village clubs in New York City when he got a *Tonight Show* booker's attention, made his first Carson appearance in January 1971. A day later, he says, he got ten thousand dollars' worth of job offers. Freddie Prinze, the nineteen-year-old Puerto Rican phenom from New York, made a legendary *Tonight Show* debut in December 1973. His routine about the Washington Heights neighborhood he grew up in (where "even the birds are on drugs" and home was a "six-floor run-up") nearly brought down the house. Carson called him over to the couch. "There's no greater thrill for me personally," he said, "than to have somebody come out here who's unknown and absolutely wipe 'em out the first appearance." Shortly after that, sitcom producer James Komack cast Prinze in *Chico and the Man*.

For most of the comics, Carson himself had a mandarin inscrutability. Aloof and uncomfortable in social gatherings, he was friends outside the show with few of the younger comics. "We talked during the commercials; that was my social life with Johnny Carson," says Robert Klein, who made more than eighty appearances on the show. (When Klein in the early '70s began coming on the show dressed in sweaters and jeans, word came from Carson's producers that Johnny would prefer he wear a suit.) "He was intimidating. He didn't mean to be. But when he walked into the room, it was like lightning—always with that cigarette, straight as an arrow." David Letterman idolized Carson, became a favored guest host, and even lived down the street from him in Malibu; yet he had virtually no off-screen relationship with him.

Even when Carson would pay a rare visit to one of the L.A. comedy clubs, he kept his distance. Jamie Masada, owner of the Laugh Factory on Sunset Boulevard, recalls one night when Johnny walked into his club and got so drunk that Masada himself had to take the wheel of Carson's Mercedes and drive him back home to Malibu. "He didn't say a word the entire ride," Masada says. When he had pulled into Carson's driveway and deposited him at his front door, Carson said good night and went inside—leaving his chauffeur stranded in the middle of Malibu without a ride home. (He wound up hitchhiking back and got picked up by a passing comedian.)

Yet it was the very blankness of Carson's public persona, his willingness to serve as the self-effacing straight man, that made his show such a flattering showcase for stand-up comics. "He was so secure in himself that he never had a problem laughing his ass off when somebody was funny," says Jeff Wald, George Carlin's former manager. The *Tonight Show* host, of course, had his peculiar tastes and prejudices. He had a frat-boy weakness for leering sex gags—the wink-wink of Art Fern and his buxom blonde assistant, played by Carol Wayne—but drew the line at comedy he felt was mean-spirited or in bad taste. Some faulted him for having on relatively few black and younger women comics. Yet he embraced much of what was happening in stand-up comedy in the late '60s and '70s. He gave Carlin and Klein an important TV platform early in their careers. And he was clearly taken with the wacky put-on bits that Albert Brooks began rolling out in the early '70s—even when he couldn't quite explain why they cracked him up.

The opportunities for a stand-up club performer in Los Angeles B.C.—Before Carson—were pretty sparse. There were a few small clubs that would book comedians—the Horn, a mainstream club in Santa Monica; the slightly edgier Ye Little Club in Beverly Hills, and the Ice House, the folk joint in Pasadena where Steve Martin developed much of his early act. Comics occasionally opened for music acts at the Troubadour, the rock club on Santa Monica Boulevard, and newcomers could try out there on Monday open-mike nights. But there was a definite void when the owner of the building that once housed Ciro's, the legendary Hollywood restaurant on Sunset Boulevard, offered Sammy Shore, a Vegas comic who used to open for Elvis Presley, the cocktail-lounge space next door rent-free.

Shore asked his friend Rudy De Luca, a writer who later worked on several of Mel Brooks's movies, what he should do with the space, and De Luca suggested they turn it into a comedy club, like the Improv in New York. Shore thought it was a great idea; they could put in a few tables and chairs, invite all their comedy friends, and call it the Sammy Shore Room. "Who's going to come to the Sammy Shore Room?" asked De Luca. "Sammy Shore," said Sammy. His wife, Mitzi, however, came up with a better name, and in April 1972, just a month before Johnny Carson set up shop in Burbank, the Comedy Store opened for business.

They charged eighty-five cents for drinks and put the word out to their friends from TV shows like *Laugh-In* and *Mary Tyler Moore*. Few of them actually got up to entertain, but there were plenty of comics willing to grab the mike: old-timers like Leonard Barr (Dean Martin's uncle); younger up-and-comers like David Brenner and Steve Landesberg; newbies like Alan Bursky, who used to park cars in the lot next door and became, at age seventeen, the youngest comic ever to do *The Tonight Show*. Barry Levinson and Craig T. Nelson, two former acting school buddies, formed a comedy team (sometimes joined by De Luca), doing satirical sketches on things like military precision drill teams and the *GE College Bowl*. "It was fun because there was no structure, no schedule," says Levinson, who went on to write and direct *Diner* and *Rain Man*, among other films. "People would just show up and go onstage. None of us really saw ourselves as performers. I saw myself as a writer. But it was a place to play around. It kept us loose."

Shore was the emcee, while De Luca tried to manage the nightly lineup. But that didn't last for long. "It was a rough job," says De Luca. "I made the decisions—ten, twelve, fifteen comics a night, comin' and goin'. It was too much for me. I couldn't handle it." After six months De Luca quit to write for *The Carol Burnett Show*, and Shore struggled for the next year or so trying to run the place on his own. Then he got a four-week engagement in Vegas and told Mitzi to mind the Store while he was gone. When he came back, she had transformed the place. "The booths had been moved around. There were plants in the ladies' and men's rooms. It had a woman's touch," says Sammy. "I came back and it was a different place."

For Mitzi, the Comedy Store was a chance to finally emerge from Sammy's shadow. They had met in 1950 at the Pine Point Resort in Wisconsin, where the former Mitzi Saidel was working as a secretary and Sammy was the entertainer. He got her pregnant, married her, and for the next couple of decades Mitzi raised four kids (among them future slacker-film star Pauly Shore) and kept track of the money while Sammy traveled the road. "She was always a good businesswoman," says Sammy. "And she learned comedy through me. She always had a good insight into material. She had a great eye."

Mitzi brought some order and business discipline to the Comedy Store. Instead of the impromptu free-for-alls of the early days, she began to set the nightly lineups in advance. Sammy wouldn't have minded, except that one comic who seemed to get left out of Mitzi's lineups was Sammy Shore. "I would walk into the Store and say I want to go on. She'd say, 'You can't. The show is booked. Call me tomorrow.'" When he insisted and grabbed a microphone anyway, she'd complain that he had disrupted her carefully planned schedule. Their fights became angrier, sometimes violent. One night, when he wanted to come to the club and see a friend perform, she told Sammy he couldn't because the babysitter wasn't available. Sammy says he went down to the club anyway and found the babysitter laughing at the show from the front row. He slapped Mitzi across the face right there in the club, so hard the bag of money she was holding flew up in the air and scattered all over the floor.

She filed for divorce. In the settlement they worked out in August 1974, Sammy gave Mitzi the Comedy Store, in return for a six-hundred-dollar-a-month reduction in his child-support payments. And that was the end of the Sammy Shore Room. "I could never have run it; it's not in my skin," Sammy says. "But she never gave me credit. Everyone forgot about me. It became Temple Mitzi on Sunset Boulevard."

She didn't see it as a temple so much as a college of comedy, where Mitzi—a pretty, petite brunette with a whiny, Roseanne-like voice that every comic could imitate—was both dean and den mother. "I love comics," she would say years later. "They needed a lot of work. And I was willing to do it."

The club developed a familiar routine. Newcomers could audition on Monday nights. On Tuesdays, all the comics would call in to find out what time slots Mitzi had booked for them during the week. The comedians she liked got the prime spots. The ones she didn't were consigned to the wee hours, or shut out altogether. Like the showcase clubs back in New York, Mitzi didn't pay her talent anything. But she helped out the ones who were hard up by giving them jobs as doormen or emcees, loaning them money, and even letting some of them live, rent-free, in the house she owned on Cresthill Road in the hills behind the Store. She gave some a more intimate form of support. She had a four-year relationship with Steve Landesberg, and another one with Argus Hamilton, a good-looking former frat boy from the University of Oklahoma who began working at the Store in 1976. There were rumors of other comics who did more than just come up with great one-liners to win Mitzi's favor.

She prided herself on nurturing new talent, but she also courted bigger-name comics who could bring in crowds and give the room buzz. When Jimmie Walker, a former Improv comic from New York who was starring in the TV sitcom *Good Times*, performed at the Store in the mid-'70s, he let Mitzi put his name on the marquee outside, and fans packed the place. Richard Pryor began using the Comedy Store to develop material for his 1978 concert tour, which became the basis for his groundbreaking first concert film, and that gave the club even more cachet. By the time Robin Williams broke out of the Comedy Store in 1978 and became an overnight star on TV's *Mork and Mindy*, Mitzi Shore's club was the white-hot center of the L.A. comedy scene.

Mitzi moved quickly to expand her comedy empire. She opened up a second Comedy Store in L.A.'s Westwood district, which became a kind of farm team for newer comics (Williams worked there when he first came to L.A. from San Francisco), and another club down the coast in La Jolla, where she booked some of her best acts as headliners. In 1976, after she nearly lost her Hollywood lease when the DJ who ran an oldies show in the big room next door wanted to take over her space, she bought the entire building—refinancing her house to raise the money. Then she refurbished the large showroom—where Ciro's had once been—and turned it into the Main Room (the original club became known as the Original Room), where she planned to book big-name Vegas comics.

The most serious threat to her dominance of the L.A. comedy scene came from a New York interloper. Budd Friedman, who had invented the showcase comedy club in New York a decade earlier, opened a West Coast branch of the Improv on Melrose Avenue in 1975. He brought out two of his best New York acts, Elayne Boosler and Andy Kaufman, to help launch it, and the club became a magnet for many of the New York comics who moved out to L.A. But in contrast to the collegial, live-and-let-live relationship he had with Catch's Rick Newman back in New York, Friedman found in L.A. a rival who wanted to play hardball. Mitzi told the comics who played the Comedy Store that she would bar them from her club if they worked at the Improv. The crusty New York club owner wasn't used to this kind of treatment. "I used to come out to visit, and Mitzi would be very nice," Friedman says. "The minute I signed a lease, I was persona non grata. Mitzi said I stole her idea."

"In the beginning I didn't care," says Mitzi. "I felt, let [the comics] work there because he's from New York, and we eventually got them all working here. But it came to a point where I couldn't have them playing both clubs." It was a power play motivated by almost maternal possessiveness. "She felt that if she developed you and took you in, like a child, then why would you go over there?" explains her son Pauly. Says Friedman: "I felt badly for the comedians. A few of them, like Jay Leno, had the balls to say I wanna work both clubs. But the weaker guys kowtowed."

With most of the comics forced to choose sides, the two clubs developed very different personalities. The L.A. Improv was home to the edgy, sardonic, East Coast observational style—Richard Lewis made it his home base when he moved to California in 1976, as did Jerry Seinfeld a few years later. The club had more of a New York feel, with a bar where the comedians could hang out. (Les Moonves, an out-of-work actor who went on to become the head of Warner Bros. Television, and later CBS, was a bartender there for, he says, "two of the most fun years of my life," in 1977 and '78.) At the Comedy Store, a somewhat forbidding stucco box painted black inside, there was only a small rear hallway for the comics to linger while they waited for their turn onstage, so they usually mingled out front, or in the parking lot in the back to smoke their joints.

Mitzi had different tastes from Budd. She liked impressionists and broad physical comics—like Gallagher, whose stunts included smashing a watermelon with a sledgehammer onstage. She was drawn to good-looking WASP types like Hamilton and Tim Thomerson, a surfer from San Diego whose premium bit was a fast-paced spoof of Hollywood westerns, packed with voices and sound effects. Yet she was also a fan of Lenny Bruce (whom she had seen perform in Miami Beach) and gave stage time to more edgy comics too—like Paul Mooney, Richard Pryor's friend and writer, who worked the last spot of the evening at the Comedy Store in the late '70s, sipping Courvoisier onstage and drawing an admiring crowd of fellow comics with his political and racial commentary. She was welcoming to ethnic comics, and when she felt female stand-ups were having too hard a time cracking the boys' club at the Store, she opened a smaller showroom upstairs, called the Belly Room, just for women. She was even known to give hecklers a shot at the mike.

"Budd sort of stuck by his old favorites and went by reputation," says Hamilton. "Mitzi was the only one who really developed new talent. Budd would give them a place to perform. But Mitzi really nurtured us. She was very much into the artistic-ness of stand-up comedy. That meant she liked creative, charismatic kids growing as artists onstage." "The great thing about Mitzi," says Thomerson, "is that she really, really believed in these young guys. She would give almost anybody a shot."

For the comics Mitzi took under her wing, it was all good. "It was just a tremendous time in our lives," says David Letterman, who quit a radio job in Indianapolis and drove out to L.A. in 1975 with his wife. He became one of Mitzi's favorites, moving quickly from Monday audition nights to a regular gig as weekend emcee; after his marriage broke up, he moved into a converted motel across the street from the club and had the time of his life. "Mitzi was a maternal influence," says Letterman. "She had this place where we could all come, and be silly and make mistakes and have fun and go home with a waitress. I left a job for what I thought could be nothing, and then found this life and friends and home and creative outlet. And without Mitzi I don't know what I would have done."

Yet she could make or break a comic's career, and she seemed to relish the power. "Everybody feared her and worshipped her," says Merrill Markoe, a comedy writer and sometime stand-up, who met Letterman at the Comedy Store in 1979 and lived with him through much of the '80s. "She was in charge of time slots, and that's all you heard from those guys—did you get your times?" To Markoe and others, Mitzi seemed obsessed with control, supportive only of the talent that she could claim as her own. She was especially tough, Markoe felt, on comics who had other means of support, such as writing. "She liked the idea of a performer who was dangling by a thread and couldn't get a job anywhere else. If you were a writer, Mitzi didn't take you nearly as seriously," Markoe says. One example was Garry Shandling, who came out to L.A. to write sitcoms in 1973 and spent five years struggling with his stand-up act at the Comedy Store. Yet Shandling, who was terribly insecure onstage, had few complaints. "I was the most inexperienced person who walked in there," he says. "I really had to struggle. Mitzi will admit she gave me the toughest time of anyone. But it sure worked for me that it wasn't easy, because it made me work harder."

After a bitter labor dispute that led most of the Comedy Store regulars to go on strike for six weeks in 1979, some thought her possessiveness got even worse. "Anybody who did anything without her OK was gonna get blackballed," says John Witherspoon, a comedian who worked as an emcee and part-time manager of the club in the late '70s. "She was the queen." One former Mitzi pet who ran afoul of her was Mike Binder, a young stand-up who came to L.A. from Detroit in 1976 when he was just eighteen. (Later he became an actor and a director of films like *The Upside of Anger*.) "Mitzi was very nice to me the first few years," he says. "But she turned very dark. She wanted to control all of us." When Binder produced a comedy special for HBO in 1985 called *Detroit Comedy Jam*, Mitzi found out and called him up in a rage. "I was expecting congratulations," says Binder. "But she was furious. She starts screaming, 'You stole that from me! I'm the one that produces specials—you do comedy!'" Bobby Kelton, who was getting regular *Tonight Show* spots in the early '80s (and was even briefly mentioned as a possible successor to Carson as host), was miffed that Mitzi refused to give him decent time slots so he could try out new material. "I told her I had done fifteen *Tonight Show*s," says Kelton. "She told me, 'That means nothing here.'"

And when a hot comedian from New York named Jerry Seinfeld came into her club in 1980, Mitzi practically turned him away at the door. "I didn't like his attitude," Mitzi says. "He didn't fit in." Seinfeld thought it was "kind of a sick culture over there, to tell you the truth. Unless you were kind of a broken-wing bird, they had no interest in you. It wasn't a healthy environment. Mitzi Shore didn't like me. I came presold from New York—people kind of told her, this guy's coming out, he's really good, you should put him on. Well, she didn't like that. She told me to my face. She felt so many people liked me, that's not good for a comedian. She wanted me to seek her counsel. She was like the kid with the drugs at school—if you want to be my friend, you'll buy drugs from me."

Seinfeld, the comedy professor from New York, was turned off by almost everything about Mitzi's club, including her taste in comedy. "There was this whole prop-act thing in L.A.," he says. "Kind of junky, gimmicky stuff. Guys that were pretty hacky. They were strong, they were crowd-pleasers, but they weren't going anywhere." He even hated the room. "There's a darkness about that place. Some people thought it was because, when it was Ciro's, there were a lot of Mob rubouts there. It's painted black, with red, like blood. It's like hell."

It was more like heaven for many of the comics who hung out at the Store during the drug-fueled good times of the late '70s. "You'd drink out in front of the club, smoke pot in the back, and snort coke downstairs," says Argus Hamilton, who admits to being one of the big indulgers. The house on Cresthill that Mitzi lent out to some of the comics became a notorious pleasure palace. The comics who didn't end their nights talking comedy at Canter's Deli on Fairfax Avenue would hit the bars and discos. "We were just as busy after the shows," says Hamilton. "On Monday nights we would go to the fifties night at a bar in Santa Monica. We'd go to Donkin's Disco on Wednesday night, Dillon's Disco on Thursday night. We didn't know we were crazy and sick and alcoholic and drug-addicted lust junkies. We were having the time of our life. We were still on the pleasure side of the equation. And it was an absolute ball."

To the comics who came out from New York, the L.A. club scene was both more freewheeling and more intense. In New York, you were allowed to experiment, and even to bomb. In L.A., you constantly had to have one eye out for the next agent or producer who might walk in the door. "It was OK to be an artist in New York. You didn't look like something went wrong with your life," says Rick Overton, a New Jersey native who worked the New York clubs before moving west in 1980. "When you go out to L.A., you smell success like a barbecue in the neighbor's yard."

The club owners would set up special showcase nights, when producers or casting agents would come in to scout out comedians for a specific part. But the comics couldn't let their guard down on any night; who knew what power broker might be sitting at a back table? "The joke is, I wouldn't dare break in new material at the Comedy Store, because you could ruin your career," says Tom Dreesen. "If you have any new material, I used to say, break it in at Caesars Palace in Vegas, where it can't hurt you."

The most important person to keep an eye out for, by far, was the comedy booker for *The Tonight Show*. For many years, that job belonged to Jim McCawley, a soft-spoken, hard-drinking Irishman who joined *The Tonight Show* in 1977 after stints in the theater and as a talent booker for a Canadian talk show. McCawley spent several nights a week in the clubs, and when he walked in the house, the stakes rose immediately. His job was to decide what comedians would please his boss, Johnny Carson. Before you could even get seen by *The Tonight Show* host, however, you had to please Jim McCawley.

Not surprisingly, the man dubbed in a *Los Angeles Times* profile "The Other King of Comedy" was controversial among the comics. Many of those McCawley championed and whose careers he boosted, like David Letterman and Garry Shandling, were warmly appreciative. Others thought he was a mediocre judge of talent whose power had gone to his head. McCawley didn't just book the comedians; he would often work on their acts with them, telling them which jokes they ought to use and in what order. "I hone their material," he bragged to the *Los Angeles Times*. "I make them jump through hoops." Shandling, for one, was grateful for the help: "Sometimes after a set [in the clubs], Jim would say, why don't you put this joke here or that joke there? I would say most of his advice was good." (After Shandling did a killer spot on his *Tonight Show* debut in the spring of 1981, Carson looked offstage as the applause was rolling in and gave McCawley a rare on-air plug: "Thanks, Jim.") Says John De-Bellis, the New York stand-up who worked for a year as a *Tonight Show* writer: "McCawley had a very specific idea of what would work and what wouldn't. And he was right a lot of the time. He knew the audience and he knew what Johnny liked."

Others weren't so sure. When Catch a Rising Star's Rick Newman came out to L.A. for David Sayh's *Tonight Show* debut in 1977, he was taken aback at how much McCawley meddled. "He would dissect your material," says Newman. "You had to follow his rules and regulations. He was very impressed with himself and thought he knew comedy better than the comedians." Jay Leno, who was snubbed by *The Tonight Show* for many years, didn't have much respect for McCawley's comedy chops. "Jim didn't understand the comic sensibility, and he could get a little bit harsh," says Leno. "It was like he went to comedy school. He wasn't a natural. He always had a Willy Loman aspect to me. His heart wasn't in it."

Mitzi Shore couldn't stand McCawley, complaining that he drank too much and passed over some of her best acts, like Louie Anderson. He was rumored to be having an affair with Maureen Murphy, an Australian comic who got a number of guest shots on *The Tonight Show* in the early '80s. (McCawley, who was married, denied they were romantically involved.) And he seemed to enjoy throwing his weight around. Larry David, who had few expectations that his quirky act would ever get him on *The Tonight Show*, remembers performing in one of the New York clubs in the late '70s when McCawley came up to him after a set and gave him an unsolicited thumbs-down. "He said, 'Hi, I'm Jim McCawley of *The Tonight Show*, and I just wanted you to know that you're not really right for the show. Johnny wouldn't like your material.' I had never auditioned for him. I had never even asked about it."

"There were a lot of complaints from the comics, who said Jim mistreated them," acknowledges Peter Lassally, the longtime *Tonight Show* producer. "He bullied people, allegedly. He was very good at his job. But the power he had maybe went to his head." (McCawley's role on the show was cut back near the end of Carson's reign. He died of cancer in 1997.)

McCawley's approval was only the first step on the gauntlet the comedians had to run to reach Carson's national TV stage. Comedians accepted that the four-letter words and off-color material they got away with in clubs would have to be toned down for *The Tonight Show*. But many felt they suffered from the show's capricious standards. Tom Dreesen had a joke about a loose Catholic girl who was so promiscuous that after confession her priest had to take a cold shower. The NBC censor thought the line was a reference to masturbation and nixed it. Bobby Kelton used the word *nipple* in one routine, got an OK from the producers for it, then saw it bleeped out when the show aired. "Johnny didn't like it," he was told. Even top comics had to tread carefully around delicate subjects. During the Nixon years, Robert Klein had a bit in which he described Vice President Spiro Agnew as "a felon." Executive Producer Fred De Cordova told him he had to drop the line. Klein, pointing out that Agnew had pleaded no-contest on bribery charges, appealed to the NBC lawyers—who backed him up.

Sometimes the comedians had better luck with Carson himself, on the rare occasions when they could break through his praetorian guard. Richard Lewis's *Tonight Show* career had a near-death experience one night when his routine about renewing a driver's license stretched way past its allotted six minutes. Despite frantic signals to cut it short, Lewis couldn't bear to stop the bit before he got to the end. He barreled ahead, for nearly eleven minutes, right through the commercial. When he walked offstage, a furious McCawley told him he'd never work the show again.

Later that evening, Lewis was having dinner with his agents at the Palm restaurant, when Carson himself came in, accompanied by his lawyer, Henry Bushkin. Lewis shot over to their table, threw himself on his knees, and blurted out a long explanation to Johnny of why he had to finish the routine. "I told him I had done this monologue for years, and there was no way I was gonna embarrass myself in front of you [by not finishing it]," says Lewis. "It was a minute and a half rant, while he was eating his lobster. His lawyer was ready to call the police." But when Lewis finished, Carson made a small nod. The next day McCawley told Lewis he was the luckiest man on the planet: Carson had given him a reprieve.

The Tonight Show could be cruel and it could be kind. It was both, at various times, to the two comics who emerged at the top of the L.A. comedy-club scene in the late '70s: Jay Leno and David Letterman.

After shuttling between the New York clubs and his hometown of Boston for a couple of years, Leno had moved to L.A. in 1974. He scrounged up a few TV and movie roles (playing greasers in *American Hot Wax* and TV shows like *Laverne and Shirley* and *One Day at a Time*), but realized that stand-up was where he belonged, and pursued it with his usual peripatetic zeal. He was one of the few comics who was friendly with both Friedman and Mitzi Shore and able to work at both of their clubs. He drove down the coast for sets at the Comedy & Magic Club in Hermosa Beach; and he went on the road for practically any place that would book him. He was a polished and charismatic stage performer, and his sarcastic observational comedy—on everything from TV commercials to gas-station restrooms—was an influence on almost everyone who worked the L.A. clubs in those years, including Letterman. "Jay was the funniest guy in that group, without question," Letterman says. "He was the valedictorian, the top of the class. What he demonstrated to me, by being onstage, was the importance of attitude."

Leno may have been valedictorian, but he still acted as if he were always running for class president. "He was the Bill Clinton of comedy," says Mike Binder, whom Leno befriended when the Detroit teenager arrived in L.A. and started hanging out at the Comedy Store. "He wanted to like everyone, and wanted everyone to like him. He needed to be at the center of everything. He was an absolute politician." Leno was the guy who taped everyone's TV appearances, helped them with their jokes, razzed them good-naturedly when they made a mistake. Leno (who met his wife, Mavis Nicholson, at the Comedy Store in the mid-'70s) was focused on his career and disdainful of the party crowd. Binder says Jay used to berate him for his drinking and drug use. "He'd say, 'Why are you hanging out with those guys? Work on your act!' He didn't want anything to do with alcohol or drugs. Behind their back, he'd say, 'Just watch— those are the ones who aren't going to make it.'"

One of the few places where Leno wasn't very popular was *The Tonight Show*. He made his first appearance on the show in February 1977—later than many of his Comedy Store contemporaries—and thought he did well. (Leno even had a rare heckler in the studio audience, whom he parried with skill.) But after he was on the show a couple of times, the *Tonight* folks stopped calling. "We didn't feel his material really worked for Johnny," says Lassally. Leno rationalized his problem with Carson as sort of the good-son syndrome: "I didn't quite fit in on the Carson show. Because Johnny was an adult. And my thing was sarcasm. But growing up in a polite family, I'd go to Johnny, 'How are you, sir?'" Binder, who accompanied Leno to his *Tonight* gigs, thought Carson's producers were insulting to Jay. "They made him feel like he was just another hack comic," Binder says. "It was clear Johnny didn't like him."

Letterman's stand-up was similar to Leno's: lampooning the little stupidities of life with derisive irony. (Markoe liked to call it the "you and me and everyone else is a jerk" approach.) But where Leno shouted in mock outrage, Letterman, with his midwestern reserve and Alfred E. Neuman grin, commented drily from the sidelines. He did a bit about commercials for dog food that claim to help constipation, for example. "If your dog is constipated," Letterman mused, "why screw up a good thing?" Or those Alpo ads that advertise "not a speck of cereal." Letterman's take: "My dog spends his day rooting through garbage and drinking from the toilet. Chances are he's not gonna mind a speck of cereal."

He was a couple of steps behind Leno in his career, but was clearly a comer. "Right away Dave had the poise, the personality," says Leno. "I think we took from each other. I got from Dave a sense of stringing words together in an interesting way. I think he saw in me—just get up there and razzmatazz the audience. He was much more the TV performer than any of us. We were all nightclub performers—the ability to be loud, and if the audience got loud, you'd get louder. Dave talked in the same voice in the club that he did on TV."

The two were opposites offstage as well. Leno was gregarious, everybody's pal; Letterman was aloof, hanging with a tight circle of comedian friends, among them George Miller, John Witherspoon, and Tom Dreesen. (Like Leno, Letterman wasn't into drugs—but he took full advantage of the free drink tickets Mitzi used to pass out to comedians at her club.) Where Leno brimmed with self-confidence and bonhomie, Letterman was brooding and ruthlessly self-critical. He claims he never had more than twenty minutes of good material at any one time and felt inadequate next to the big crowd-pleasers at the Comedy Store like Gallagher and Tim Thomerson, who really took over a stage. "When these guys would get on-stage," Letterman says, "that's when I realized, I didn't have what people were paying for." Says Markoe: "He was stressed-out, paranoid, worried all the time. And he was always in a panic. That's one of his orientations in life—that he has no material, that he's going to fail, that everything's going to come apart." Markoe helped out by feeding him jokes of her own—which led to some awkward moments. One night Markoe did one of her lines at the Comedy Store early in the evening—then watched in horror as Letter-man came in later and did the very same line. As the audience looked puzzled, she sat in the back of the room and cringed.

Leno was a glutton for the road, a comic who never met a crowd he didn't want to win over. Letterman never liked performing outside of the comfortable cocoon of the Comedy Store. A weeklong gig in Denver in the summer of 1976, opening for Leslie Uggams, was torturous for him. "The first show went pretty well," Letterman recalls. "So now I think, great, this is gonna be an easy week. The second show: dead silence. They sent a limo to pick me up for the first show. After the second show I never saw the limo again." By the end of the engagement he was filling out his sets by moving from table to table asking people where they were from. One patron lost patience. "He says to me, 'I'm from Denver. He's from Denver. We're all from Denver. *You're in Denver*.' I said, 'Oh. All right. Fair enough.' It was one of those deals for ten days your stomach hurt."

He spent another depressing three weeks at the Sahara Hotel in Lake Tahoe, opening for Helen Reddy. One night he got so few laughs that his twenty-five-minute set was over in fifteen minutes. After saying good night and beating a fast retreat for his room, he bumped into Reddy's manager and husband, Jeff Wald, rushing out of the dressing room. "Jeff Wald says, 'What the hell is going on? I'm downstairs putting on my pants and they tell me you're done!' I said, 'I'm sorry. They didn't laugh.' You take the laughs out of your act and time really flies." Markoe remembers sitting with him in the hotel dining room near the end of one depressing Tahoe gig, when a fan who had seen his show came up and said, "Are you Dave Etterman?" The *L* in his name had fallen off the hotel marquee.

Letterman decided he wasn't meant for nightclubs. In Indianapolis he had worked for a local TV station as an announcer, weekend weatherman, and late-night horror-show host. His comedy was more influenced by Steve Allen's TV show than by any of the stand-up comics, like Jonathan Winters, he had loved growing up. When Jack Rollins, the respected comedy manager, signed Letterman as a client, it wasn't because of his stand-up prowess. "Doing stand-up was an artificial project for him," Rollins says. "The material was not there. I looked at this guy and said, if he belongs anywhere, it's on television." In November 1978, three years after arriving at the Comedy Store from Indiana, Letterman made his debut on *The Tonight Show*. After just three appearances on the show, he was guest-hosting.

The Letterman-Leno saga after that is by now familiar TV lore. After winning attention for his *Tonight Show* hosting stints, in 1980 Letterman was given his own morning show on NBC, which was canceled after just nineteen weeks, and then a late-night talk show in the time slot following Carson in 1982. There he began booking his old Comedy Store comrade Jay Leno, whose appearances (with Letterman playing the expert straight man to Leno's "What's My Beef?" routines) were such a success that *The Tonight Show* took notice and put Leno back on the guest list. Leno eventually became the show's permanent guest host and, when Carson retired in 1992, beat out Letterman for the ultimate prize as Johnny's successor.

The two went on to become twin ambassadors for the 1970s stand-up tradition to a new generation of TV viewers. Oddly, it was Leno, the sarcastic loudmouth from the East Coast, who softened his edge and became the celebrity-friendly voice of Middle America on *The Tonight Show*. Meanwhile, Letterman, the midwesterner turned Californian with the likeable, made-for-television style, moved back to New York and developed the edgy, ironic, self-parodying voice—a talk show host who made fun of talk shows—that became the armor for hip comedians through the end of the century and beyond.

CHAPTER 9

Extremists

This isn't working. I have no business being here, and I'd like
to thank you all for showing me where I'm at.

—Andy Kaufman

The Carnegie Hall concert began, appropriately enough, with the
National Anthem—delivered, less appropriately, by the oily Vegas lounge-
show entertainer Tony Clifton. He was followed by a wholesome, Up with
People–type singing group known as the Love Family, who performed a
medley of songs from *Hair* and *The Sound of Music* before getting booed
off the stage. Finally the star of the show, Andy Kaufman, came out and
did a bouncy but anemic rendition of "Oklahoma!," then introduced his
special guest for the evening: a little old lady who was sitting quietly on a
sofa at one corner of the stage.

It was his grandma Pearl, Kaufman said. He explained how as a boy he
used to have long talks with her about his dreams for a show business career. She told him he was wasting his time. He insisted that one day he was
going to play Carnegie Hall. "And when that day comes," Andy said, "I'm
gonna give you the best seat in the house." So there was Granny, at Andy's
big Carnegie Hall debut in April 1979, not just in the house but right up
there on the stage.

She sat quietly during the entire two-hour-plus concert, laughing a little, dozing occasionally. Through the "It's a Friendly, Friendly World"
sing-along, and Andy's Elvis Presley routine, and his performance of an
old Caspian folk song, with conga accompaniment and a melody that
sounded suspiciously like "Alouette." She watched as he showed a clip
from an old western two-reeler, with a cowgirl quartet singing "Jingle,
Jangle, Jingle"—and then brought out the last surviving member of that

quartet, a sweet old gal whom he coaxed into doing a reprise of her movie number. The aged cowgirl hopped around on a broomstick horsie, pushed faster and faster by the music, until she got so overheated that she keeled over and dropped dead on the stage. At which point Andy went off and returned wearing a dime-store Indian headdress, performed a spirit dance, and miraculously brought her back to life.

And when the concert was over and Andy was taking his bows, he asked Grandma to come over to join him. Underneath the wig and makeup was Robin Williams.

A more unlikely comedy team would have been hard to imagine. Williams, the improvisational dervish who awed people with his performing virtuosity; Kaufman, the conceptual comic whose big joke, most of the time, was that he didn't have an ounce of talent in his body. For the comedians who worked with them in clubs during the 1970s, the only thing that seemed to link the two was the impossibility of following either one onstage. Williams's manic, mile-a-minute act could leave a room sucked dry of energy. Kaufman's affectless, sometimes droning routines—reading *The Great Gatsby* aloud, say, or leading the audience in "One Hundred Bottles of Beer on the Wall," from beginning to bitter end—were more apt to leave the room sucked dry of people.

They were the two great extremists of 1970s stand-up. Williams took the improvisational, stream-of-consciousness style of Lenny Bruce's later years and supercharged it into a frenetic, almost abstract barrage of voices, sound effects, ad-libs, quick-change characters, and pop culture references. Kaufman, on the other hand, took the anti-comedy of Albert Brooks and Steve Martin and turned it into something more like anti-entertainment. Williams was stand-up's most dazzling pure performer; Kaufman its most daring performance artist.

Their comedy was an expression of two divergent camps in the counterculture-lifestyle revolution. Williams, a big drug user at the time, delivered wild, nonlinear comedy riffs that reflected the freewheeling, mind-altering spirit of the drug years. Kaufman did carefully worked-out, high-concept bits that varied little from performance to performance, reflecting the self-discipline of a teetotaler who was into health foods and transcendental meditation. Williams was a perpetual-motion machine who sweated for the audience's love. Kaufman posed alternately as a childlike naïf and an abusive sleazebag, and he seemed to love nothing better than when the audience hated his guts.

Both took stand-up further away from the social-political commentary of Carlin and Pryor and Klein. Williams, a child of the Bay Area counterculture, would slip an occasional Reagan joke or antiwar gibe into his run-on monologues, but nothing carried any weight on his splatter-paint canvases. Kaufman's stand-up act seemed almost entirely disconnected from the world of political and social events—even from the world of adults. Yet both were satirists of a media-saturated culture that was beginning to overwhelm us. Williams's comedy (intentionally or not) showed how it was turning into mindless cacophony, making us crazy. Kaufman showed how it had perverted our values, turned the performer into an imbecile and the audience into lemmings.

Their radical comedy had unremarkable personal origins—more similar to those of their baby boomer fans than any of the comedy pioneers who preceded them. Carlin and Klein grew up on the streets of New York City; Pryor came from the Peoria ghetto; Brooks was the product of a Hollywood showbiz family; and Martin, for much of his childhood, was steeped in show business's idealized version of Middle America, Disneyland. But Williams and Kaufman were the products of relatively stable, upper-middle-class families from the suburbs—two nice, middle-American kids who pushed stand-up comedy to the limits.

Williams was born in Chicago on July 21, 1951, the son of a Ford Motor Company executive who moved the family to the tony Detroit suburb of Bloomfield Hills when Robin was in grade school. An only child, he spent a lot of time by himself in the family's thirty-room mansion, devising elaborate battles for his toy soldiers in the attic. He wore a jacket and tie to his fancy private school—a nerdy, overweight kid who got himself in good enough shape to make the school wrestling team as a freshman, only to dislocate his shoulder and have to quit. Just before Robin's senior year in high school, his father retired, and the family moved to Marin County, north of San Francisco. Transplanted to the Bay Area at the height of the hippie years, Robin adapted quickly: he dumped the blazers and briefcase for jeans and Hawaiian shirts, took "gestalt history classes" at his laid-back high school, and experimented with drugs.

He went to Claremont Men's College, outside of Los Angeles, to study political science. But his grades slid when he discovered theater, and after a year he transferred to the College of Marin, near home, to study drama. He played Fagin in *Oliver!* and Snoopy in *You're a Good Man, Charlie Brown*, and took workshops at the Committee, the San Francisco improvisational-comedy troupe. Then in 1973 he went to New York City on a scholarship to Juilliard, where he took classes in acting, movement, and fencing and did mime on the steps of the Metropolitan Museum of Art. But he quit before graduating and moved back to the Bay Area, to be with a girlfriend.

The two soon broke up and Williams had trouble finding acting work, so he tried stand-up comedy. At a time when comedy clubs were starting to pop up in cities outside of New York and Los Angeles, San Francisco had a thriving alternative-comedy scene, and Williams began working at little clubs like the Holy City Zoo, a joint on Clement Street that held about eighty people. "Stand-up was an easier platform to get seen," he says. "Especially at that time. It was kind of like a new resource. It paid the bills. It really gave me a sense of independence. And to be honest, it was a great way to get laid."

His stand-up was different from the start. Influenced by his work with the Committee and by the multivoiced improvisational riffs of his idol Jonathan Winters, Williams did a scattered, stream-of-consciousness act—jumping from topic to topic and voice to voice, wandering into the audience, breaking the fourth wall, heckling himself. "My style in the beginning, especially in the smaller clubs, was not to be on mike," he recalls. "Because if you were on mike, you invited the standard thing where people could kind of lose track. So if I didn't go on mike, they were immediately listening." He entered a San Francisco comedy competition run by Frank Kidder, who taught a comedy workshop in the city. Williams finished second (to a conventional joke-joke comic named Bill Farley) but was the crowd favorite. "I remember his energy and his obvious presence," says Paul Krassner, editor of the *Realist* and onetime friend of Lenny Bruce, who was one of the judges. "He wore a cowboy hat, had a hairy chest, and sweated a lot. People in the audience were angry he didn't win." Harvey Myman, a Bay Area newspaper editor who was another judge, says Williams was clearly the best in the competition, "different from any comedian I'd ever seen," but figures he got penalized for running too long.

He got noticed elsewhere quickly. In 1976 he moved to Los Angeles with his new girlfriend, Valerie Velardi, a Mills College dance instructor he had met at the Holy City Zoo. At his first paying gig, at the Laff Stop in Orange County, the mikes went dead, which unleashed Williams. Jay Leno, who was also on the bill, was so impressed that he talked up the wild kid from San Francisco to Mitzi Shore at the Comedy Store. Soon Williams was a regular at her club in Westwood. He took a comedy-improvisation class taught by actor Harvey Lembeck and caught the eye of Larry Brezner, a talent manager for Rollins and Joffe, whose wife, Melissa Manchester, was also in the class. "I was watching stuff I had never seen before—the energy onstage, and a mind working outside the parameters of anything I'd encountered on this earth," says Brezner, who became Williams's manager.

Dressed in flowered shirts and suspenders, Williams was a free-associating whirligig, almost literally bouncing off the walls. He had a repertoire of characters that became familiar staples of his act: the drawling redneck, the lockjawed Brahmin, the California surfer dude ("ferr-sherr"), the Southern-fried TV evangelist ("*Be-LIEV-a!*"), the Soviet stand-up comic ("I wish to begin by doing one quick suppression for you . . ."). His burly, squarish body and thick, hairy arms could turn fey and limp-wristed in an instant—as a swishy Broadway choreographer, say, at Custer's last stand: "Opening number for the Indians, pasties and tomahawks only, let's go—Shoot, shoot! Scalp, scalp!" The Juilliard-trained comic could do long extemporaneous riffs in mock-Shakespearean verse: "The moon, like a testicle, hangs low in the sky . . . Ah, my sister Hernia, what news?" He rummaged through his pop culture memory chest—a snatch of *The Wizard of Oz*, a smidgen of Peter Lorre, the tiny "Help me!" cry from the last scene of *The Fly*. And if he flubbed a line or started to lose the crowd, Williams was ready for that too—turning into his own superego, issuing orders inside his brain as if he were on the flight deck of the *Starship Enterprise*: "Move into dynamite second routine . . . Phase in now, sequence A . . . Ego check . . . All system overload . . . Mayday! Mayday!"

The audience had never seen anything like it. Neither had his fellow comics. "He made everybody check your wallet," says David Letterman, who was a couple of years ahead of Williams at the Comedy Store. "Because we were all accustomed to doing it one way, in which you stood at a microphone and told your jokes. And he not only didn't stand at a microphone; he didn't stand on the stage. He made us all feel pretty insecure." He generated a little resentment among the comics too—not just of his obvious talent, but of his over-the-top sets that sometimes ate into their time and could leave the audience spent. "Guys were jealous of him from the beginning," says the Improv's Budd Friedman. "He was all over the place."

Williams described his style as "part conscious, part survival mechanism"—he wasn't much of a writer, but his quickness and incredible performing resources could get him through any tight spots. "People wrote me letters, thinking I had ADD. But it was more, sample this, sample that. It was my stream of consciousness combined with, in the early days, a little help of alcohol. I mean, I didn't drink a lot onstage, but sometimes a glass of wine would certainly loosen things up. And it was dictated by the audiences, kicking them off balance. Plus, this is the edge of the drug days, so you have people ready to talk about wild shit, a little less linear—people going, wow, I'm OK with that."

The performances didn't stop when he was offstage. Around the clubs, says Letterman, Williams used to affect a Scottish burr for no apparent reason. When Brezner started to send Williams on acting auditions, an unhappy casting agent at Universal called him to complain; why, she wanted to know, would they send over a Welshman for the role? "That's when I realized that auditions may not be the answer for Robin," says Brezner. Williams insists he wasn't doing shtick. "Sometimes in those days I would sound almost English or Scottish," he says. "Maybe after coming from Juilliard, my voice had a certain precision about it."

Television found him fast. Producer George Schlatter, who was casting for a new version of *Laugh-In*, his comedy hit from the late '60s that launched stars like Goldie Hawn and Lily Tomlin, saw Williams at the Westwood Comedy Store and was knocked out by the wild kid in the overalls, beard, and straw hat. "I remember he hung the microphone over the audience and said, 'I'm fishin' for assholes,' Schlatter recalls. "He was hysterical. I told him we're doing this show and whenever you want to clean up your act, stop saying 'fuck,' and come on in, you've got a job."

Williams was hired for the ensemble cast of the new *Laugh-In*, which also included comics like Ed Bluestone and Lenny Schultz. Williams was easily the standout—doing Jonathan Winters–like improvs as he picked through a bin of hats, ad-libbing with guest stars like Bette Davis and Frank Sinatra. But the show tanked in the ratings and aired only sporadically through the 1977–78 season. "It was supposed to be the cast of tomorrow," says Merrill Markoe, a writer on the show. "The people who are going to rule comedy in the future. You never heard of any of them again except Robin Williams. Everybody loved him." He was cast in another ill-fated TV comedy hour, *The Richard Pryor Show*, that same season. In an overpopulated ensemble cast (including Marsha Warfield, Tim Reid, and Sandra Bernhard), and with Pryor himself getting most of the spotlight, Williams had less of a chance to show his stuff before the show imploded after just four weeks in the fall of 1977.

Williams's TV career was famously turned around by Garry Marshall's eight-year-old son. Marshall was the producer of the hit sitcom *Happy Days*, and his son, after seeing *Star Wars*, told him he thought it would be funny if Fonzie met an alien. Marshall scoured the city for a comic to play the role of Mork from Ork; Williams was brought in for an audition at the last minute, after the initial choice, John Byner, didn't work out. On his way into the audition, Williams passed Richard Lewis just coming out, grumbling, "I don't speak Norwegian." But Williams won over the producers—standing on his head in the audition to demonstrate his Orkan spirit—and got the role in a *Happy Days* episode that aired in February 1978. It did so well in the ratings that the episode was spun off into its own series, and when *Mork and Mindy* debuted the following fall on ABC, it was an instant top-10 hit.

The sitcom was a perfect showcase for Williams, almost an extension of his stand-up; the writers played off his ad-libs during rehearsals and created scenes to showcase his voices and impressions. But the show also gave Williams something few of his stand-up contemporaries or predecessors had to deal with: overnight, almost overwhelming fame. When he walked into the comedy clubs now, the waters parted, and that wasn't entirely a good thing for a young stand-up still developing his act. The other comics looked at him differently: "It was like, 'What are you doing here?' I'd say, 'I just want to go on like you.'" The crowd reaction changed too. "You'd get the jolt of adulation," he says. "It was a little scary because all of a sudden they laugh at everything."

The jolt proved hard to resist. Williams would stop into the clubs two or three nights a week, even after long days of *Mork and Mindy* rehearsals, then sometimes party for hours after that. He and Valerie (whom he married in June 1978) were living in Topanga Canyon, west of Los Angeles, but his managers had to rent an apartment for him near the Paramount lot in Hollywood, just to make sure he showed up for work in the morning. His drinking and drug use spiraled upward, and his marriage began to fray. Williams blamed it on his hectic schedule. Valerie tried to defuse rumors of his infidelity. "I believe that there are certain people in this world that belong to everyone," she told *People* magazine. "When it comes to women, they've always liked Robin. His success hasn't changed that."

Even more than Carlin or Pryor, two other big coke users during those years, Williams's stand-up seemed to express the trippy, liberating spirit of the time. In his first HBO special, taped at the Roxy Theatre in Los Angeles in October 1978 (just after the debut of *Mork and Mindy*), he goes from 0 to 60 in seconds and never takes his foot off the gas. He enters through the crowd, wearing an engineer's cap and suspenders, in his drawling redneck character: "Billy Bob, I'm on TV! Marlene this is for you!"—then squeals as he mimes humping a pig. "Is anyone here on drugs?" he shouts to the crowd, then puts on space goggles with feathers and mimes a slow-motion run through molasses: "Iffff yoouu arrrrre, it's oookaaay . . ." He points to his fly: "I'd like to start off with something that I'm very proud of." Peering inside his pants, he shouts "Ready, Simba?" and imitates an elephant's roar. He wades into the crowd, grabbing a carafe of wine from one table—"I'm

Laurence Olivier for Ripple wine"—then works his way to the outside door: "We'll get lots of people in here—*free cocaine*!" Back onstage, he dances up the steps like Fred Astaire, vaults over the railing into the box seats, and turns into Quasimodo. When someone in the crowd whistles, he stops on a dime: "Cab?"—he quickly grabs for his back pocket—"Too late!" When one of the cameras follows him in the audience, he wheels around and becomes a *National Geographic* photo subject, breaking into an aboriginal dance and chant—which morphs into "Stayin' Alive."

It is dazzling but exhausting. Even Williams, looking back, thought it was a little out of control. "That was kind of in the crazy days, more scattered, running all around," he says. "Later I had more material, actually talking about stuff, more in control." It wasn't all improvised craziness, however. You could see, from performance to performance, the same recurring "ad-libs" ("Are there any Hell's Angels here?" he'd call out suddenly to the crowd. Then after a few seconds of silence, sotto voce: "Those pussy-whipped faggots"). The management team at Rollins and Joffe spent a lot of time working with him. "He wouldn't say 'good evening' or 'thank you' onstage. He just jumped right in," says Buddy Morra. "He was hysterical, but he had no idea of where he was going. We got a court stenographer to take down all his words. Then we worked it out afterward and honed it with him." His unpredictability made him one of the few major stand-ups of the era who had trouble getting on *The Tonight Show*, because Johnny Carson felt uncomfortable with him. (Andy Kaufman was another.) "We didn't know what to do with him," says Peter Lassally. "Johnny wasn't sure he was gonna work on the show at all." Williams didn't appear on *The Tonight Show* until 1981, well after his first flash of fame.

Only when *Mork and Mindy* was canceled (after just four seasons, a fad hit that dropped quickly in the ratings) did Williams return for a second HBO concert, in March 1983. It's probably the best undiluted sample of Williams's stand-up at its peak. Taped at the Great American Music Hall in San Francisco, the act is better shaped, the riffs more developed and sustained. He does a long bit in which he acts out the conception and birth of a baby—playing the sperm getting ready to fertilize the egg, swooshing through the snow like Jean-Claude Killy—and another one on the difference between cats and dogs, an old reliable for Carlin and other comics but made fresh by Williams's physical inventiveness and grace. "You never see a cat in a major park going, 'Hey, a Frisbee!' " he says as he bounces straight upward, paws perched in front of him. He throws in a couple of Reagan jokes ("I think Nancy's been dubbing him for years. Ever notice he doesn't speak while she's drinking water?") and some gag impressions (Elmer Fudd doing Springsteen: "I'm dwivin' in my cahhh / I tuhn on the wadiooo . . ."). Even his drug humor has a well-crafted through-line:

> Going to bed with coke—you feel like a vampire on a day pass. You're lying in bed in a big pool of your own sweat, with Buddy Rich on your heart going, *yakatayakatayakatakayakata* . . . You have conversations like this: 'Yeah, I'm fine, redundant, redundant, redundant, redundant, yeah, redundant, redundant, redundant . . .' And then you think, I'll take a Quaalude, I'll be fine. Taking a Quaalude—that's like throwing bricks in the Grand Canyon. It's such an anti-evolutionary drug. So strange, you see a girl who's taken two or three Quaaludes in the lipstick room going [*woozily drawing all over his face*]. You can always save money on Quaaludes: just take a hammer and go [*hits himself in the head*] *BAM!* Has the same effect, makes English optional. Then you make the ultimate mistake—you walk outside, and every animal in the world knows that you're fucked up. Even the birds are going [*slow, menacing beating of wings*] *Akkk! Akkk!* [*Suddenly fighting off the birds in his face*] Mr. Hitchcock, please!

By this time, however, stand-up had become a part-time vocation for Williams, who was getting major movie roles—starring in Robert Altman's *Popeye* in 1980 and *The World According to Garp* in 1982. His wildness onstage was in sharp contrast to the serious and soft-spoken man off it: a voracious reader ("dust jacket literate," he liked to say) and history buff, politically liberal and popular in Hollywood. Still, there were two things that were hard to ignore about Robin Williams's comedy. One was the drugs. The other was the charge that he stole material.

Williams's coke use was hardly unique among the L.A. comics in the late '70s and early '80s. "Robin could afford a better version of what we were doing," says his friend Rick Overton. "A cleaner, nicer, healthier version—less cut, better connections. Did it help him onstage? Yeah, sadly. That's the bitch." When he cleaned himself up a few years later, Williams freely confessed to his lavish cocaine use, though he claims he never performed on the drug. "It was only afterwards," he says. "Never onstage. You'd be too fuckin' paranoid." For a hot young star running around with a fast crowd in those years, coke was hard to avoid. "The thing about those times were, you never really had to pay for it," he says. "The amount of times I bought it were like minimum, compared to the amount of times—the old thing, hey, you want a bump? The place across the street from the Comedy Store, a hip Chinese restaurant called Roy's, people could close the curtains and just blow in the booths. Backstage it was everywhere. I remember once Redd Foxx came in and he had a mason jar. He opened it and it was just blow. I remember people comin' back there and it was like 'Scarface, the Musical.' "

The event that finally sobered him up, as it did many in Hollywood, was John Belushi's death in March 1982. Belushi, though never a stand-up himself, was friends with many of the comedians and a frequent visitor to the L.A. comedy clubs after he left *Saturday Night Live* and got into movies. As his drug use mounted, some in the crowd saw signs of trouble—at least in retrospect. Overton says he watched Belushi walk into the Improv with Williams and Richard Belzer the night before his death: "He looked gray. Looked like pigment was giving out, layer by layer, on his skin, like onion skin. You feel like you lost a couple of years when he walked past. It chilled us to the bone. Because he's doin' a version of what we're doin', just so much more of it." Mitzi Shore says she saw Belushi sitting by himself at a table at the Comedy Store earlier on the night he died, "looking very forlorn, watching the show. I could just see the darkness around his face."

Later that night, Williams ran into a friend at a bar who said Belushi wanted to see him at the Chateau Marmont. Williams thought it was odd, but went over to Belushi's suite, where he found no Belushi, but two people he didn't know. When Belushi came back, says Williams, "he was pretty out of it. And I thought ludes or whatever. And he says, 'What are you doing here?' I said, 'I thought you wanted to see me.' He said, 'Not at all—but hey, you want a bump?' " Williams says he turned it down and drove home. The next day, on the set of *Mork and Mindy*, Williams learned that Belushi had been found dead of an overdose.

Williams was forced to testify later at an inquest into the death. He was never implicated, and he suspects the whole encounter at the Chateau Marmont may have been orchestrated as part of a police sting to nab some Hollywood celebrities. But Belushi's death shook him up and spurred him to kick his cocaine habit. He wasn't alone; for many of the fast-lane comics at the time, like Overton and Belzer, Belushi's self-destruction was a rude awakening that signaled the end of the drug-fueled free ride of the '70s.

Williams also had to defend himself through much of his career against charges that he took material from other comics. There were stories of young stand-ups who were crushed to see their best bits turned into jokes on *Mork and Mindy*. Some of the stories were undoubtedly exaggerated.

Tim Thomerson, one of the hot Comedy Store acts in the mid-'70s, was said to have punched out Williams over some stolen lines. Thomerson says he merely had a testy encounter with Williams's manager after Thomerson was quoted in a newspaper article calling Williams "the Milton Berle of comics"—a reference to Berle's reputation for stealing gags. "Robin's manager came up to me and he got in my face," says Thomerson. "And my manager called this guy up and had some words. But I think it got romanticized."

But some comics had real gripes. David Brenner says he was so furious when Williams did a chunk of his material on HBO that he called up Williams's reps and warned, "Tell Robin if he ever takes one more line from me, I'll rip off his leg and shove it up his ass." Bob Shaw, a stand-up in the New York clubs in the mid-'70s, confronted him directly when he heard Williams do one of his bits: talking about snorting coke through a dollar bill, Shaw would mime the portrait of George Washington holding his fingers in an OK sign. "I said, you're funny enough on your own; you don't need that," says Shaw. "I confronted him, and he never did it again." Robert Klein was taken aback by a more egregious incident at an all-star AIDS benefit, where he and Williams were among the hosts. During the dress rehearsal, Klein introduced the Latino comic Paul Rodriguez with an ad-libbed riff from *West Side Story*: "A boy like that / He kill your brother." During the live broadcast, Klein says, Williams leaped up first and did the same bit before Klein could open his mouth.

Williams's general response to such charges was that any stealing was unintentional, part of his "sampling" style of comedy. His supporters liked to describe him as a sponge, soaking up material from everywhere, almost unconsciously. "Hanging out in those clubs for that long, it was like hearing it and sometimes not even knowing," says Williams. "Being absorbent. And then if you're riffing, it comes out." When confronted by an aggrieved comic, Williams would apologize and often pay for the material. After a while, though, he began to feel taken advantage of. "I was like the First Bank of Comedy for a long time. People were making a good living off it. In the beginning there were a couple of guys and I said, yeah, I got it; thank you. After a while, I went, fuck it. It became a myth. It became a way of just sticking somebody." Not all the comics bought his explanation.

It was hardly his individual jokes, however, that made Robin Williams one of the decade's most important comedians. It was the free-association onslaught of them, his deconstruction of our overstimulated, media-dominated culture. Carlin and Pryor helped free stand-up from its inhibitions about sex, drugs, race, political correctness. Williams helped free it even from the requirements of linear thought. "He kind of eliminated the need for the segue," says Paula Poundstone, who a few years after him worked in some of the same San Francisco clubs where Williams got his start. "In the old days you had to have a story to lead up to everything. Robin would just turn and say something—it wasn't attached to anything."

What was missing from his comedy was anything beneath the scintillating surface—a voice behind the virtuosity, apart from the cacophony of voices. Even when he would drop his characters and talk as "Robin Williams," he'd affect a tensed-up, self-mocking, highfalutin performance-voice. Williams was a huge fan of Richard Pryor, but he seemed to recognize that his comedy couldn't approach that level of candor and intimacy. "He has this incredible ability to recognize the most basic human truths, to talk about deep-seated fears," he once said of Pryor. "I've never been able to talk personally about things . . . That's such a Pandora's box. Once you open it, can you deal with it?"

Williams never opened it up, never let us inside. It was one thing he shared—one of the few things, aside from that moment at Carnegie Hall—with his fellow comedy extremist, Andy Kaufman.

Andy was a strange kid from the start, the oldest of three children in a close-knit Jewish family in Great Neck, New York, where his father ran a costume-jewelry business. Nine months after he was born, in January 1949, little Andy was reaching through the bars of his crib to play children's records on his portable Victrola. He was an unusually withdrawn child—his parents had him in and out of shrinks' offices from the age of four—who would open up only when he was alone in his bedroom, doing make-believe television shows for himself. In grade school, while the other kids were playing at recess, he would go off by himself, enacting an entire monster movie or playing Dick Clark and all the singers on *American Bandstand* for an audience of one. At age fourteen, he took his private act public, when he began entertaining at children's parties—leading sing-alongs, doing silly magic tricks, and showing clips of old *Little Rascals* shorts.

In high school, Kaufman grew his hair long, smoked dope, and hung out with a crowd of school pranksters who dubbed themselves F Troop. After graduation, he drove taxis and delivery vans in Great Neck for a year, then enrolled at Grahm Junior College in Boston to study television. One summer break he took a trip to Los Angeles, where he stayed with a family friend, Sam Denoff, one of the original writers of *The Dick Van Dyke Show*. Infatuated with Elvis Presley, Andy got on an all-night bus and rode to Las Vegas to see if he could meet his idol. He dressed in a pink suit and hung out in a kitchen backstage at the International Hotel until Elvis and his entourage passed through. Kaufman handed the King a pile of manuscript pages—a novel he had written in college called *God*, about an Elvis-like figure's rise to the top—and told him he intended to be famous. Elvis uttered a few words of encouragement and patted him on the shoulder. Andy was thrilled.

Back at Grahm Junior College, a girl convinced Andy to try out for a school talent show. He adapted some of his old children's-party bits and for the first time discovered he could make adults laugh too. He began performing in coffeehouses around campus, and did a fifteen-minute show for the campus TV station called *Uncle Andy's Fun House*, featuring a theme song to the tune of "It's Howdy Doody Time" and characters like Mr. Bee Bop, a beatnik puppet. On a talk show hosted by another student, Burt Dubrow (later a producer of talk shows for Mike Douglas and Sally Jessy Raphael), Andy appeared as a guest, playing a terrible stand-up comedian. When no one laughed at his jokes, Andy started blubbering about how badly he needed the work, then suddenly pulled out a gun to shoot himself. As the host lunged for him, the show abruptly went to a commercial. After the break, they were back, Andy sitting calmly in the guest seat, making no mention of the outburst.

The seeds of his subversive comedy were planted. Kaufman moved back to New York City and made an assault on the comedy clubs. He introduced himself to Budd Friedman in the guise of a meek, wide-eyed foreigner, who claimed to be from "an island in the Caspian Sea." He played the same character onstage, shifting his eyes nervously, botching his jokes ("Take my wife—please, take her") and doing bad "eemeetations" ("De Archie Bunker: 'You stupid! You meathead! Get out of de chair!' "). As the audience tittered uncomfortably, wondering whether he was for real, he would announce his impression of Elvis Presley—then turn around, comb his hair, grab a guitar, and reappear with a terrific (for real) impression of the King. After the applause died down, Kaufman would then seal the gag with a final, bashful, "Tenk you veddy much."

He did other bits, taking silly children's songs and turning them into deadpan minimalist stunts. He led the audience in sing-alongs of "Old MacDonald's Farm" and "The Cow Goes Moo"—no jokes, just Kaufman cheerily orchestrating the moos and oinks. He lip-synced the voice of a father leading his kids in song on a recording of "Pop Goes the Weasel"—an enthusiastic punch of his fist for each "pop." He put on a record of the theme song from *Mighty Mouse*, then stood silently on the stage through most of it, jumping in only to lip-sync Mighty's one-line refrain—"Here I come to save the day!"—one hand pointed lamely at the sky, one leg jiggling to the beat.

Sometimes he'd come out as himself—his voice thin, musical, almost effeminate—and tell jokes that purposely bombed. When he realized that the crowd was laughing in all the wrong places, he would start to panic, then grovel in self-pity: "This isn't working . . . I have no business being here, and I'd like to thank you all for showing me where I'm at." Then he'd begin to cry, and the tears would grow into great, heaving, hiccuping sobs—at which point he would sidle over to the conga drums, turning his sobbing jag into a rhythm number.

Kaufman was the latest comedian to make show business itself the object of satire—creating comedy so bad it was good. But there was a difference. Steve Martin's "ramblin' guy" hack entertainer and Albert Brooks's desperately bad mimes, jugglers, and ventriloquists were blithely unaware of how dumb they were—but the audience was hip to the put-on. Kaufman's game was to play the audience for fools too. In his "foreign man" bit, the surprise Elvis impression at least gave you the release of a joke. But many of his routines had no payoff at all: Mighty Mouse saved the day, and the cow went moo, and that was it. Brooks and Martin were satirizing a debased show business culture, where idiots could pass as entertainers. Kaufman wanted to make the audience feel like idiots too—unsure of what was real and what was a put-on.

Other stand-ups of his generation were inspired by Lenny Bruce or Robert Klein. Kaufman's heroes were the kids' show hosts and professional wrestlers he grew up watching on TV. The only comics he ever mentioned as influences were Laurel and Hardy. He had little if anything to say about his major stand-up contemporaries. "I don't even watch comedians nowadays," he told *Rolling Stone* in 1981. "It's hard for me to watch a stand-up. When I saw Richard Pryor at Philadelphia Hall in 1974, I couldn't understand it. It was all over my head. I didn't laugh once."

Around the comedy clubs in New York, Kaufman would drop his put-ons once he was offstage. But the real Andy—shy, childlike, unfailingly polite—didn't seem all that different. "A little strange, but a very sweet guy," says Buddy Mantia, who used to get rides with him when Kaufman would drive back to Great Neck. "I once asked him where he came up with all that stuff. He said, 'It's the same stuff I was doing when I was eight years old in my bedroom.'" At the Improv Kaufman became closest with Elayne Boosler, whom he dated until he moved out to California in 1975. She played characters with him in public, indulged his quirks, helped him develop some of his bits, like his Tony Clifton character. He, in turn, helped encourage Boosler, a hostess at the Improv when he first started coming in, to develop her own stand-up act. (Boosler dated other comics at the club too, like Ed Bluestone, but she and Kaufman remained close through the end of his life.)

Kaufman found another comedy soulmate at the Improv, a comic from Chicago named Bob Zmuda. A fan of the anarchist stunts of Yippie leaders Abbie Hoffman and Jerry Rubin, Zmuda had been part of a radical theater group in Chicago called the No Name Players, who specialized in subversive street-theater performances: running through the zoo screaming that the lions had gotten loose, or boarding a bus en masse and breaking into spasms of coughing as if poison gas had been released. Zmuda moved to New Jersey to get into acting and wound up partnering with another struggling actor, Chris Albrecht, in a comedy team they dubbed Comedy from A to Z. When the act didn't go anywhere, Albrecht quit to help Budd Friedman run the Improv and eventually became the club's manager. Zmuda, meanwhile, latched onto Andy Kaufman.

The two shared a taste for somewhat sadistic pranks. When Zmuda introduced himself to Kaufman after seeing his act at the Improv for the first time, Kaufman told him he had a bad back and got Zmuda to help him load all his props—conga drums, puppets, a 16-mm projector—into the trunk of his car. Then Kaufman told him his back was fine and drove away laughing. Zmuda, in turn, told Kaufman stories about his Chicago street-theater days and about a bizarre job he had for an eccentric Hollywood screenwriter, Norman Wexler (*Saturday Night Fever*, *Serpico*), who hired Zmuda to assist him in man-on-the-street pranks, a kind of do-it-yourself *Candid Camera*. One time, for example, Wexler was unhappy at having to wait in line at a bakery for a glazed doughnut, so he took out a briefcase full of money and bought up the store's entire stock of baked goods, then offered hundred-dollar bills to employees if they'd strip off their clothes. When he left, as Zmuda tells the story, the workers were in their underwear and Wexler had cleaned out the store's entire inventory—except for one glazed doughnut left in the display case. Kaufman thought it was genius.

Zmuda became Kaufman's writer and best friend. Many of their collaborations were similar street-theater pranks, performed in public for an audience of two. They would climb into the roller coaster at Coney Island, say, and Kaufman would break into hysterical sobs as Zmuda tried to calm him down. They worked on new bits for Kaufman's act, testing how far they could push an audience. In one, Kaufman adopted a British accent and announced he was going to read aloud from *The*

Great Gatsby. Which he did, droning on mercilessly, until the crowd
hooted for him to stop. Zmuda came up with the gag's ending. After fend-
ing off the audience revolt, Kaufman finally asked if they would rather he
put on a record. They cried yes—even "Pop Goes the Weasel" would be
better than this. He put the needle on his phonograph record—and it was
Kaufman's own voice, picking up the *Gatsby* chapter exactly where
he had left off. "Andy would always watch the audience," says Zmuda.
"The theatrical moment for him was not onstage, but what's taking place
in the crowd."

Kaufman's stand-up experiments got a national audience relatively fast,
thanks to Lorne Michaels, who saw him at Catch a Rising Star and gave
him a spot on the very first *Saturday Night Live*. He was one of a surfeit of
stand-up comics booked on that first show—along with Billy Crystal and
Valri Bromfield, as well as host George Carlin—but even when the show ran
long, Michaels let Billy Crystal walk off rather than cut Kaufman's Mighty
Mouse routine. "I had taught at an art school, and there was this sort of
stuff happening in the art world—conceptual art," says Michaels. "So there
was something sort of cool about what he was doing that wasn't traditional
comedy. He was the only person who was not cuttable in that first show. Because, I thought, nobody's ever seen anything like this."

Kaufman did several guest shots that first season, and *Saturday Night
Live* transformed him from an underground curiosity into a TV star. He
moved to Los Angeles, got a regular spot on *Van Dyke and Company*, a
short-lived 1976 variety show hosted by Dick Van Dyke, did warm-ups
for *Laverne and Shirley*, and got himself a manager, George Shapiro, a
former William Morris agent who had heard about him from Carl Reiner
(Shapiro's uncle) and Improv owner Budd Friedman. "My hesitation in
signing him was that I thought he may be too crazy, you know?" says
Shapiro. "And I didn't know what kind of a guy he was. But we had lunch
and dinner a couple of times; he talked about his family, his grandma
Lillie. He seemed to be a warm kind of a person, a hamish kid. Even
though he was totally bizarre.

"When Andy talked about the bits he wanted to do, he was very normal," adds Shapiro, who became a confidant and something of a father figure to him. "Basically, he liked to create things that were different. He said
he wanted the audience to be off guard. He didn't want to be predictable."
Shapiro let Kaufman do his thing, but tried to temper it with a traditional-
ist's concern for the audience. They would negotiate over material—like
how long Kaufman would cry during his "bombing" routine before he
turned it into a conga solo. Kaufman wanted ten minutes; Shapiro one. "I

said, no one will be left in the audience. I wanted them to be there for the conga drums and the dancing and the uplifting part of the act."

Kaufman's experiments—a mix of deadpan showbiz parody and dadaist performance art—continued through the late '70s. At the Improv in L.A., he hosted a mock talk show he called "Midnight Snacks," where he sat in a chair perched three feet higher than his guests and introduced segments like Has-Been Corner, where he interviewed washed-up celebrities. (Real-life has-beens like former *West Side Story* costar Richard Beymer came on as guests.) One time he had a refrigerator delivered onstage; when audience members came up to open the door, Kaufman was inside balancing his checkbook. Another time he charged audience members a dollar apiece to touch the boil on his neck. When he played Carnegie Hall in April 1979, he not only convinced Robin Williams (with whom he had become friendly and who was a big fan) to sit onstage for two hours disguised as his grandmother; he hired a fleet of buses to take the entire audience after the show to a cafeteria at the New York School of Printing, where they sat at kiddie tables and were served milk and cookies.

Most notoriously, he would disguise himself in a black toupee, mustache, and sunglasses and become Tony Clifton, a crass Vegas lounge entertainer who abuses the audience as he assaults them with smarmy renditions of "My Way." As Clifton, Kaufman was merciless. He would come out onstage and ask the crowd, "How ya doin'?"—then, if he didn't get a fast enough response, berate them: "Let's get one thing straight: when I ask a question, I want an answer!" He would bring audience members up and insult them, or dunk pitchers of water on their head (Zmuda was usually the shill). "I'm not up here for my health!" he'd snap if he didn't get enough applause. The bad entertainers that Martin and Brooks made fun of were deluded idiots. Clifton was a menace—Kaufman's corrosive satire of the sadomasochistic underbelly of show business. Clifton tested the limits of what the audience would put up with, even in the name of put-on. At a concert in San Francisco, where Clifton was booked as the opening act for Rodney Dangerfield, the crowd reportedly got so angry that they began throwing beer bottles at the stage. Clifton fled behind the curtain for safety—and sang three more numbers from there.

Tony Clifton became Kaufman's obsession. When in Clifton guise, he would never break character. Even in interviews with reporters, Kaufman refused to admit he and Clifton were the same person. To keep up the ruse that Kaufman and Clifton were different people, sometimes Zmuda would don the toupee and sunglasses and play Clifton himself. (He did so once as a guest on David Letterman's show, fooling both the host and the producers.) In 1978, when Kaufman was offered a role in the sitcom *Taxi* as Latka Gravas, a part based on his foreign-man character, Kaufman said he would take it only if Clifton was also given four guest appearances on the show. Clifton even had a separate contract, which stipulated that he get his own dressing room and parking space on the Paramount lot.

When he arrived for his first *Taxi* rehearsal, Clifton showed up with two bimbos on his arm, swigging a bottle of Jack Daniels and throwing insults at the cast. Though the cast and crew tried playing along with the stunt, he was so disruptive that, even before the episode was shot, the producers told Shapiro they'd have to fire Clifton—for real. When Shapiro told Kaufman later, he agreed on the condition that the firing be done in front of everyone on the set. The result was a shouting mêlée, with Clifton being bodily escorted off the lot by security—all of it recorded by a *Los Angeles Times* reporter, who was, by coincidence, doing a story on the show. After the incident, out of his Clifton makeup, an ecstatic Kaufman told Shapiro: "George, this may be the greatest day of my life. This is truly what I stand for."

Kaufman, sans Clifton, stayed with *Taxi* for five years. He always felt inhibited by the show, and reduced the number of episodes he did in the later seasons. "He wanted to be on the cutting edge," says Zmuda. "He felt all of TV was a sellout. We couldn't tell the difference between *Full House* and *Saturday Night Live*." He made one TV special of his own, *Uncle Andy's Fun House*, which had the distinction of being killed twice—on two different networks, ABC and NBC—by the same executive, Fred Silverman. After *Taxi* became a hit, ABC finally aired the show, which collected many of Kaufman's early bits and whose highlight was a special guest appearance by one of Andy's idols, the real Howdy Doody.

Kaufman's stage antics and I-dare-you-to-hate-me comedy were not always popular with his fellow club comics. "We used to think what he did was astonishing. We would all show up to see it," says Rick Overton. "But it could mess up a show. Everyone at the back is not watching him chase everyone out of the club and saying, 'Wow, performance art!' They're saying, 'Dude, that's my spot next.'" They would play along with his put-ons—Overton once had a pitcher of ice water dunked on his head by Clifton—but only up to a point. When Clifton was emceeing at the Improv one night, Tom Dreesen, taking the stage after his introduction, made the mistake of thanking "Andy" as he took the mike. Budd Friedman yelled at him afterward: "Goddamn it. Andy went home, because you called him 'Andy'!" Jay Leno was so creeped out by Kaufman's refusal to drop his Clifton put-on that he made a game of trying to crack it.

One night he told Clifton he had seen someone in another club doing his act. "Where?" asked Kaufman, suddenly dropping out of character. "Gotcha," said Leno.

Kaufman's obsessiveness extended beyond his comedy. He was fanatic about cleanliness, washing his hands dozens of times a day and rinsing off the utensils in restaurants before he would eat with them, according to Zmuda. He used a different toothbrush for every day of the week, except for Sunday, when he wouldn't brush. When they checked into a hotel on the road together, Zmuda had to scout out the hallway in advance, banging a saucepan with a mallet; if Andy could hear the noise from his room, they'd switch rooms, or even hotels. Despite his anodyne, childlike affect, he had a sexual appetite impressive even in the promiscuous '70s. When Kaufman played Harrah's in Reno, according to Zmuda, he paid a visit to the Mustang Ranch, the famed Nevada brothel, and vowed to sleep with all forty-two girls in the house before the end of his weeklong run. He accomplished the feat just under the wire, Zmuda says.

And then there was his wrestling. In clubs and concerts, Kaufman began dressing up in long johns and challenging women in the crowd to wrestle him. Imitating the villains from the TV spectacles of his youth, he would play the male-chauvinist pig, taunting the females in the crowd that all they were good for was scrubbing floors, peeling potatoes, and having babies. When a woman would finally take his dare, they would get in the ring for a full-contact grapple, which would usually end with Kaufman pinning her for the victory. He began advertising himself as the world's "inter-gender champion" and staging matches at all his concerts. (Sex was one attraction; Kaufman would frequently bed his female combatants after the show.) Against the advice of Shapiro, who feared that his antifeminist rants might not go over so well on TV, Kaufman convinced *Saturday Night Live* to let him wrestle on the show. Shapiro was right: after his second wrestling appearance, in December 1979, Kaufman stopped getting invited as a guest.

Losing his *Saturday Night Live* platform was a blow. When Dick Ebersol—the NBC executive who had first discovered Kaufman at Catch a Rising Star and told Lorne Michaels about him—came back to run the show, Kaufman proposed a new idea: a "feud" with Ebersol, which would start when a Kaufman guest spot was canceled at the last minute, supposedly because Ebersol thought he was no longer funny. The two even staged a shouting match backstage to fuel the ruse. Then Kaufman convinced Ebersol to hold a call-in poll on the show, asking viewers to decide whether he should be allowed back. The vote was held on November

20, 1982, and Kaufman lost. To his dismay, Ebersol really *didn't* invite him back on the show.

Shapiro was furious, claiming that Ebersol had assured him that Kaufman would be asked back no matter how the vote turned out. Ebersol says he made no such promise; indeed, when he figured Kaufman would probably lose the vote, he tried to convince the comedian, on the night before the show, to call off the stunt. Ebersol felt the results had to be respected; viewers were paying fifty cents apiece to vote, and if it turned out to be a sham, he thought it would amount to something close to fraud. When Shapiro pleaded that Kaufman was losing bookings because of the *SNL* snub, Ebersol suggested that the comedian buy some thirty-second ads on small NBC stations to plead his case; Ebersol would then run one in front of the studio audience to see if it "engendered any warm feelings." But when he ran one of Kaufman's ads, it drew boos instead—which convinced Ebersol that *SNL*'s fans were fed up with Kaufman. "He was well aware that he had begun to wear out his welcome in a lot of places," says Ebersol. The *SNL* rejection "wounded Andy badly," says Zmuda. Some put-ons went too far, even for Andy Kaufman.

Meanwhile, he went across the street to ABC's new *Saturday Night Live* imitator, *Fridays*, where he pulled off another of his metacomedy stunts. He was appearing in a sketch in which a group of friends at a restaurant sneak off one by one to smoke dope in the restroom. Halfway through the sketch, in the midst of a live broadcast, Kaufman stopped the scene, claimed he "felt really stupid" playing the role, and said he couldn't continue. The cast looked confused; one of them, Michael Richards, threw the cue cards in a fury. Kaufman tossed a glass of water in Richards's face—at which point the show's producer, Jack Burns (George Carlin's old sidekick), rushed onto the set and called for a commercial. Once again, press coverage raised the question of whether it was real or fake. The answer was fake—the producers knew about Kaufman's plans but didn't tell the cast—but Kaufman fueled the ruse by coming back a week later to read a sober on-air apology, which he claimed had been forced on him by ABC.

After 1981, Kaufman was performing almost entirely under the national media radar—in wrestling rings across the South, and no longer just with women. A Memphis wrestler named Jerry Lawler, upset at Kaufman's obnoxious behavior in the ring, challenged him to wrestle someone his own size, and the feud led to a vigorously hyped match between the two. In the days leading up to it, Kaufman upped the stakes by taping commercials in which he taunted the people of Memphis as hicks and bragged about his Hollywood connections.

A capacity crowd of twelve thousand packed the Mid-South Coliseum in Memphis on November 23, 1982, to see Kaufman get his comeuppance. Kaufman scurried in and out of the ring in terror, before Lawler invited the comedian to put him in a headlock, then picked him up and slammed him to the mat with an illegal hold called a pile driver. As Kaufman lay motionless and apparently unconscious on his back, he was declared the winner by disqualification—and rushed to the hospital.

"It was all staged, choreographed," says Shapiro, who was at the match. "They took him to the hospital in traction, but he was totally faking. He had a bruise on the top of his head, but he didn't get knocked out. I knew. His parents weren't so lucky—they heard it on the news." Yet Kaufman, as usual, played it for all it was worth, wearing a neck brace for months. He and Lawler even appeared together on David Letterman's late-night show to try to resolve the feud. Kaufman whined that the whole thing had been a joke but the injury all too real. Lawler listened scornfully, then stood up and gave him a hard, open-handed slap across the face. After a quick cut to a commercial, Kaufman came back to spew a torrent of bleeped-out invective at Lawler, vowing to "sue you for everything you have." Letterman reacted with a few nervous jokes; though he had learned to be ready for anything when Kaufman came on the show, the outburst flabbergasted him.

Kaufman continued to wrestle—carrying on his feud with Lawler, teaming up with other wrestlers in tag-team matches, always taunting the "hicks" who came to see him in towns across the South. His great discovery was that, in much of Middle America, the most hateful villain of all is the Hollywood star—arrogant, entitled, surrounded by lawyers. "I'm from Hollywood!" Kaufman would scream at the TV audience. "I've got the brains!" But even longtime friends (including Shapiro, who never liked the wrestling and wasn't involved in booking the matches) thought the joke had gone too far. The matches may have been rigged, but the body slams were real.

Kaufman and Shapiro were discussing a cable show, *Andy Kaufman's Wrestling and Variety Emporium*, when Kaufman was diagnosed with lung cancer in December 1983. The first thing he told Shapiro after getting the news was that he wanted to go on Letterman's show one more time. When Dave asked him what he got for Christmas, he would say, "Cancer." But five months later, on May 16, 1984, after flying to the Philippines to try various new-age cures, he died. Many of his fans assumed it was just another gag.

To the end, Kaufman never spoiled the purity of his put-on comedy.

"The critics try to intellectualize my material," he told *Time* magazine in 1979. "There's no satire involved. Satire is a concept that can only be understood by adults. My stuff is straight, for people of all ages." Kaufman wasn't being straight even then; pretending to be without irony, of course, was part of the irony. But Letterman, for one, respected him as a performer because he knew where to draw the line. "He wouldn't take you too far into the woods," Letterman says. "He was always protective of me on the show." After his appearances, Letterman says, Kaufman would whisper, "Send me the hate mail."

The hate was important to him. Kaufman may have been about as far as stand-up could travel from the politically and socially engaged monologues of Lenny Bruce and his followers. But he carried on the Bruce tradition of shaking up the audience, challenging their complacency, testing how far they could be pushed. He made them question the very notion of what constituted entertainment—and when the entertainment stopped and real life began. He provided a template for put-on comedy for years to come, from *Punk'd* to *Borat*.

Yet his comedy was a detour from the main road that stand-up was traveling. Stand-up comedians of the '70s created an intimate art form by emphasizing how much the performer and the audience had in common. Even Brooks and Martin elicited a kind of crackpot empathy. Kaufman kept his distance, creating comedy out of the gulf between the artist and his audience. Sooner or later, stand-up had to return to the business of making people laugh by inviting them in rather than shutting them out.

And one important place to start was with that vast segment of the audience—half of it, in fact—that had largely been ignored during the '70s stand-up explosion. Women, who had to endure Kaufman's taunts during those inter-gender wrestling matches, eventually would get up off the mat and start talking back. It just took a little longer.

CHAPTER 10

Women

*Sometimes I just don't feel wanted. Last night I went out with
a guy who faked premature ejaculation.*

—Elayne Boosler

Sex may have been a hot topic for stand-up comedians in the 1970s, but gender was not supposed to be an issue. The old, sexist "take my wife, please" jokes were gone, and the feminist movement was fighting for women's rights everywhere from the workplace to the abortion clinic. There should have been no reason why female comics couldn't take their place alongside men at the stand-up mike.

And yet, oddly, the 1970s turned out to be something of a black hole for women in stand-up. A few troupers from an older generation—Phyllis Diller, Totie Fields, Joan Rivers—had achieved stardom comparable to the top male comics in the 1950s and '60s and continued to work through the '70s. By the mid-'80s, a new wave of women comics—Roseanne Barr, Paula Poundstone, Ellen DeGeneres, Rosie O'Donnell, and others—had emerged for the first time to create a stand-up force as potent as the best male comics. But in the thriving comedy-club world of New York and Los Angeles through most of the 1970s, women comedians were scarce. Good ones were even scarcer. Good ones who had anything close to the popularity of their male counterparts were pretty much nonexistent.

The one woman who made it to the front ranks of the club comedians of the '70s, Elayne Boosler, was a true gender pioneer, a comic with a strong, independent, female point of view who did jokes without putting down her sex or playing into men's stereotypes. Yet she never matched the success of many of the men—like Richard Lewis, Jay Leno, and Andy Kaufman—who started out with her at the New York Improv in the early '70s. *The Tonight*

Show barely noticed her; she didn't get a big sitcom or major movie roles; she was never awarded the young comedian's imprimatur of success, her own HBO special. (She wound up on Showtime, the also-ran cable network.) Indeed, the roster of comedians who were featured in HBO's influential *On Location* concerts in the late '70s—so important in showcasing the work of comedians like George Carlin, Robert Klein, and Robin Williams—is starkly revealing. Of the forty-three specials aired between the first one, on New Year's Eve in 1975, and the end of 1980, exactly one was headlined by a woman: that old stalwart Phyllis Diller.

Why were women missing in action in the 1970s? Explanations usually start with the conventional wisdom that women are less suited by nature to stand-up comedy, an aggressive, take-charge art form. Men who were just getting accustomed to the feminist movement may not have been ready for them either. Boosler used to claim that men simply weren't comfortable laughing and being turned on at the same time. Christopher Hitchens, in a January 2007 *Vanity Fair* article called "Why Women Aren't Funny," floated another theory: that only men have the cynical, downtrodden view of the world needed for comedy—an understanding "that life is quite possibly a joke to begin with," in contrast to nurturing women, who "would prefer that life be fair, and even sweet, rather than the sordid mess it actually is." Which still, of course, wouldn't explain why so many more of those sweet, nurturing women defied the stereotype and became stand-up stars in the '80s and '90s, but were largely sitting on the sidelines in the '70s.

Ironically, some of the problems women comics faced in the '70s might be traced to the very movement that was supposed to be liberating them. Though Betty Friedan had written *The Feminine Mystique* in 1963, and women were at the front lines of the late '60s protests, the major advances of the feminist movement were still quite new in the '70s. The Equal Rights Amendment was passed by Congress in 1972 (and failed when not enough states ratified it); *Ms.* magazine made its debut that same year; the Supreme Court's decision legalizing abortion in *Roe v. Wade* came a year later. Oppressed groups still fighting for equality are generally not in the mood for jokes. Joan Rivers, a groundbreaker of the prefeminist era, argues that the feminist movement imposed a political agenda that denied women the right to speak truthful comedy. "The next generation after me, in the women's lib years, had a very difficult time," she says, "and no major women [comedians] came out of that time, because they weren't going to talk about fundamentals: 'I wanna get married, I wanna be attractive, my boyfriend left me,' that kind of stuff. They were saying, 'I'm a liberated woman,' and weren't talking about that. So they had nothing to talk about. They went against everything they really believed in." Well, everything Rivers believed in.

Perhaps more important, they faced a show business establishment that was not yet ready to fully accept them. Women in the comedy clubs of the '70s had more to deal with than tables full of drunk guys from the outer boroughs; they were at the mercy of the agents, talent managers, TV bookers, and other largely male power brokers, many of whom still thought it peculiar to see a woman onstage doing jokes. "So many industry folks had no interest in female comedy," says Catch a Rising Star owner Rick Newman. "I remember some would literally be getting up to go have a drink at the bar while women were on. They didn't want to accept women in that world."

The comedy-club world itself didn't seem particularly welcoming to women either. Hanging out at the bar all evening, waiting for a chance to get onstage, trading gossip over burgers late at night at the Green Kitchen—it took a determined woman to crack that late-night boys' club. When Joy Behar, a single mom from Queens, was having trouble getting on at the Improv in the early '80s, Silver Friedman, who then ran the place, told her she really needed to be camped out at the bar every night. Behar couldn't; she was raising a daughter by herself and had a full-time job. "For women to do stand-up comedy, it was a major production," says Behar. "You felt like an outsider."

It got worse on the road, sharing accommodations in the local "comedy condo" with a couple of other comics, almost always guys. The men romanticized the seedy glamour; women were more likely to resent the cramped, often run-down accommodations. "Some of the guys just didn't give a shit," says Paula Poundstone, who started doing stand-up in San Francisco in the early '80s and toured through the decade. "If they had a waitress run a vacuum cleaner before you came, you were lucky." Says Zane Buzby, who worked in a sketch group at Catch a Rising Star in the early '70s before becoming an actress and TV director (of HBO's first *Women of the Night* comedy special, among other shows): "At some point I realized that, even at the top of my game, I would be alone in a club or at a bar in some hotel. It's not a great life for a woman."

Most of the few role models for women comedians, meanwhile, were made obsolete by the feminist consciousness-raising. The women who succeeded as stand-up comics in the prefeminist era had to do it by telling jokes and adopting attitudes that weren't threatening to men. Phyllis Diller, with her freaky outfits, electroshocked hair, and braying laugh, made fun of her looks, her sex life, and her ineptness at housework. Totie Fields, with her roly-poly figure and Vegas-friendly one-liners, would come out on *The Ed Sullivan Show* stage dressed in a blousy muumuu and preen self-mockingly: "Aren't I precious?" (Typical Totie line: "I'm a firm believer in exercise. I mean, that's how I stay firm.")

One of the few exceptions was Jean Carroll, a sophisticated blonde who dressed in fancy cocktail dresses and did adult jokes about men and marriage—jokes that emanated from a position of power, not self-mockery. "It was one of those triangles," she cracked about one old boyfriend. "He and I were both in love with him." Or: "My oldest celebrated his birthday the other day. He's forty-seven. My husband." Carroll, who appeared frequently on *The Ed Sullivan Show* in the 1950s, was an inspiration to a Detroit youngster named Lily Tomlin, who would dress up in angora sweaters and do Jean Carroll routines at home when she was ten. But after a relatively brief period of popularity in the '50s (including a short-lived sitcom, *Take It from Me*), Carroll got out of show business in the 1960s and was largely forgotten.

The key transitional figure, the woman who bridged the gap between the self-deprecating jokesters like Diller and the liberated women comics of the feminist era, was Joan Rivers. Born Joan Molinsky, a doctor's daughter and Barnard graduate from Larchmont, New York, she scandalized her family by moonlighting as a stand-up comic in the Village, while taking temp jobs as a secretary during the day. She worked in strip joints, under the stage name Pepper January, went to Chicago for a stint with the Second City troupe, and was part of a sketch-comedy trio called Jim, Jake, and Joan. The group did fairly well, but Rivers thought their revue-style humor was too sophomoric and artificial. So after a few months she returned to solo stand-up and started talking more frankly about her own life. For inspiration, she looked not to other women like Fields or Diller, but to the same comic outlaw who had influenced so many of her male contemporaries, Lenny Bruce, whom she first saw at the Village Vanguard in 1962. "He was so beyond anything else at the time," she says. "He told the truth. I thought, he's saying what I'm thinking."

The truth about herself didn't sound, superficially, all that much different from Phyllis Diller: cracks about her looks and her troubles finding a man. But there was a big difference. Diller tossed off joke book one-liners, synthetic pieces of cleverness with rim shot attached (she used writers; Rivers for a time was one of them). "I once had a peek-a-boo blouse," said Diller. "People would peek, and then they'd boo." Or: "My mother always wanted me to have a hope chest. Of course, with my chest, there's no hope." Rivers's style was more conversational, with jokes that emerged more organically from her own life and insecurities. "I'm the last single girl in Larchmont," she quipped. "My mother's desperate. She has a sign up: 'Last Girl Before Thruway.'" She was so unpopular in high school, Rivers said, she had to get her cousin to take her to the prom: "Think of the humiliation. And my cousin—she didn't want to take me either." She talked about her gay hairdresser, Mr. Phyllis, and her affair with a married professor in college, and Queen Elizabeth's dowdy wardrobe. "Can we talk?" became her catchphrase, and it was her way of announcing that she was telling uncomfortable truths, like Lenny Bruce. Even such mild self-revelation "was very radical in those days," says Rivers. "I never thought I was pushing the edge. But I was saying things you dare not say. Jack Lemmon came to see me at the Duplex, thought I was disgusting, and walked out. I was so hurt."

Rivers struggled for years, driving in from the suburbs in her broken-down Ford, lugging a Wollensak tape machine to record her act. She watched contemporaries like Bill Cosby and George Carlin, whom she worked alongside and got to know in the Village, break through on television, while she continued to plod along, undiscovered. She was past thirty, and agents and managers were giving up on her. "You're too old," said Irvin Arthur, the agent for whom she had once worked as a secretary. "Everybody's seen you. If you were going to make it, you would have done it by now." Some of the few words of encouragement came from Lenny Bruce himself, who saw her act at Upstairs at the Downstairs and left her a note: "You're right and they're wrong." Says Rivers: "That kept me going for a year and a half."

Jack Paar had her on his show once and hated her. She auditioned seven times for Johnny Carson, and kept getting turned down. Finally, after Bill Cosby put in a word for her, *The Tonight Show* booked her in February 1965. She was shoehorned into the last ten minutes, billed not as a comedian but as a comedy writer. But that meant she could just sit and talk with Johnny, which showcased her intimate, conversational style. Carson laughed so hard he was wiping his eyes at the end, and *The Tonight Show* asked her back eight more times in the next eight months. She began getting headline bookings at hip clubs like the Bitter End and the hungry i. Charles L. Mee Jr., profiling her in the *New York Times*, called her "a prime example of what's new in comedy," comparing her not to Phyllis Diller but to Woody Allen: "The style is personal, an autobiographical stream-of-consciousness. And they both, somehow, always come out with the short end of the stick."

Yet Rivers, as it turned out, also came out with the short end of the stick as a pioneer in women's stand-up. She broke through just a couple of years before the feminist movement began to take hold. By the late '60s, when she was the leading female comedian in America, her desperate-for-a-man jokes were already sounding dated. The women who followed her into stand-up in the 1970s may have been inspired by her lonely battle for success in a man's world, and her willingness to talk honestly about herself onstage. But they didn't want to sound like Joan Rivers.

And so there was a void. The few women comics who could be found on the stage of the Improv in the late '60s and early '70s, when it was the premier spot for stand-up comics in New York, tended to be impressionists, like Nancy Parker, or sketch performers like Emily Levine, a founding member of the New York Stickball Team improvisational group. But Parker, whose impressions included a knockout Bette Davis, was more comfortable as a cabaret performer. And Levine, unhappy at the kind of roles she got as the only girl in the sketch group, went off to create a one-woman show for herself. "All I was being cast as was ditsy," she says. "And I was concerned about becoming ditsy as a result."

Lily Tomlin, who had come to New York from Detroit in 1965, fell somewhere in between. Though she mainly performed in revues at clubs like Upstairs at the Downstairs, and was a regular on Garry Moore's short-lived variety show in 1966, she would sometimes drop by the Improv to work on a stand-up act. Budd Friedman's most vivid memory is of her being deposited in front of the club one night by a limo; later she confessed that she had paid a driver waiting outside a Broadway theater five dollars just to drive her around the block. She did offbeat character pieces; in one she played a woman who has a rubber fetish—eating the soles of shoes and the erasers off pencils. "It was tough for her at the Improv because people weren't used to her," says Friedman. "Still, she did very well." But she didn't stay long. In 1969 *Laugh-In* producer George Schlatter—who had first seen her auditioning on the stage of the Ed Sullivan Theater doing a barefoot tap dance—hired her to join the cast of his hit NBC show.

Tomlin pretty much left stand-up behind after that, turning to longer scripted character pieces that became the basis for her one-woman Broadway shows. Some of her later monologue material, to be sure, had elements of confessional stand-up:

When I was growing up in Detroit, my mother told me lots of things that later turned out not to be true. She told me only tramps get their ears pierced. She told me the people in Washington wouldn't be there if they didn't know what they were doing. She told me enough is enough. And she told me whatever makes you happy will make me happy.

But as wonderfully written and performed as it was, her work did not have the conversational spontaneity (or at least the illusion of it) that lies at the heart of the stand-up art. Tomlin was a widely influential comic actress (with a movie career that was the envy of many), and she created the model for the autobiographical stage monologues of women from Whoopi Goldberg to Sarah Silverman. But the job of blazing a trail for female stand-ups in the '70s fell to another performer—not a singular comic artist like Tomlin, but a more practical role model for a new generation just discovering that women could do stand-up comedy and still respect themselves in the morning.

With her brassy manner and giant head of teased-out hair, Elayne Boosler was the quintessential '70s New York single gal, as tough and ballsy as any of the guys. Her material was smart, urban, unmistakably female, but not stridently feminist. For women in the audience who were used to laughing at what their dates laughed at—men talking about chasing girls, sleeping with girls, breaking up with girls—here, at last, was someone talking to them.

She joked about the desperate scene in singles' bars late at night, where "five minutes before closing even Frankenstein could walk in and get lucky." (Monster: "Rrrrggghhh." Girl: "Smooth talker!") She lamented her troubles with guys, balancing vulnerability with hard-won cynicism. "Sometimes I just don't feel wanted," she said. "Last night I went out with a guy who faked premature ejaculation." She talked about the everyday trials of being a single woman in New York. Apartment buildings, for example, where you delude yourself into thinking the eighty-year-old doorman is there for protection. ("Don't shoot!" she imagines him crying at the first sign of trouble. "I'll tell you where the young ones live!") Or waitressing in restaurants where the men insist on ordering for "the lady." Boosler: "It made it seem like there could be only one lady. 'The lady will have coffee.' 'OK, the slut'll go get it.' "

Boosler was born in August 1952 in Sheepshead Bay, Brooklyn; her father was in the tool-and-die business, and her mother was a former dancer. After some college in Florida, she came back to New York to be a Broadway singer. Hoping to be discovered, she got a job as a waitress and hostess at the Improv, where, if the hour was late and the audience sparse, she could get onstage and sing. Vocalists in the club typically got three numbers, but

Boosler would do only two, using the extra time for comedy patter. Pretty soon the comedy took over. One night, when there was a gap in the show, she went onstage and talked for nearly an hour. Richard Belzer and Freddie Prinze, watching her from the back of the room, initiated her into the boys' club by walking up to the stage and pretending to piss on her.

At the Improv, Boosler became part of the boys' club because that was the only club to be part of. Chris Albrecht, who eventually became manager of the club, admired Boosler because she would ask for all the tough spots—after the top acts, like Jimmie Walker or Freddie Prinze. She got more hecklers than the men ("Take it off!" "What's with the hair?"), but could counterpunch like the best of the guys. "She didn't take any crap," says Nancy Parker, who worked alongside her at both the Improv and Catch a Rising Star. "She could be as tough up there as any man. And yet she was still a woman." By 1975 she was a strong enough act that Budd Friedman brought her out to L.A. (along with her boyfriend Andy Kaufman) to help launch his new branch of the Improv there.

Richard Lewis called her "the Jackie Robinson of our generation," but Boosler always resisted efforts to cast her as a standard bearer for the women's movement. "Talking about things [feminists] want me to is just as bad as doing pots and pans," she told *New York* magazine in a 1976 profile. "And not even as funny. I'm a woman who's a comic, not a woman comic." She saw herself in the same progressive stand-up tradition as the men she worked alongside. "Lenny Bruce had already made a fissure in the status quo," she said. "But for my generation, the ones who really changed things were Robert Klein and Richard Pryor. They changed the role of the stand-up comic into that of a town crier delivering the news about life and growing up. Like all the young men who were starting out at the same time—people like Andy Kaufman and Jay Leno and Richard Lewis—I picked up from there." She refused to do interviews for articles where she would be lumped together with other women comics. She thought it demeaned her achievement—and was a bad career move as well. "The more you separate yourself from the mainstream, the less opportunity for work there is," she told Alan King in a cable TV interview. "It's not so much political as being thought of as a certain type of comedian that can only entertain one aspect of the population."

For women comics who came along after her in the 1970s, Boosler was the key pathbreaker. "Elayne was like a meteor at the time," says Carol Leifer, a Long Island optometrist's daughter who was attending the State University of New York at Binghamton when she read about Boosler in *New York* magazine. "She did break down a big door. She was doing it like the guys were doing it. I never wanted my act to be, 'Am I right, ladies?' Elayne didn't do that. It was very inspirational to me." Merrill Markoe, who became friends with Boosler later in Los Angeles, says: "The big discussion at the time was that the old [women's] comedy was very self-deprecating. And then Elayne was doing jokes that had a certain ego and pride of ownership to them. They were observational, in the way that Leno and Letterman's were. But told from her point of view, a female point of view."

In the clubs, as in her comedy, Boosler didn't seem interested in being part of the sisterhood. "She wasn't the kind to sit around with the girls' club," says Nancy Parker. Later on, among some of the younger women who were coming up when Boosler was top dog, she was viewed as somewhat aloof. Sandra Bernhard, who was starting out at the Comedy Store in L.A. in the late '70s, found Boosler "kind of distant and standoffish. She was really good friends with the guys." When she would come back to New York and make a cameo appearance at the Improv or Catch a Rising Star, Boosler didn't talk much to the younger comics, or stick around to watch their acts and offer advice. Some of the younger women defended her. Tokenism was still a reality of the stand-up world, and Boosler had worked hard for her seat on the bus. "Because people would decide to have one woman on the bill, there may have been more of a rivalry between [women] than may have been between some of the guys," says Paula Poundstone. "It's not like you wish anybody any ill. But when there's one spot—gee, I'd like to have it. Elayne had that slot for a long, long time, so I can understand her wanting to protect it."

Boosler's difficult road gave her a tough shell. She reacted angrily to perceived slights and would hold grudges. She worked for liberal political causes and refused what she felt were career compromises. She got a reputation for being difficult. "She could have been a major star," says Caroline Hirsch, the owner of Caroline's, a headliner comedy club in New York that opened in 1981. "But she was too difficult to deal with. Every time she came to work for me, there was a problem." Once, according to Hirsch, Boosler was so unhappy about her opening act, Emo Philips, that she walked out and refused to finish her weekend engagement. George Shapiro, the avuncular manager who handled her friend Andy Kaufman, took her on as a client in the '80s, but gave up after she walked away from projects, including a sitcom that would have paired her with Phyllis Diller as mother and daughter comedians. "She has very strong opinions," says Shapiro. "She follows her own drummer." Alan Bursky, who toured with her in the early '90s, doubling as her opening act and road manager, got in a shouting match with her outside her dressing room; it ended when Boosler smacked him across the face.

Some of that prickliness could probably be traced to her career frustrations. Johnny Carson wasn't a fan, and she was denied the regular *Tonight Show* spots that helped boost many of her contemporaries to stardom. "The brief on her was that she wasn't feminine enough, which was horrendously unfair in many ways," says Emily Levine. "First of all, there was a bias in the definition of 'feminine,' which hurt on a deep level, I'm sure. And so what if she weren't—why was she forced to be 'feminine'? Was Woody Allen 'masculine'? It limited her and it was destructive to her. And to watch other women who she didn't feel were as talented as she get breaks that she should have had was extremely difficult."

Boosler bristles at the suggestion that she wasn't supportive of younger women comics—many of whom she befriended, toured with, and in later years gave work to in her TV specials—and felt she never got the credit she deserved as a trailblazer. For thirteen years she scratched out a living, touring up to fifty weeks a year, without even an apartment of her own. When HBO refused to give her a special, she used her small nest egg of cash (she didn't have a credit card) to produce one on her own, *Party of One*. No one would run it, and it sat on the shelf for a year while Boosler contemplated retirement, before Showtime finally aired it in 1986. The following year HBO began its series of *Women of the Night* specials, devoted to female comics. Boosler was proud of the breakthrough—even if the name, typically, made the women sound like hookers. She once did a routine on the disparaging term "comedienne," which she hated; when asked the difference between a comedian and a comedienne, Boosler replied, "Ten thousand a week."

By the end of the 1970s, thanks largely to Boosler, women were no longer a rarity in clubs. Far from being discriminated against, they felt welcomed. "I always felt it was a big advantage," says Leifer, "because there were so few women comics. There was a novelty element to it." Adrianne Tolsch—a New York stand-up whose father had snuck her in to see Lenny Bruce in the Village when she was a kid by claiming she was a midget—was a Catch a Rising Star regular in the late '70s when Kelly Rodgers, an emcee at the time, asked if she'd fill in for him on a night when he had another gig. Rick Newman chewed him out later for doing it without his approval, but Tolsch became the first woman to be a regular emcee at Catch. "The hecklers could be more vicious, but there were great things about being a woman," Tolsch says. "The bottom line is, they couldn't ignore you if you were funny."

The opportunities for women should have been even better in Los Angeles; after all, the leading comedy club in town was run by a woman, Mitzi Shore. But Mitzi, disappointed that more women weren't getting onstage at the Comedy Store (never mind that she was the one doing the picking), felt they needed some affirmative action help. So in 1978 she refurbished a lounge space upstairs, decorated it with flowers, and christened it the Belly Room, where only women could perform. "Down here [in the Original Room] it was too hard for them," she says. "They were fighting all the comics in the world. This was like the sharks—you better have it together, or you're gonna get bit. The room was tough for them, so I said let them go into the Belly Room. You could do anything you wanted up there, with a freedom of spirit." Lotus Weinstock, Lenny Bruce's last girlfriend, was the room's first emcee. ("Develop your sense of humor instead of your breasts," went one of her femme-friendly lines. "It won't sag as much after childbirth.") Sandra Bernhard, a former manicurist who was discovered by Paul Mooney, Richard Pryor's writer and consigliere, was another regular, doing a mixture of music, fashion commentary, downtown attitude, and sexual innuendo. A few years later, Whoopi Goldberg, fresh from her movie debut in *The Color Purple*, used the room to develop the character sketches that she would later turn into her one-woman Broadway show. "It was perfect for me, because it was like a little theater," she says. "Mitzi made folks grow. She watered us."

Yet the Belly Room was regarded as a mixed blessing by some of the women comics, who felt it ghettoized them. A few of the established women, like Boosler, could still get time slots in the Original Room, but the rest were shunted to the separate-but-unequal accommodations upstairs. "It was a gimmick," says Bernhard. "A small room—there was no threat to her business. And if there was an overflow from the other rooms, then she'd send people up there, so a lot of times the audiences really weren't very interested. I think they felt they got stuck with, you know, the chicks." Indeed, the more progressive women comics like Bernhard and Markoe never felt they had much of a supporter in Mitzi Shore. She preferred impressionists and old-fashioned joke-joke comics. "The women she liked best were a group that have all vanished," says Markoe. Bernhard says Mitzi was "totally freaked out by me. I think she liked men. That was the bottom line. She just wanted to be surrounded by men who were paying homage to her. And she just kind of took women for granted."

But if the Belly Room was a patronizing gesture, at least it was a gesture. "Mitzi had some old-school ideas about women," acknowledges Emily Levine, another Belly Room regular in the early years. "But even more hats off to her for making the attempt." Outside of Mitzi Shore's club, after all, life did not get any easier for women stand-ups. Though things had improved some since those early days at Catch a Rising Star, when the male agents would move to the bar when the women came on, female comics still faced big hurdles. And one of the biggest, in the opinion of many, was the TV host who provided the launching pad for so many of their male counterparts: Johnny Carson.

The Tonight Show host didn't much like assertive women comics. He confessed as much in a 1979 *Rolling Stone* interview that was probably more revealing than he intended. "I think it's much tougher for women," Carson commented. "You don't see many of them around. And the ones that try, sometimes, are a little aggressive for my taste. I'll take it from a guy, but from a woman, sometimes, it just doesn't fit too well." The only female comic Carson had on his show regularly in the 1970s was Joan Rivers, whose self-deprecating one-liners were no threat. (He even made her a permanent guest host—until she got her own show, which he treated as a betrayal.) He had Boosler as a guest once in 1977, but after that she was booked only with guest hosts like Helen Reddy and David Letterman. Producer Lassally acknowledges that Boosler "was not much on Johnny's radar," but denies there was any antiwoman bias on the show. Nevertheless, many of the hipper and more contemporary women comics didn't feel welcomed. "I was never as big a fan of *The Tonight Show* as Dave was, because it didn't ever have women who looked like me on it," says Markoe, whose boyfriend Letterman idolized Carson. "I always had the feeling that Carson, if he ever met me, wouldn't like me. Carson never had much in the way of brainy women on. Dave saw him as your great, cool, wacky uncle, who you were so glad you got to hang with. And I saw him as a guy who liked Carol Wayne"—the buxom object of Art Fern's double entendres in Carson's "Tea Time Movies" sketches.

The dearth of women comics on Carson's show in the 1970s, of course, was in part a reflection of the scarcity of women comics across the board. But the chicken-and-egg question remains: Did Carson not book many women comics because there were so few of them? Or were there so few because Carson wouldn't book them? Even in the '80s, when a cadre of new female comics was emerging from the clubs, Carson's show was slow to embrace them. A 1984 *New York Times Magazine* story on women comics noted that in 1983 *The Tonight Show* had on only five women comedians all year. Two of them, Gilda Radner and Andrea Martin, were primarily sketch players, from *Saturday Night Live* and *SCTV*, respectively. A third, Sandra Bernhard, was promoting a movie, *King of Comedy*. The other two were Victoria Jackson—later a regular on *Saturday Night Live*, who affected a spacey little-girl manner and did comedy acrobatics—and Maureen Murphy, the Australian stand-up who did impressions and was close friends with Jim McCawley, the show's comedy booker.

It was fitting that the woman Johnny Carson embraced most enthusiastically in the '80s was a whiny, overweight housewife from Denver, who became an overnight star with her *Tonight Show* debut in August 1985. Roseanne Barr had grown up in Salt Lake City, got married and moved to Denver, and began entertaining in bars after she had her consciousness raised in a women's reading group. She had a radical postfeminist take on the women's movement, which she thought had ignored the economic realities faced by most American housewives. But her frumpy appearance and snappy one-liners made her easy for an old-schooler like Carson to like.

"I've been married for thirteen years, and let me tell you, it's a thrill to be out of the house," Roseanne said when she walked out on *The Tonight Show* stage. She complained, in her bored nasal whine, about husbands who won't lift a finger to clean up ("Is lemon Joy kryptonite to your species?"), husbands who can't find anything in the house without their wife's help ("Like they think the uterus is a *tracking device*"), and husbands who "all the time wanna talk" ("'Roseanne, don't you think we should talk about our *sexual problems*?' Like I'm gonna turn off *Wheel of Fortune* for that!"). Roseanne upended the power relationship and turned the prefeminist housewife into the most ballbusting feminist of all.

Roseanne was just one of an eclectic parade of new women comics to break through in the early and mid-'80s. Paula Poundstone, who began her stand-up career on a women's-only night at Boston's Comedy Connection in 1979 before moving to San Francisco, expressed her working-girl insecurities with dry, Letterman-esque irony. On other drivers berating her, for example, when she tries to parallel park: "They yell at me. Like I'm therapy for everyone. I'm mad too. I roll down my window and get into it with them. 'Hey, what the hell do I think I'm doin' here? Am I gonna get this piece of shit outta here or what? *Where'd I learn to drive anyway—Sears?*'" Rita Rudner, a willowy ex-dancer with a spacey, singsong manner, delivered existential one-liners about the sexual divide: "I was reading: Men reach their sexual peak at eighteen. Women reach their sexual peak at thirty-five. Do you get the feeling that if there is a God, he's into practical jokes?" Carol Leifer adapted Robert Klein's animated improvisational style

to the travails of a single woman in the city, talking about dating and cooking and filling up your first apartment with your parents' old furniture (tell-
tale sign: serving wine in a Flintstones glass). Sandra Bernhard, meanwhile,
curled her Mick Jagger lips and delivered sexually loaded come-ons to men
in the audience:

> I like you. I like you a lot. And yet . . . I'd like to hurt you. I'd like to
> smack your fuckin' beard off, mister. I'd like to make your life miserable
> tonight. I feel very open with you. I feel very close. I feel very vulnerable.
> I wanna share things with you. I wanna show you things. I wanna show
> you my breasts. And yet I'm frightened . . .

For women, the stand-up revolution of the 1970s finally arrived, a decade late. The old-school agents and managers were being replaced by
younger guys (and even some gals) who were receptive to the more assertive, feminist-era comics. New television outlets—cable, syndicated
shows, hipper network talk shows like *Late Night with David Letterman*—
gave them more outlets, breaking the hammerlock of the Carson show.
The rise of the ensemble comedy shows of the '70s and early '80s, like *Saturday Night Live* and *SCTV*, provided a showcase for women comics
who, even if they weren't traditional stand-ups, left no doubt they could be
full partners with men.

And as the gains of the women's movement were solidified and female
comics became more commonplace, the pressure to be a spokeswoman or
a role model was relieved. There was a place for Joan Rivers and Elayne
Boosler too, and no one had to apologize. And when the '80s comedy
boom kicked into high gear, everyone could enjoy the ride.

CHAPTER 11

The Boom

*If you guys see me working on the yard and stuff around
the house next week, would you do me a favor? Kill me!
Strangle me, shoot me, run me over,
whatever it takes! . . . I'M IN HELL!*

—Sam Kinison

For the stand-up comics who had spent years giving away their jokes
for free at Mitzi Shore's Comedy Store, the Norma Rae moment came late
one night at Canter's Deli. A few of the Store regulars were lingering in a
booth when Jay Leno walked in and cried, "What is this bullshit?"

The line had had a long setup. Ever since getting custody of the Comedy
Store in 1974, Mitzi Shore had stuck to her policy against paying the comedians who put customers in the seats. In this she was no different from her
counterparts in New York, Budd Friedman and Rick Newman. They regarded their establishments not as ordinary nightclubs but as workshops,
where comedians could try out new material, hone their acts, and be seen by
people in the industry. The comics were getting as much out of the clubs as
the clubs were getting out of them; besides, the owners claimed, paying all
the acts—a dozen or more a night—would have been financially prohibitive.
But for Mitzi, the issue of whether to pay the talent was more personal. She
saw her club as a college of comedy, an "artists' colony," and it wasn't just
her bottom line that would suffer if that talent were to earn a few bucks for
their effort. It was the very integrity of the art form.

The comedians may not have bought into this, but for most of the '70s
they tolerated it. They worked for no pay at the Comedy Store because
that's how they got seen by the agents and bookers and producers who
could be their ticket to the real paying jobs—a TV guest shot, a club gig

out of town, maybe even a part in a sitcom or movie. Landing good time slots at the Comedy Store was too important to risk alienating the club owner who put together the nightly lineups.

But by early 1979 the comics were growing restive. For one thing, Mitzi Shore's little artists' colony was the center of a growing comedy empire. Along with her two clubs in the L.A. area and another one down the coast in La Jolla, she had started a college concert tour featuring comics from the Comedy Store and signed a creative-consultant deal with ABC to develop TV projects. She had expanded her original club as well, opening a second showroom, dubbed the Main Room, where she intended to feature (and pay for) top comics from Vegas and TV.

But many of the big-name comics she tried to hire for the Main Room turned her down, and the ones who did work there weren't doing much business. "Mitzi was just crestfallen," says Argus Hamilton, the young comic from Oklahoma who was her errand boy and confidant at the time. "She had built that room for Buddy Hackett, Don Rickles, Shecky Greene, Bob Newhart—all those guys, her ex-husband's generation, who were ruling the roost in Vegas at the time. They refused to play the Main Room because they thought it would hurt their Las Vegas draw." Hamilton and another comic, Biff Maynard, suggested that Mitzi instead try to fill the room with a bill of her Comedy Store regulars. So she put together a squad of her best acts—among them David Letterman, Jay Leno, and Robin Williams—and crowds packed the place. Even better, at least for Mitzi, because they were her very own "showcase" comics, who worked for free in the Original Room, she didn't feel the need to pay them. And that's what ticked off Leno and his pals. If hot young comics from the Original Room were good enough to fill the house in the Main Room, they reasoned, why shouldn't they get paid just like the Vegas headliners?

A labor movement was born. Tom Dreesen, who had been in the Teamsters Union when he worked on the loading docks in Chicago, became the comedians' chief organizer and spokesman. A former G.I. who was a few years older than most of the youngsters at the Comedy Store, Dreesen had little affection for the college kids who had protested the Vietnam War, but he provided an articulate voice for their working stiffs' complaints. He tried to appeal to Mitzi's sense of fair play. "I told Mitzi, you pay the waiters, you pay the waitresses, you pay the guy who cleans the toilets. Why don't you at least pay the comedians?" Many of the struggling kids who were helping her clubs thrive, he argued, couldn't even afford to buy groceries. On New Year's Eve he had run into one of them, on a high after finishing a set at the Westwood Comedy Store. "He said, it was fantastic, I killed 'em, had the best show I ever had. And then he said, 'Tom, can you loan me five dollars for breakfast?' I told Mitzi that story and she said, 'Well, he should get a goddamn job.' I said, 'Mitzi, he has a job. He worked for you on New Year's Eve.' "

The comics formed a quasi-union, the Comedians for Compensation, and held meetings. The first one was mass chaos, says Dreesen, "Everybody's talking at the same time. Gallagher's yelling, 'Why don't we burn the fucking place down!' It was insanity." David Letterman was there, along with his good friend George Miller, who was particularly outraged because his mother used to work as a bookkeeper for Mitzi Shore—and thus knew how much money she was socking away. Leno came too, though Letterman thought he made something of a spectacle of himself. "Jay, bless his heart, couldn't sit still," he says. "He was behaving like a hyperactive child. Jumping up and down, being funny and distracting, to the point where everybody sort of thought, well, maybe we shouldn't tell Jay about the next meeting." Dreesen eventually took over the meetings, running them according to the Robert's Rules of Order he had learned when he used to chair meetings of the Jaycees.

Mitzi was willing to relent on the comedians' most reasonable demand, the one that had sparked the whole uprising, agreeing to pay the comics who performed in the Main Room one half of the cover charges. But while that was fine for the top tier of comics big enough to play the Main Room, it meant the vast majority of lesser names would still be working for nothing in the Original Room. So the comics turned it down and dug in for a fight.

Dreesen went back to Mitzi and tried to negotiate a plan for paying all the comics, not just the Main Room elite. He suggested what he thought would be a painless solution: simply add $1 to the $4.50 cover Mitzi was charging at the time, and split that extra dollar among the comedians. If a couple hundred people were in the club on a given night, that meant $200 split among the comics; it wasn't much, but it was a start, and even those few bucks could mean a lot. But Mitzi turned him down flat. "She said no, they don't deserve to be paid," Dreesen recalls. "I knew then that we were in trouble. I thought it was about money. It was about control."

In late March of 1979, with the talks at an impasse, the comedians went on strike. A picket line was assembled in front of the Comedy Store on Sunset Boulevard, the strikers carrying placards with slogans like NO MONEY, NO FUNNY and THE YUK STOPS HERE. The spectacle of stand-up comedians, many of them well known from television, recasting themselves as extras in *F.I.S.T.*, was an irresistible national story. Johnny Carson made jokes about it on *The Tonight Show*. Some of the more established comics were scornful

("This strike is the biggest joke I've ever heard come out of the Comedy Store," quipped David Brenner). But among the younger comedians it was a serious matter, and the vast majority of the 150 or so who worked at the Comedy Store walked off the job. Some of them had careers outside the club and didn't need the money, but supported the strike nevertheless. In the midst of the walkout, Letterman filled in for Johnny Carson as guest host of *The Tonight Show*. Immediately after finishing the show he drove to the Comedy Store and joined the picket line. "This was the umbilical cord for a lot of guys, myself included," says Letterman. "Money wasn't necessarily an issue for me, because I had a couple of bucks in the bank. But for these other guys, this was it. This was sustenance." Richard Lewis, who had moved on to concerts and television, wouldn't join the picket line but thought the cause was just. "I didn't want to picket, because I didn't want to say to the owners of the clubs, 'I need your twenty bucks.' To me, it trivialized my goal," says Lewis. "But once I saw the bigger picture, that people were making no money, I said, this is bullshit. I was totally pro-strike."

Budd Friedman, who was just as much of a tightwad as Mitzi Shore and had struggled for years to keep his club afloat in New York, didn't pay his comedians either—in New York or L.A.—but he smartly positioned himself as a friend to the strikers. His L.A. club had been severely damaged in a fire just before the strike began, but he set up a makeshift performance space in the bar area of the club and continued to operate, promising to abide by whatever agreement the comics reached with Mitzi. Meanwhile, with most of her talent on strike, Shore shut down the Comedy Store for a couple of weeks, then reopened it, using the few loyalists who crossed the picket line, like Hamilton and Maynard, as well as several neophytes who saw the strike as an opportunity to get stage time. But she was shocked and hurt that so many of the comics she had nurtured, and in some cases helped out financially, were now turning against her. "The people who stabbed her in the back were people she fed and gave places to live," says Alan Bursky, the former stand-up who had become an agent—and who ostentatiously crossed the picket line just to show his support for Mitzi.

She was crushed the night Letterman—one of her favorites, the kid from Indiana whom she took under her wing and, she claimed, had talked into staying when he wanted to go back home—showed up on the picket line. "I watched him in the bay window here," Mitzi would recall years later. "I was taken aback. I was crying. Three and a half years working with him, every night. I called him that night at his apartment. I was totally choked up. And he said, 'Those comedians are my friends. And they'll be my friends for the rest of my life.' I said, 'I'm sorry to hear that, David.' " Says Argus Hamilton: "It broke her heart."

Hamilton began negotiating as her representative and presented her with a proposal to pay the comedians twenty-five dollars per set in the Original Room. She rejected it flat out. "She was so hurt over David Letterman that she continued to dig her heels in," he says. "She just absolutely refused. It cost her her greatest strength: her cool rationality." As the strike dragged on, Mitzi tried to lure the comics back with a promise to pay them twenty-five dollars per set on weekends only. Garry Shandling, one of the club's top acts at the time, thought it was a reasonable offer and went back to work.

Shandling's decision to cross the picket line came as a blow to the strikers. The other comics who had kept working were mostly close friends of Mitzi's or young kids who didn't know any better. Shandling was different. "This wasn't a hick off the street," says Letterman. "You could tell that Garry was a real talent." Dreesen calls his move "unconscionable." Shandling says he felt the strike had simply dragged on too long, and claims he got private support for his position from other striking comics, who felt the same way but were afraid to cross the picket line. "I called up Dave Letterman—I didn't know him—and I said, what do you think? And he said, 'I think the whole thing is silly; I'm not involved in it one way or the other.' My sense of it was he wasn't taking any position." (Letterman doesn't recall the conversation, but says he was fully supportive of the strike. "I don't remember giving my blessing to cross the line," he says. "If I actually thought that way, I would have gone back.") "I think there was a lot of good that was accomplished by that strike," says Shandling. "I certainly didn't cross the picket line just to work. But I thought it could have been resolved. It did not need to be dragged out."

Tensions between the strikers and nonstrikers grew. Dreesen and John Witherspoon—a stand-up who also worked as a doorman and sometime manager of the club—acted as marshals on the picket line, protecting the strikers from harassment by Mitzi loyalists. One night, the bad blood got out of hand, as one of the antistrike comics tried to drive a car through the picket line, brushing some of the comics and knocking Jay Leno to the pavement with a loud thud. Dreesen ran over to him, panicked that Leno had been seriously injured. Leno gave him a wink; he was only feigning an injury and had thumped the car with his hand. But he got hauled off to the hospital in an ambulance anyway, and the incident seemed to sober up both sides.

"Mitzi called me ten minutes later and said, let's settle this thing right now," says Dreesen. On May 4 a settlement was reached, on essentially the same terms that Mitzi had rejected earlier—twenty-five dollars per set for all but a few specified hours during the week reserved for newcomers. After a six-week walkout, the Comedy Store comics went back to work, claiming victory.

The settlement was hard for Mitzi to swallow. "It was against my basic philosophy and the principles of the Comedy Store that this settlement was made," she told the *Los Angeles Times*'s William Knoedelseder. "You might say I was unionized into a corner." Mitzi got a fig leaf of satisfaction three years later, when an administrative law judge for the National Labor Relations Board ruled that the comedians, as independent contractors, could not be unionized. "In my personal view, workman's comp, benefits—those were always in the back of Mitzi's mind as something that would break the Comedy Store," says Hamilton. "I was thrilled," Mitzi says of the ruling. "It meant they never had to pay taxes to the government."

But the strike left a bitter legacy. Some of the activists, like Leno and Dreesen, never worked in the Comedy Store again. Some who crossed the picket line later regretted it. "There were a lot of personal attacks on Mitzi, and I felt protective of her," says Mike Binder, a protégé of Leno's, who continued to work during the strike. "But it was a mistake. I didn't understand the magnitude of it. She was a bad horse to back." Mitzi, complaining that she could no longer afford to keep all her showrooms open on slow nights, shut down her Westwood club on weekdays and reduced the number of time slots at the Sunset Boulevard club—which meant less work for the comics.

Some of the strikers complained that Mitzi was taking retribution against them. One of them was Steve Lubetkin, a New York comic who had moved west and gotten close to Mitzi but wound up joining the picketers. After the comics went back to work, he complained that Mitzi would no longer give him any time slots. He appealed to Dreesen, who was getting ready to go back on the road. "He came up to me and said, Tom, don't leave; she'll retaliate. I said, she can't; it's in the contract. He said, I've called in two weeks in a row and she won't give me a time. He looked so forlorn. I grabbed his arm and said, Steve, I give you my word. I won't go back until you go back. How's that?"

Another two weeks went by, and Lubetkin still heard nothing from Mitzi. On a Friday afternoon in early June, a distraught Lubetkin walked into the Continental Hyatt House next door to the Comedy Store, climbed to the roof of the fourteen-story building, and leaped to his death. His suicide note read: "My name is Steve Lubetkin. I used to work at the Comedy Store."

It was a tragic punch line to a story that had turned darker than anyone had bargained for, and it added to the bitterness against Mitzi. When she walked into her office the day after the suicide, Mitzi found a poster of Lubetkin propped up on her couch, and the words "Got the Message" scrawled in Magic Marker on her wall. Lubetkin's girlfriend had left it.

Lubetkin's troubles clearly went beyond Mitzi Shore and the strike. "He obviously had some deep-rooted psychological problems," says Richard Lewis, a friend since their days together at the Improv in New York. "Also an unbearably bad run of luck." Lubetkin had missed out on several TV opportunities, including a heartbreaking mishap with *The Tonight Show*. After he had been booked to make his first appearance on Carson's show, Lubetkin was cutting up onstage late one night at the Comedy Store when a *Tonight* producer happened to be in the audience. The producer didn't like what he saw, and Lubetkin's guest spot was canceled.

The strike worsened his relations with Mitzi. While it was underway, Lubetkin was scheduled to work a five-night engagement at the La Jolla Comedy Store (which was not affected by the strike), but he showed up late on opening night and Mitzi canceled the gig. Lubetkin said his car broke down; Mitzi was upset because he had stopped off first at the Sunset club to walk the picket line. But after his death, she angrily denied any implication that she bore some responsibility. "I was very close with Steve Lubetkin," she says. "I loved him. He was my best friend. I was in La Jolla at the Comedy Store and when I got the message [of his suicide], I threw glasses around. I had a fit, that he would do a thing like that." She claims Lubetkin was under too much pressure because of the organizing duties he had inherited after Dreesen left town. "He couldn't handle what they were giving him to do," she says. "He had definite problems. But the pressure of getting that responsibility was too much for him." Dreesen says he doesn't know what she's talking about.

The Comedy Store strike, with its tragic coda, was a turning point for stand-up comedy in the 1970s. In later years, the L.A. comics romanticized it as the end to an age of innocence, the dividing line between an era of happy camaraderie and a more complicated one of competing factions and big business. But it had a more important, if less obvious, impact around the country. Pictures on the evening news of stand-up comedians walking the picket line in L.A., and the news of their victory in the strike, raised the profile of a profession that was growing fast in popularity, not just on the

two coasts, but in the heartland as well. The strike helped fuel the nationwide comedy club boom of the 1980s.

The first repercussions were felt in New York, where the comics who
had put up with the same no-pay policy for years sought to match the financial gains of their counterparts in Los Angeles. The owners of the three
showcase clubs in town—the Improv, Catch a Rising Star, and the Comic
Strip—balked at first. Says Jimmy Brogan, who was among the comics
who attended a meeting with the owners at the Central Park Boathouse:
"They just beat us up. Rick Newman particularly wouldn't budge. Larry
Miller got sick to his stomach and didn't come back for any more meetings." The comics, moreover, weren't as united as they had been in L.A.
"There were established comics, who didn't want to upset Rick Newman,
and they were against us," says Brogan. "And there were late-night comics,
who were afraid there would be fewer spots [if the owners did what Mitzi
Shore had done and reduced club hours] and they would kind of be cut out
in the process. And we're saying, 'This is going to help you.' It was just a
huge battle." But after some back-channel negotiating with the help of
Chris Albrecht, the former stand-up who managed the Improv, a deal was
struck to pay the comedians twenty dollars a set on weekends—less than
the L.A. comics had won, but achieved without the trauma and disruption
of a strike.

Back in L.A., new comedy clubs opened up, trying to capitalize on the
ill will between the comics and Mitzi Shore. Jamie Masada, an Iranian Jew
who had immigrated to the United States as a teenager two years earlier
and worked as a dishwasher and sometime stand-up at the Comedy Store,
got backing from a producer friend and opened his own club, the Laugh
Factory, down the street on Sunset Boulevard. He set out to make it a more
talent-friendly place, promising to split the cover charges among the comedians who appeared each night. (After Richard Pryor performed on
opening night, Masada handed him his share, which came to two dollars.
Pryor gave him a hundred-dollar bill and told him to pay his rent.) He
gave the comedians gifts on Christmas, served dinners to the homeless on
Thanksgiving, and even proposed that the club owners provide health insurance for the comics. Masada says he got a call from Budd Friedman,
complaining, "You're gonna ruin the comedy business."

Across the country, meanwhile, the strike settlement had a financial ripple effect, upping the price comics could command on the road.

Taking an act around the country, to clubs and college auditoriums and
concert halls, had long been a comedian's surest route to a steady income.
Carlin and Klein had opened up the college market for stand-ups in the

early '70s, and comics like Albert Brooks and Steve Martin had done com-
bat duty trying to entertain drugged-out crowds as the opening act at rock
concerts. But by the end of the '70s, stand-up comics were finding a new
outlet in the growing circuit of comedy clubs across the country, patterned
after the showcase clubs of New York and Los Angeles.

For a New York club comic in the '70s, touring usually started small,
with an occasional paying gig at a bar in the wilds of New Jersey or Long
Island. "We'd pile into a '67 Nova, no shocks, three comics in the back
seat, a mike stand and amplifier in the trunk," recalls Larry Miller. "We'd
go to a place called Mustache Pete's, in southwestern New Jersey. Very rural. It was like Delaware in the 1800s. It took us several times before we
could get them to turn off the pinball machine that was right at the side of
the stage." At a slightly higher level, comics could take a train down the
eastern corridor to clubs in Philadelphia or Washington and make a weekend of it. Then, when the clubs began to multiply and the owners would
spring for transportation, a comic could get on a plane and feel like a big-
time entertainer. "My theory for why the boom happened is People Express
airlines," says New York comic Bill Scheft, who toured in the mid-'80s.
"Starting in 1981, comedy club owners could fly comics cheaply up and
down the East Coast—Atlanta, Pittsburgh, all the People Express cities. It
was as if Reagan had deregulated comedy."

Before long, even comics with no national reputation could get almost
continual touring gigs—and make decent money at it. The clubs had a
fairly consistent format: an opening act, who doubled as the emcee (sometimes a local comic), a middle act, and a headliner. At the start of the
1980s, the top comic could pull in fifteen hundred dollars or more for a
weekend, especially if he had a few TV credits. But even the journeyman
who got the middle spot could make six hundred or eight hundred dollars.
That was a lot better than waiting around at Catch a Rising Star or the
Comedy Store all night for a twenty-five-dollar set.

But for the comics, it was a tradeoff. Going on the road, particularly for
the L.A. comics, meant you weren't getting your face in front of the agents
and talent scouts who could land you the really big jobs—roles in movies
or TV sitcoms. "The big battle was, they need you here for auditions,"
says Rick Overton. "Agents are screaming at you: 'Stay in town for auditions.' Another agent is booking you on the road. Same agency. You're
saying, get on the phone, you two!" Once the showcase clubs started paying, however, the calculus changed. "After the strike a comedian could
make two, three, four hundred dollars a week in L.A.," says Dreesen.
"Why go all the way to Tulsa to make that same money?" To induce the

comics to travel, the clubs in the hinterlands had to boost their pay scale. That lured more of the top comics out on the road—which, in turn, drew more customers into the clubs.

An evening at the comedy club was perfect entertainment for a baby-boom generation that was just hitting its peak dating years. You could take a date to the movies, but the conversation had to wait until afterward. The discos were too noisy. At a comedy club you could talk during the show, gauge each other's reactions, see what your date laughed at—or was grossed out by. The relatively placid Reagan years, moreover, were perfectly suited to the personal, relatively noncontroversial stand-up that most of the club comics were doing. Comedians from Richard Pryor to Steve Martin had shaped a generation's attitudes on everything from race to show business; now, here were comedians your own age, providing a running commentary on the whole traumatic experience of moving from adolescence to adulthood. You might not get your mind expanded or your assumptions challenged, but you walked out feeling smart, up-to-date, and maybe a little better able to cope.

Television played a big part in fueling the boom. Some of the L.A. comics credit one syndicated show, *Make Me Laugh*—which had a high-profile eleven P.M. time slot in Los Angeles in the 1979–80 season—with providing a crucial early boost, giving journeyman stand-ups (who competed on the game show to make contestants laugh) a big-time TV credit and thus making them more marketable around the country. Cable showcases for young comics like Showtime's *Big Laff-Off* and HBO's *Young Comedians Special*s gave them even more important national exposure. Beginning in 1981, Budd Friedman hosted a syndicated show taped at his L.A. club called *An Evening at the Improv*. It died after two years but was resurrected on the A&E cable channel (with Milton Berle and Phyllis Diller among the early hosts) and lasted for more than a decade, making the brick-wall backdrop as familiar to TV viewers as the Eyewitness News weather map. With most of the old-line nightclubs gone and rock concerts more mammoth than ever, comedy clubs were the place where you could have an up-close-and-personal encounter with big-time show business—right in your own hometown.

Much of the credit for the boom, claims Paula Poundstone, belongs to a single Johnny Appleseed: Robin Williams. When he was the biggest superstar in stand-up comedy, touring concert halls around the country, Williams would frequently drop into local clubs unannounced. "Everywhere he went, if there was a little hellhole nightclub somewhere, he would show up," says Poundstone. "There's not a comedy club in the entire country that does not have a photograph of Robin Williams on their stage, and a club owner who would breathlessly tell you how exciting it was when he came there. So there was always this feeling, all over the country, that Robin Williams might stop in. It's why people went out a lot of times to comedy clubs."

For the comics, life on the road was a combination of college spring break and showbiz hell. Accommodations in the comedy condo—an apartment set up by the club owners for the visiting talent—were communal and anything but luxurious. Typically, the headliner got the big bedroom, and the middle act or opener might have to bunk on the couch. The maid service often consisted of nothing more than a waitress from the club coming by once a week to vacuum and change the sheets. "They were like Superfund sites," says Jerry Seinfeld. "You go in this little apartment, and you could tell there wasn't one square inch of it where someone hadn't had some kind of peak physical experience."

One of the first and most notorious of these pleasure palaces was in Fort Lauderdale, Florida, where the owners of the Comic Strip opened a branch of their New York club in 1979. Nude girls in the swimming pool helped distract the comics from the wet-bathing-suit stains on the couch and a rat that became so familiar the comics named it Arthur. "Oh my God, the parties we had there," says Rick Overton. "Inexplicable stains everywhere. Waitresses who go, 'I can't believe I'm doing this,' then when you're looking for a condom, say, 'It's in the third drawer.'"

The easy sex was a big attraction, at least for a while. In some towns, the club waitresses would plan out their weekends in advance by picking which visiting comics they intended to sleep with. "Comedy was hot," says Kelly Rodgers. "The girls would go crazy. 'You're a comic?' Then after a while it became, 'You're a comic? Oh, my cousin's a comic.'" Says Paul Reiser: "You'd get to a new club and you could meet girls easy. The waitresses were receptive. A year later you'd go back to the same club and the waitresses were hardened. They were just over it. They'd seen it and been hit on by so many asshole comics. And you're saying, ah, it's all over. Paradise has been ruined."

By the time the boom hit its peak in the late 1980s, there were at least three hundred full-time comedy clubs in the United States and, according to one estimate, fifteen hundred people making a "comfortable living" doing stand-up comedy. The New York clubs that started it all went national: the Improv had as many as sixteen outposts around the country at one time; Catch a Rising Star had nine. New chains spread, with names like Zanies, Giggles, the Punch Line, and Funnybones. Chinese restaurants and bowling alleys began booking stand-up comedians. Discos stopped the music and turned on the punch lines. Jay Leno, king of the road, told of working places like the Rodeo Lounge in Atlanta, where he performed inside a cage of chicken wire as drunk patrons threw beer bottles at him, and another gig in the middle of a Canadian lake, where the audience had to be rowed out in a skiff four at a time. Towns as small as Ozark, Alabama, and Kalamazoo, Michigan, had their own comedy clubs. Big cities had enough of them to foster their own local stand-up communities, traditions, and stars. Atlanta's roster of clubs expanded to six during the peak years of the '80s. The Boston-Cambridge area boasted ten, four of them within 150 yards of each other on "Comedy Row" along Warrenton Street.

A glut was inevitable. As the TV shows and clubs multiplied, hundreds of onetime class clowns were inspired to dump their job at the insurance agency and try to tell jokes for a living. For the founding fathers of the stand-up revolution of the '70s, the overexpansion was a sorry sight. "I think what happened in the eighties, it pancaked," says Robert Klein. "It made a lot more work for a lot more comedians. And a lot of the core people felt that this wasn't only kind of taking away their livelihood; it was thinning the product. A lot of fringe people were getting up there." The club pros from New York and L.A. were appalled too when they reached some of the backwaters of the comedy world. "As clubs expanded around the country, more people came up," says Kelly Rodgers. "Smarmy, jerky guys—hacks, we called them. But the clubs were packed for whoever was there. So the owners figured, why fly in Seinfeld when you can get Lenny from the gas station for fifty dollars and still fill the place?"

With so many comics tripping over each other on the road, quality control began to suffer, as did pride of ownership. Stealing other comics' material had long been a problem in the communal environment of the New York and L.A. comedy clubs. But in the Wild West of the road, there was no way of policing things. "You could see certain jokes and bits of business that would just stay in the club," says Reiser. "The emcee would steal it—jokes about tipping waitresses, selling T-shirts, things that were eminently stealable. You'd go into a club and see one of your friend's bits, and later you'd ask him, 'Were you here recently?' There used to be these rules of honor. Guys would say, all right, I'll only do that joke out of town. I won't do it in New York. And that actually became a recognized demarcation point—I'll just do it on the road."

Yet the nationalization of the stand-up boom did not mean that homogenization was inevitable. The house style of the New York and L.A. clubs that was being exported around the country—the observational bits about dating and commercials, doing your laundry and riding on airplanes—had, by the start of the '80s, become so rote and familiar that some of the most distinctive new voices in stand-up were coming from the provinces.

In Boston, for example, a thriving comedy scene grew up in the early '80s around Lenny Clarke and a band of high-energy working-class comics, who performed in clubs like the Comedy Connection and a Chinese restaurant called the Ding Ho. Yet when *Tonight Show* producer Peter Lassally paid a visit in early 1982, the comedian who caught his eye was the one oddball in the group, a frizzy-haired sad sack named Steven Wright, who delivered off-center, absurdist one-liners in a droning monotone:

—"If you were in a vehicle and you were traveling at the speed of light, and then you turned your lights on—would they do anything?"
—"It's a small world. But I wouldn't want to paint it."
—"One night I stayed up all night playing poker with Tarot cards. Got a full house and four people died."
—"You can't have everything. Where would you put it?"

Wright made his *Tonight Show* debut in April 1982. "That's wonderfully inventive stuff," Carson raved, as he brought his new discovery over to the guest couch. Wright's stand-up was something of a throwback to an old-fashioned style of disconnected verbal witticisms, with obvious echoes of Woody Allen. But in the raucous '80s club world, he was a quiet, haunted original.

At the opposite end of the spectrum was a former traveling evangelist from Houston, who beat the club loudmouths at their own game. Sam Kinison was the son of a Pentecostal preacher who moved the family to Peoria, Illinois, after he was kicked out of his church in Yakima, Washington. At age eighteen, after his father died, Kinison began preaching on the revival circuit with his two brothers. But he was better at telling jokes on the pulpit than raising money, and after seeing Richard Pryor, a fellow Peorian, at the Comedy Store in L.A., he decided to give up the ministry and try to become a stand-up comic. But he moved to Houston after reading a newspaper ad for a comedy school there, and over the next two years became a hot attraction at Houston clubs like the Comedy Annex; he was voted the Funniest Man in Texas two years in a row, in 1979 and '80. Then he moved to Los Angeles, where he worked his way into the Comedy Store lineup.

Dressed in a baggy, park-flasher overcoat and beret, Kinison turned the cadences of his revivalist sermons into eruptions of comic hellfire. Typically, his routines would start with sweet reasonableness, then suddenly burst into piercing primal screams. You could detect the lapsed preacher in one of his early bits, a phone conversation with his parents, complaining that they won't send him any more money:

> I called them and said, "Mom, get Dad on the phone too—wake him up. I know it's late, but I want you both to hear this. You know, before I was your little son, before I was your baby . . . I was a free spirit in the next stage of life. I walked in the cosmos, not imprisoned by a body of flesh, but free, in a pure body of light. There were no questions, only answers, no weaknesses, only strengths, I was light, I was truth, I was a spiritual being. I was God . . . But you had to FUCK and bring my ass down HERE! I didn't *ask* to be born! I didn't call and say, 'Hey, please *have* me so I could work in a fuckin' Winchell's someday!' Now you want me to pay my own way? FUCK YOU! PICK UP THE FUCKIN' CHECK, MOM! PICK IT UP!"

It was Lenny Bruce updated and amplified for the heavy-metal era. Like Carlin, Kinison considered it the comedian's job to tell uncomfortable truths; like Pryor, his confessional outbursts had an almost masochistic honesty. But his profane, politically incorrect rants were even more incendiary. His tirades against marriage were cries of the damned—as a pussy-whipped husband, for example, telling his friends that his wife won't let him out of the house:

> If you guys see me working on the yard and stuff around the house next week, would you do me a favor? [*Screaming:*] Kill me! Strangle me, shoot me, run me over, whatever it takes! . . . I'M IN HELL! AAUGHH! AAUGHH! AAUGHH!!

His infamous rant on famine in Africa is even more shocking today than it was back then:

> You really want to help these people? Stop sending them food! Send them U-Hauls! Send them luggage! Send them somebody like me, who'll say, we just drove seven hundred miles with your food, and it occurred to us that there wouldn't be world hunger if you people would live where the FOOD IS! YOU LIVE IN A DESERT! YOU LIVE IN A FUCKIN' DESERT!

At the Comedy Store, Kinison at first was too dangerous for prime time, and Mitzi Shore relegated him to late at night. But he steadily built an underground following, and in 1985 got his big TV break—a six-minute spot on an HBO *Young Comedians Special*, hosted by Rodney Dangerfield. From then until his death in a car accident in 1992, Kinison was stand-up's outlaw rock star: drinker, drug addict, wild man on the stage, and Lenny Bruce's last great spiritual heir as a stand-up comedy provocateur.

His over-the-top comedy raised the stakes, and the sound level. He opened the door to even crasser, dumbed-down "shock comics" like Andrew "Dice" Clay. Even Carlin, hearing Kinison in the mid-'80s, decided he needed to raise his voice to get attention. Yet Kinison was perhaps the last real rebel at a time when the rebellion was rapidly getting co-opted by the mainstream. The goal of most stand-up comedians, moving from the '70s into the '80s, was not finding new ways to challenge taboos and upset the status quo. It was making the stand-up revolution palatable for a mass audience. And for that, the model was not a shrieking wild man from Texas, but a soft-spoken young comic from Massapequa, Long Island.

CHAPTER 12

Mainstream

*Milk-estimation skills—so important. What do you do when
you get to the bottom of the bowl and you still have milk left?
Well, I say, put in more cereal!*

—Jerry Seinfeld

By the mid-'70s, Richard Lewis was feeling pretty good about
himself—at least, as good as a professional neurotic trying to make people laugh every night for virtually no money could feel. Four years after
getting discovered by Budd Friedman on open-mike night at the New
York Improvisation, Lewis was one of the hot comics at the club and at its
rival across town, Catch a Rising Star. He was getting TV guest spots,
and even had a *Tonight Show* appearance under his belt. Lewis thought
of himself as a pioneer, one of a relatively small band of comics working
side by side every night in New York who were developing a new style
of stand-up. Pacing outside the Improv in those days, you could hear him
mutter, "We're in the top seventeen . . . the top seventeen."

But Lewis didn't know what making it as a stand-up comic really
meant until the night Jimmie Walker came back. Walker, a kid from the
South Bronx who got his start at the Improv in the early '70s, had moved
to L.A. and landed a role as J.J., the oldest son in a Chicago ghetto family
on Norman Lear's sitcom *Good Times*. His string-bean, jive-talking character was less than beloved among many African Americans (including his
costars, John Amos and Esther Rolle). But Walker, with his "Dy-no-
mite!" catchphrase, was the breakout star of the show, which vaulted into
the Nielsen Top 10 at the start of its first full season, in the fall of 1974.
So when he came back to New York for a return appearance at the Improv,
there was a genuine star in the house.

"It was a night I'll always remember," says Lewis. "A limousine stopped out front, Jimmie walked out, and he was like a shadow—the thinnest human being I've ever seen. He walks in, and when Budd introduced him, the place went fuckin' nuts. Before he opened his mouth. I was just sitting there in the back, one of the hot young comics then, broke, but still learning my craft and proud that I was making it in New York, and I remember thinking to myself, I'm never quitting. Until I hear a Budd Friedman say, 'Ladies and gentlemen, Richard Lewis,' and they're already applauding."

Television had long been the ticket to fame and fortune for stand-up comedians. In the 1950s and '60s, they aimed for guest shots on the top variety and talk shows—exposure that could raise their profile, and thus their fee, in Vegas and the best nightclubs around the country. Starting in the 1970s, however, an even more lucrative TV avenue opened up for them: the situation comedy. This was due, at least in part, to a radical overhaul that the genre had undergone after the success of Norman Lear's *All in the Family*. That show, which debuted on CBS in January 1971, wasn't just a breakthrough in subject matter—in contrast to the farcical or sentimental comedies that preceded it, it focused on a realistic working-class family dealing with real-world issues of race and class and economic disparity. It also represented a significant change in style. Unlike sitcoms of the past—which were typically shot on film, using canned laughter and featuring actors from movies or the Broadway stage—*All in the Family* was videotaped in front of a live studio audience, and its scripts were packed with gag lines and jokey interplay between the characters, to keep that audience laughing. All of this put a premium on performers who had experience in putting across a joke in front of a live audience.

So producers and network programmers went looking for the people who did that best: stand-up comics. Redd Foxx, the raspy-voiced veteran of Vegas lounge shows and racy "party records," was handed a new career as junk dealer Fred Sanford in Lear's first post–*All in the Family* sitcom, *Sanford and Son*. Gabe Kaplan, a Catch a Rising Star regular in the early '70s, was cast in *Welcome Back, Kotter* as a high school teacher trying to tame a class of cutups in his old Brooklyn neighborhood, based on Kaplan's own experiences. And Freddie Prinze, the Puerto Rican teenager who had jumped from the New York clubs to an acclaimed debut on *The Tonight Show* in December 1973, became an overnight star playing a Chicano mechanic who partners with the Anglo owner of an East L.A. garage in *Chico and the Man*.

Getting a TV sitcom, however, was a Faustian bargain for any stand-up comic who was serious about his art. On the one hand, it could make you famous beyond your wildest dreams. On the other, it neutralized your best talents by putting you at the service of formulaic scripts, ensemble casts, and network restrictions on language and content. You might get an ovation when you walked back into the Improv, but it wasn't necessarily deserved. The skills of live stand-up needed constant maintenance; it wasn't easy to pick up again after you stopped doing it regularly. Neither Kaplan nor Walker had notable stand-up careers after the end of their network sitcoms. Prinze's life took a more tragic turn: at the height of his TV popularity, he shot himself to death in his Beverly Hills hotel room.

Prinze's fast rise and fall were seen by many as a Hollywood morality tale: the tragic story of a street kid who couldn't handle Hollywood success and fame. "He stepped into a subway going to the Bronx and got out in a limo in Beverly Hills," says David Brenner, who used to work on Prinze's material with him when he was starting out. Prinze's drug problems, volatility, and obsession with guns dated back to his New York club days. Jay Leno recalls the time he let Prinze stay at his Boston apartment and came home later to find the living room full of bullet holes. At the height of Prinze's TV fame, according to his close friend Alan Bursky, he was sucking down three grams of coke and ten quaaludes a day; shooting out streetlights and hotel rooms with a .357 Magnum; and slipping into paranoid fantasies. He would order Bursky to wipe his fingerprints off anything he touched in Prinze's hotel room, and once made him strip naked when he thought Bursky was hiding coke from him. "One time he gave me a call at midnight—'Meet me on Mulholland Drive at four A.M.,'" Bursky recalls. "When I got there, he was in the woods with a flashlight and a gun: 'Anybody follow you?' I thought he was fuckin' with me." In December 1976 Prinze's wife filed for divorce, sending him deeper into depression. He was living in a Beverly Hills hotel in late January 1977 when, a few days after performing at Jimmy Carter's inaugural ball, Prinze made some good-bye phone calls to family and friends and then shot himself in the head. He died the next day in a Los Angeles hospital.

Few comedians, of course, had to worry about superstar meltdowns like Prinze's. For them, the chief dangers of television were the mundane, everyday compromises that could turn even the boldest stand-up warrior into a prime-time nincompoop. Carlin and Pryor, their radical comedy still gestating, both could be seen in the summer of 1966 wearing straw hats and joining in song-and-dance medleys with host John Davidson on Dean Martin's summer show. When Richard Lewis was lured out to Hollywood by Sonny and Cher (with whom he was touring as an opening act) for a regular spot on their CBS variety show, the crowd back at the Improv in New York cringed along with him as they watched Lewis, barely recognizable in hokey sketches dressed as pieces of fruit.

"I did two shows and had one line," says Lewis. "I went from being one of the hip young comics in New York to, like, the ninetieth banana on the Sonny and Cher show. My mom would call me—which one were you, the Roman soldier or the banana peel? It was like a Halloween show every week. One day I was standing there, spray-painted as a Greek god. At CBS they had these gorgeous twenty-by-twenty-foot mirrors, and I looked at myself in the mirror, and I said, 'I'm quitting this shit. I didn't come to Hollywood to do this.' And Sonny Bono's manager was standing there, and for whatever reason—I don't know if he was putting me on—he said, 'This is the biggest mistake of your life.' "

Lewis eventually got his own sitcom, costarring with Jamie Lee Curtis in *Anything But Love*, a romantic comedy set in a Chicago newsroom that had a middling three-year run in the early '90s. But for stand-up comics who had hits earlier in their careers, TV stardom could be life changing. *Mork and Mindy* turned Robin Williams into an instant superstar, leading to a movie career and bringing him a huge audience for his still-evolving stand-up. Billy Crystal, a New York club comic who (like Williams) had the powerful Rollins and Joffe management team behind him, was cast as network TV's first openly gay character on the sitcom *Soap* in 1977. Crystal later had some regrets about his four-year run with the show ("If I had a choice to do it over again," he says, "I would have said no to *Soap* and continued to develop my stand-up"), but it propelled him to a successful movie career and enabled him to return to stand-up a more confident and seasoned performer.

These TV successes, however, were only a preview of the real gold rush for stand-ups, which began when *The Cosby Show* became a surprise hit in the fall of 1984. The comedians who had starred in sitcoms in the 1970s were, for the most part, actors cast in roles that had been developed by others (even if, as in *Mork and Mindy*, the role was later shaped to fit their peculiar talents). But Cosby's show, in which he played a pediatrician and patriarch of an upper-middle-class black family in New York City, was something different: a sitcom built from the ground up to showcase one comedian's persona and stand-up material. *The Cosby Show* was such a monumental success (during its peak years 35 percent of all the TV households in the nation were watching it Thursday nights on NBC) that it set off a talent hunt for other comedians whose act could be transformed into a sitcom. A string of stand-up-generated hits followed, making stars of relatively little-known comics such as Roseanne Barr (*Roseanne*), Brett Butler (*Grace Under Fire*), and Tim Allen (*Home Improvement*).

The TV sitcom changed the dynamics of the stand-up profession. It drew comedians from New York to Los Angeles faster than ever. It encouraged them to develop clean, family-friendly routines that would be palatable to a mass TV audience. And it altered their career ambitions. The goal was no longer simply to develop a stand-up act good enough to make you a big draw in Vegas or in concerts or at colleges. The game now was to develop a six-minute block of A material that could put you on the fast-track to Carson's *Tonight Show*, and then to a prime-time sitcom. Comedians began to treat stand-up not as an end, but as a road to something else.

At the start of the '80s, moreover, solo stand-up was being eclipsed at the cutting edge of comedy by the sketch-based satire of *Saturday Night Live* and its network cousins, *SCTV* and *Fridays*. These shows were less interested in comedians who stood alone in front of a mike and poured out their private angst than in comics who could fit into an ensemble, do impressions, and develop characters that could be brought back week after week. They found most of their new talent not at Catch a Rising Star or the Improv, but in improvisational theater companies like Second City in Chicago and Toronto and the Groundlings in Los Angeles.

A few stand-up comics made the transition. One was Eddie Murphy, a cocky teenager from Roosevelt, Long Island, who began hanging out at the Comic Strip in New York when he was still in high school. In the fall of 1980, *Saturday Night Live* was looking for a black cast member to help rebuild the show's ensemble after the departure of Garrett Morris and the original Not Ready for Prime Time Players. When the first comic hired didn't work out, Bob Wachs and Richie Tienken, the Comic Strip's owners, sent over Murphy, and he was brought on as a featured player for $750 a week. In a rebuilding season that was mostly a disaster (one cast member, Charles Rocket, was fired after saying "fuck" on the air), Murphy was one of the few highlights. By the following season he was the show's breakout star, and Wachs and Tienken became his managers.

"His material wasn't very good," says Wachs of Murphy's early stand-up, "but he had great attitude, tremendous confidence." His comedy showed the obvious influence of his idol, Richard Pryor: he did a routine on the names like Buckwheat that white people thought up for black kids on the *Our Gang* comedies (which would later evolve into his popular Buckwheat bits on *SNL*), and another on the different ways black and white audiences react to scary movies (a bit Pryor also did). Still, when he made his first *Tonight Show* appearance in early 1982, after his *Saturday Night Live* success, Murphy was allowed to do something that even Pryor couldn't get away with. In a bit he had used in clubs, Murphy instructed the studio audience, on the count of three, to all scream the word "nigger!" "It's all right, you got my permission: I ain't gonna hurt nobody," he said with a grin. "Just wait for me to count to three. Because last time I was out here, they screamed it before I asked 'em."

Wachs, who accompanied Murphy to the show, was surprised the NBC censors okayed the bit, but Carson went crazy for it, and Murphy proved that his boyish charisma and horse-whinny laugh could win over mainstream white audiences—something he would prove more emphatically in the next few years in movies like *48 Hrs.* and *Beverly Hills Cop*. On the flight back to New York after his Carson debut, Murphy looked at the unappetizing tray of airline food in front of him, turned to Wachs, and said, "This is the last time we fly coach."

For young stand-up comedians in the late '70s and early '80s, the role models were no longer the determined outsiders of the decade past—comedians like Carlin and Pryor, Martin and Brooks, who invented themselves and made the mainstream audience play catch-up. They were the comics who got so good at their job that they could leave it behind—for movies or a TV series. In the '60s it would have been called selling out. In the '80s it simply meant that stand-up was losing much of its urgency and vitality, a sense that it was central to what was happening in the culture and the country.

Which made the achievement of the last great stand-up comic to emerge in the 1970s even more impressive. Though he went on to star in one of the biggest stand-up-inspired sitcoms of them all, Jerry Seinfeld was no short-timer or stand-up dilettante; he was as dedicated to the craft as any practitioner in history. And if he seemed to represent the final trivializing of a revolution that had begun with the committed, socially relevant comedy of Carlin and Pryor, he did as much as anyone to transmit the gospel of stand-up to the next generation and beyond.

Jerry Seinfeld was born in Brooklyn, New York, on April 29, 1954, and grew up in the Long Island suburb of Massapequa, where his father owned a commercial sign business. Jerry logged the usual milestones for a middle-class Jewish kid—bar mitzvah at thirteen, a summer in Israel between his junior and senior years of high school. Shy and too small to play sports, he spent his time studying comedians on *The Ed Sullivan Show*, listening to Bill Cosby records, and entertaining his friends with bits from

Rowan & Martin's Laugh-In. From the age of seven he wanted to be a stand-up comedian.

He went to college at the State University of New York at Oswego, but after two years, beginning to think seriously about a comedy career and feeling he needed to be closer to New York City, he moved back home and finished up at nearby Queens College. A theater and communications major, he appeared in a few plays, like *One Flew over the Cuckoo's Nest*, but was bored by acting. "Frankly, it wasn't challenging enough," Seinfeld says. "A lot of standing around while other people talked. I only liked the funny parts." For a socially uncertain, self-disciplined college student, a devotee of health foods, yoga, and Zen meditation (and later, for a brief time, Scientology), stand-up comedy was an important creative outlet. "Any art works best when it's the only pinhole of expression that a human being has," he says. "Everything that they want to express gets forced through that little hole. As a young person I just felt closed off—closed off socially, closed off to the world, closed off for an avenue to relate. And there was a lot going on in my head. I was not insecure. Anybody who stands on a stage and tells people what to think, you're not insecure. I had no avenue."

To celebrate his graduation from college in 1976, Seinfeld worked up a comedy routine and went into the city to try it out on open-mike night at Catch a Rising Star. It was an inauspicious start. Nervous, he froze up onstage, jumping from one joke to the next by simply announcing the subject: "The beach." "Driving." "Shopping." When he was done, emcee Elayne Boosler cracked, "That was Jerry Seinfeld, the king of segues."

"A friend made me drink a glass of Scotch before the show, because that's what Bogie would do," Seinfeld remembers. "I couldn't drink, but I'm forcing the Scotch down at the bar next door. It was pretty much a disaster. I was completely unprepared for how difficult it really is when you first go on. I hadn't really memorized it. I thought I could just get up there. I could always make my friends laugh, and I thought maybe it won't be that difficult a transition."

The debacle sent Seinfeld back to the drawing board. He wrote new material, memorized it, and began performing at a less-intimidating place—a restaurant on West Forty-fourth Street called the Golden Lion Pub, where they'd make a space for the performers by removing one table and rigging up a spotlight out of a single lightbulb with a can around it. The preppie-looking kid with the toothy grin got his first big laugh with a riff on being left-handed. "Why are 'left' words always negative?" Seinfeld mused. "Two left feet. Left-handed compliment. On TV, ever see a crook named Righty? You go to a party, there's nobody there, where'd everybody go? 'They left.' " Jackie Mason came in one night and told him, "You're gonna be so big it makes me sick."

The comedian he modeled himself after was Robert Klein—the first stand-up he heard who sounded like his own friends, not his parents' friends. He liked Klein's intelligence, and his willingness to talk above the audience's head without seeming smug or insular. "I thought I could get into that attitude, that same vein of observation," he says. "More than Woody Allen, working in the Village, which I always thought about as preaching to the choir—talking about your therapist, and everyone in the audience has a therapist. Klein was a hipper guy, but he was talking to unhip people, and getting them to laugh. If I could sum up my entire philosophy of comedy in one sentence, it is to be hip without excluding. That's the key: staying on the front of the curve, without leaving the mainstream audience behind."

Emboldened, Seinfeld went back uptown and passed the auditions at Catch a Rising Star and at the Comic Strip, where the less-pressured atmosphere and a crowd heavily populated with Long Islanders like himself made it a more comfortable place to call home. "Catch was the cool place; the Comic Strip was lame," Seinfeld says. "It was almost a suburban place. But that room really rang. It had a great, strong sound to it."

At first he commuted in from his parents' house in Massapequa. But when he turned twenty-three, Seinfeld got his own studio apartment on West Eighty-first Street. Every day he and his friend Larry Miller would ride the bus across Central Park to the East Side clubs (using a discount pass given to them by their friend George Wallace, a comedian who worked for a company that sold ad space on the city buses). Seinfeld and Miller would hang out together all day, eat burgers at the Comic Strip, often for both lunch and dinner, and get free T-shirts there too. Seinfeld held various part-time jobs—selling lightbulbs over the phone, hawking costume jewelry on the street, and waiting tables at Brew Burger. But when he got a job emceeing at the Comic Strip two nights a week for sixty-five dollars a week, he could focus entirely on his comedy. "I had my lunch. I had my dinner. I had T-shirts," says Seinfeld. "Then all I had to pay for was my jeans. Rent is two hundred dollars a month. I'm making sixty-five dollars a week, so that left me fifteen dollars a week to play with. I was on my way. I'm golden."

Seinfeld was at the center of a tight circle of Comic Strip regulars, most of them Long Islanders like himself, including Miller, Mark Schiff, Paul Reiser, and Carol Leifer—the latter two State University of New York at Binghamton graduates who were dating and who auditioned for Jerry on the same night at the Comic Strip. (Leifer later went out with Seinfeld for a year.) Next to the fast-living Catch a Rising Star crowd, the Seinfeld group were like the class nerds; instead of hitting the discos or doing drugs after the shows, they'd convene at the Green Kitchen and talk about comedy. (Though he worked at Catch as well, Seinfeld was never part of Rick Newman's cool crowd. When the comics and the club owners held a meeting in 1979 to talk about getting paid after the L.A. Comedy Store strike, Seinfeld piped up with a comment. According to one of the participants, Newman snapped, "Who the hell are you?")

Seinfeld was known among his friends as the professor of comedy. He studied jokes and worked diligently on new material. He made sure he spent at least an hour a day writing, compiling his ideas on a pad of yellow lined paper. "Jerry was the first one I saw who understood the importance of craft," says Larry Miller. "He would write every day. I only started doing that about three years in." "His life was always very efficient and clean and uncluttered," says Reiser. "He used to have a wallet that had one credit card and however many crisp bills he needed. And one piece of paper of one-word ideas he wrote down that day. He'd try out that stuff. Jerry did new stuff regularly and methodically. Larry used to keep his act on cocktail napkins and matchbooks, in a drawer. And Jerry always had the same-sized yellow legal pad, the Bic pen. He was just methodical."

He became known for "observational" comedy—the somewhat misleading term given to comedy that wasn't about politics or social issues or the comedian's own autobiography, but simply about everyday life. Seinfeld seemed to delight in taking the tiniest things and inflating them into giant soap operas. Like his fantasia on the secret life of socks:

> I admire socks. They have great ambition, great drive. How many times you do a big load of laundry, you go to the dryer, you take out your socks, you count them up—one of them got out! He escaped. He took off on his own. What are his chances out there? I don't think they're good. Sometimes you see a dirty sock by the street there, just one sock. It's a sock that didn't make it. I don't know how they escape. They have their own ideas. Sometimes they'll hang on a sweater—that's like a freight car to them . . .

Or his critique of men's pajamas:

> Pajamas have got to be the world's funniest clothes. Who designed them to look that way? Like a little tiny suit. Little collar, buttoned down.

And a breast pocket—*there's* a useful item. Anybody using the breast pocket on your pajamas? What, you put a pen in there, you roll over in the middle of the night, you kill yourself!

Seinfeld didn't do characters, or act out his routines like Klein. He delivered everything in the same voice—a lightly sarcastic New York whine that seemed to poke fun equally at the little absurdities of everyday life and the comedian compulsive enough to make an issue over them. He never talked about current events, or sex, or his own relationships in any serious way. Except for some early lapses, his material was free of X-rated language. On a 1979 Showtime *Big Laff-Off* special, it's a shock to hear the *f*-word in his riff on the old *Superman* TV series: "The *Daily Planet*, supposedly the largest circulation newspaper in the entire city—they got three reporters. And each week two of them are stuck in a fuckin' cave somewhere." Later he scorned such four-letter helpers and scrubbed his material clean. "They're an easy way out, a crutch," he says. "And once you get a word into your act, you cannot get it out."

But in language that was colorful, concise, and colloquially spot-on, Seinfeld chronicled the unending battle between the poor schlub and the People Who Make the Rules. He could get up in arms over blank greeting cards, for example: "No words, no message, nothing. It's like Hallmark is saying, 'Hey, we don't know what to tell her. *You* think of something, pal. For sixty-five cents—*I don't want to get involved*.'" Or the wanted posters at the U.S. Post Office: "What do they want you to do about it at the post office—write the guy?" He talked about his first time scuba diving ("another of those pointless activities where your main goal is to not die") and obsessed over how to gauge the right amount of milk to put in your cereal: "Milk-estimation skills—so important. What do you do when you get to the bottom of the bowl and you still have milk left? Well, I say, put in more cereal!" A dozen comics could have thought that up. It took Seinfeld to add the priceless "I say"—the hint of self-mockery that gives it the comedic oomph.

Compared with Carlin's jeremiads or Pryor's self-revelation, this was utterly weightless stuff. But that doesn't mean it was any less personal or authentic, the confessions of a Long Island Jewish narcissist who could make a joke of his own fetish for cleanliness, order, and logic. Seinfeld may have removed the edge from stand-up comedy, but not the honesty: his voice onstage, you felt, was exactly the voice you'd get if you were sitting with him over a bowl of cereal. Seinfeld acknowledged, later on, that some criticized his comedy for not "dredging up deep pain." But he told an interviewer in 1991: "Anyone who's seen what I do knows I am revealing how my mind works. All right, so I talk about cereal, and not existentialism or drug addiction. I work with the material that's natural to me."

In the late '70s Seinfeld was one of the most popular stand-ups in New York, widely admired by fellow comics for his work ethic and the speed of his ascent. He was the unrivaled star of the Comic Strip and was the first of his group to start touring. "He was always sort of one step ahead," says Paul Reiser. "Doing those gigs, opening for people—and the next year we would be doing the same gigs." But after four years, he packed up and made the move so many of his fellow New York comics had already made—to the West Coast. "I was at the top of the food chain in New York," he says. "I didn't like everybody looking up to me. I figured that wasn't good for my growth."

But he had a harder time in L.A. than he expected. Mitzi Shore, resentful of the well-hyped star from New York, wouldn't put him on at the Comedy Store. He landed a role in the TV sitcom *Benson*—as a messenger who tries to write jokes for the governor. But after only three episodes, he showed up for a script reading and was told his character had been dropped and he was out of a job. (His agent had forgotten to give him the message.)

So Seinfeld put all his energies into stand-up. He bided his time before doing *The Tonight Show*, fearful of repeating the nasty experience of David Sayh, the Catch a Rising Star phenom who made a smash *Tonight Show* debut in 1977, only to fizzle afterward because he didn't have enough material. When Seinfeld made his first *Tonight Show* appearance on May 7, 1981, a year after arriving in L.A., he looked confident and in control, doing bits about driving in L.A., security checks for drugs at the airport, and fourteen-hundred-pound Bob Hughes, listed by the *Guinness Book of World Records* as the world's fattest man: "Ladies and gentlemen, the man has *let himself go.*" Johnny didn't call him over to the desk or come over to shake his hand, as he had with Sayh, but the little OK sign Carson flashed was validation enough that Seinfeld's hard work, patience, and PG-rated self-discipline had paid off. It was the most important night of his career.

In the '80s Seinfeld became one of the most successful touring acts in comedy, making up to three hundred live appearances a year in clubs and concert halls. While other comedians kept one foot in L.A., to be available for network auditions, Seinfeld disdained them. "He never hung around for pilots," says George Shapiro, who became his manager shortly after his arrival in L.A. "He was dedicated to doing stand-up. Being your own writer, director, choreographer, star—for him there was nothing like it." And when he finally did get his own sitcom on NBC in 1989, it was on his own terms. He teamed up with Larry David—who had been in the class ahead of him in the New York clubs during the late '70s, though the two were not especially close—to create a sitcom about himself, a stand-up comedian living in New York. They eschewed conventional sitcom story lines, with their two-act plot structure and heartwarming dénouements ("no hugging, no learning" was the Seinfeld-David mantra). Instead, the show was a dense weave of stand-up premises and complications, carried out to their logical extreme, like a series of comedy routines, each with a punch line payoff. After struggling in the ratings at first, the NBC series became the most popular sitcom on television and one of the most critically acclaimed in all of TV history, climaxing its nine-season run with a finale in May 1998 watched by seventy-six million viewers.

Seinfeld represented the audience-friendly capstone to the stand-up revolution of the 1970s, the culmination of its journey from rebel art form to mass-audience entertainment. After the challenging social commentary of Carlin, the incisive character sketches of Pryor, the antiestablishment barbs of Klein, the showbiz parody of Brooks, the anti-comedy of Martin, the head games of Kaufman and the high-wire performance art of Williams, Seinfeld ushered stand-up comfortably into the Reagan era: his material was apolitical, squeaky clean, easy to take, safe for everyone.

Though Seinfeld was no innovator or social provocateur, he was a worthy ambassador for another part of the '70s stand-up revolution: the comedian as truth-telling everyman, exposing our secret thoughts and airing our dirty laundry—even when it's just laundry. Seinfeld's stand-up may have seemed trivial, but it was never phony or forced. It was the personal statement of an artist using stand-up to comment on the little guy's battle for sanity in a crazy world. And no one showed more dedication to the art form—something he put on film, memorably, in the 2002 documentary *Comedian*, which chronicled Seinfeld's attempt to resume his stand-up after the end of his TV sitcom. Traveling from club to club, trying to write a new act after a nine-year layoff, he expressed the eternal predicament of the stand-up comic, even those who become huge stars. "You can't be bigger than me," he told one crowd when he was having a bad show, "and look, I'm still shit."

Yet Seinfeld's longevity—his ability to stay remarkably fresh and funny in a stand-up career that spanned thirty years—was partly a function of his conservatism. Most of the great innovators of '70s stand-up, like avant-garde artists of many eras, faced the problem of watching their outsider art become part of the mainstream culture—robbing them of their originality and their raison d'être. Pryor's once revelatory confessional comedy began to look relatively tame when black comedians and rap artists cranked up the anger, the misogyny, and the street profanity. Klein's hip counterculture attitude grayed awfully fast, when even Johnny Carson let his hair grow long and middle-aged swingers were smoking grass. Steve Martin's manic put-ons didn't look so wild and crazy when fifteen thousand fans in the audience were doing them along with him.

Some, like Martin and Brooks, met the challenge by simply putting a period on their stand-up days and never looking back. Pryor got a second wind from his own personal troubles in the early '80s, but ultimately gave in to the more comfortable rewards of Hollywood. Klein would have liked to do the same, but settled instead for the role of stand-up elder statesman, doing jokes about Viagra and colonoscopies. Carlin managed to hang on and maintain his edge into his seventies, but with increasing strain—and an occasional trip to rehab.

Provocative stand-up comedy hardly died out after the 1970s. Following Sam Kinison, Bill Hicks, another rabble-rouser from Texas, was perhaps the most committed to carrying on the Lenny Bruce–George Carlin mission of attacking the status quo and the sacred cow. Before his death in 1994, at age thirty-two, he delivered sharp, fearless commentary on America's war culture, the L.A. riots, antismoking activists, and (perhaps the surest sign of a comic with a career death wish) a ruthless riff on "my favorite cultural train wreck, *The Tonight Show* with Jay Leno." But with most of the taboos shattered and the sacred cows defiled, stand-up comedians had to raise their voice, and twist themselves into increasingly strange contortions, in order to have the same shock effect. Chris Rock adapted Pryor's racial attitude but ratcheted up the volume and the confrontational posturing. Lewis Black took on the role of angry Howard Beale, flying into X-rated rages about everything from designer water to governmental corruption. Dave Attell aired the forbidden musings of the skankiest guy in class, from amputee sex to priest pedophilia. ("There is a problem in the priesthood. These little kids will not keep their mouths shut.") Sarah Silverman skated to alt-comedy stardom with an original, if sometimes exasperating, comic character: the brazenly self-centered, politically incorrect Jewish American princess. Dane Cook cast himself as the populist outlaw-hero with his sick-joke flights of fancy—the joy of shoving an ice cream cone into a kid's face, say, or watching a pedestrian get hit by a car—and, in 2005, released the first number-one-ranked comedy album since Steve Martin's *Wild and Crazy Guy.*

The comedy clubs, meanwhile, have staged an improbable comeback, after the '80s boom suddenly imploded in the '90s, when at least a third of all the clubs nationwide shut down. The run-of-the-mill comics who fill these clubs (and the stand-up wannabes who play out their backstage angst for the cameras in the TV reality show *Last Comic Standing*) still sound mostly like Seinfeld—doing casually ironic observational bits, though with a sexual and scatological candor in the clubs that Seinfeld never would tolerate. But political satire, too, has enjoyed a resurgence, as the Iraq War and the follies of the second Bush administration brought out the kind of artistic dissent not seen since the Vietnam era.

The news headlines from Washington and Hollywood, meanwhile, are filtered through the irreverent and ironic sensibility introduced by the stand-up comics of the '70s—and today on display everywhere from the monologues of Letterman and Leno and Conan O'Brien to the satiric newscasts of *Saturday Night Live*, Jon Stewart, and Stephen Colbert (whose pompous, relentlessly ironic talk show host owes as much to Steve Martin as to Bill O'Reilly). On the Internet, bloggers do stand-up routines in the guise of commentary, wisecracking in real time about presidential speeches and candidate debates. Candidates for office know that their political fate rests on how they perform in the late-night comedy crucible—where they go to announce a presidential bid or put their spin on a brewing scandal, or simply show that they're down-to-earth folks who can laugh at themselves. Even the president himself gets up at the annual White House Correspondents' Dinner and proves his mettle by trying to outdo the stand-up comedian who has just cut him down to size.

And while issues of war and peace, of crime and scandal, are turned into fodder for comedy, stand-up itself has become serious business. Richard Pryor's death in December 2005 prompted the kind of reverent tributes that Pryor himself, the ghetto survivor who made fun of self-important preachers, might have had fun with. Michael Richards, the former *Seinfeld* costar, loses his cool with some hecklers at an L.A. comedy club and has to apologize for his racial slurs, like a political prisoner in a Stalinist show trial, in front of David Letterman and a national TV audience and with his friend Jerry Seinfeld standing by for support. Comedians are honored with sober testimonials at the Kennedy Center. Steve Martin, getting his Mark Twain Prize in 2005, at least took his in the right spirit; he pulled objects out of his fly.

Stand-up comedy in the '70s helped create the world we live in, and the way we look at it. It made us more cynical about our leaders, and more suspicious of authority of all kind. It forced us to take a close, skeptical look at the media world that has overwhelmed us. It made us more open about ourselves, and more willing to tolerate differences in others. It freed up our language and showed that our most embarrassing memories are nothing to be ashamed of, because others share them too. It made us observant and questioning and smart. It taught us not to sit still for anything, but to talk back.

And if you get a laugh, you're golden.

Acknowledgments

I am enormously grateful to all of the people—comedians, managers, agents, club owners, and many more—who talked with me for this book and helped me tell the story of this remarkable era:

Danny Aiello, Chris Albrecht, Jimmy Aleck, Irvin Arthur, Michael Ashburne, Chris Bearde, Pat Benatar, Joy Behar, Richard Belzer, Conan Berkeley, Sandra Bernhard, Mike Binder, Larry Bishop, Ed Bluestone, Marvin Braverman, David Brenner, Larry Brezner, Bernie Brillstein, Jimmy Brogan, Albert Brooks, Jack Burns, Alan Bursky, Zane Buzby, John Byner, Maple Byrne, George Carlin, Dick Cavett, Tommy Chong, Paul Colby, Billy Crystal, Larry David, Rudy De Luca, John DeBellis, Tom Dreesen, Dick Ebersol, Bob Einstein, Cliff Einstein, David Franklin, Budd Friedman, Michael Fuchs, Sandy Gallin, Whoopi Goldberg, Bob Golden, Merv Griffin, Charles Grodin, Argus Hamilton, Jerry Hamza, Hugh Hefner, Caroline Hirsch, Charles Joffe, Monica Johnson, Craig Kellem, Bobby Kelton, Dennis Klein, Robert Klein, Mark Krantz, Paul Krassner, Mike Langworthy, Peter Lassally, Norman Lear, Carol Leifer, David Letterman, Emily Levine, Jay Leno, Barry Levinson, Richard Lewis, Bill Maher, Buddy Mantia, Cheech Marin, Merrill Markoe, Steve Martin, Jamie Masada, Kelly Carlin McCall, John McEuen, Lorne Michaels, Bette Midler, Larry Miller, Paul Mooney, Les Moonves, Buddy Morra, Robert Morton, Herb Nanas, Rick Newman, Rick Overton, Nancy Parker, Joe Piscopo, Christopher Porterfield, Paula Poundstone, Jennifer Lee Pryor, Rain Pryor, Rob Reiner, Paul Reiser, Joan Rivers, Kelly Rodgers, Jack Rollins, Manny Roth, Arlyne Rothberg, Bill Scheft, George Schlatter, Jerry Seinfeld, Garry Shandling, George Shapiro, Bob Shaw, Harry Shearer, Mitzi Shore, Pauly Shore, Sammy Shore, Stu Smiley, Tom Smothers, Bob Stane, David Steinberg (comic), David Steinberg (manager), Judy Steinberg, Tim Thomerson, Richard Tienken, Adrianne Tolsch, Rocco Urbisci, Bob Wachs, Jeff Wald, Fred Weintraub, Fred Willard, Mason Williams, John Witherspoon, Bob Zmuda, and Alan Zweibel.

Among the many others who helped provide background material, I'd especially like to thank Jim Bradley for tracking down early tapes from *The Merv Griffin Show*; Tobe Becker for filling my constant requests for HBO tapes; Loretta Ramos and Amy Douthett of the Paley Center for Media (formerly the Museum of Television and Radio) for giving me access to the museum's invaluable archives; Paul Slansky for turning over his precious tape of old Albert Brooks TV appearances; Jeff Sotzing of Carson Productions; and Jim Oberman, along with the rest of the *Time* magazine research staff, who helped me track down articles. For their help in smoothing the way to some of the book's key sources, I would also like to thank Jeff Abraham, Cindi Berger, Jude Brennan, Elizabeth Clark, Sarah Fuller, Michelle Marx, Mike Miller, Marcia Newberger, Alan Nierob, Steven Rubenstein, and Gil Schwartz.

I owe a great deal to my editors and colleagues at *Time* magazine, who put up with a rather substantial side project over the past three years, especially Steve Koepp, Jim Kelly, Rick Stengel, and Josh Tyrangiel, as well as Daniel Eisenberg, Howard Chua-Eoan, Rebecca Myers, Tony Karon, Catherine Sharick, Mark Rykoff, and the entire staff of Time.com.

My editors at Bloomsbury, Colin Dickerman and Nick Trautwein, made the experience of doing my first book far less traumatic than I had feared. I thank them for their confidence in me and their close attention every step of the way. For their work on the book, I'd also like to thank Mike O'Connor, Amy King, John Candell, and Maureen Klier.

My agent, Kristine Dahl, was incredibly patient over the years as I groped, in fits and starts, toward the idea for this book. Once I embarked on it, she was unfailingly supportive and kind.

Other friends who provided me with feedback, advice, and in some cases specific help during my work on the book included Lorenzo Carcaterra, Roger Director, Tom Houck, Dan Klores, Harvey Myman, Peter Newman, Steve Oney, Jeff Ressner, Jeff Ross, and Claudia Wallis. In addition, Richard Gurman provided invaluable counsel all along the way, from first germination of the idea to the final product. Dennis Klein went far beyond the call of duty in offering to read the entire finished manuscript, and I'm grateful for his perceptive comments and corrections throughout.

Finally, my wife, Charla Krupp, was more than just a patient sounding board during the writing of this book (even as she was finishing her own). She was the toughest and most astute editor a writer could want, critiquing an early draft and setting the book on the right course. She also made sure the women got a fair break. I couldn't have done it without her.

A Note on Sources

All of the quotations in this book come from my own interviews, except where otherwise specified. What follows is a list of the chief books and articles that supplemented my own research (matched with specific quotes when they're not cited in the text), as well as some notes on the major interviews. One book that deserves a special mention is Phil Berger's *The Last Laugh: The World of Stand-up Comics* (Cooper Square Press, 1975; Limelight Editions, updated 2004), which provided insights into several of the comedians I discuss as well as general background and inspiration, with its flavorful and immensely engaging behind-the-scenes look at stand-up comics plying their trade.

Chapter 1: After Lenny

Any attempt to reckon with Lenny Bruce's life and work has to begin with Albert Goldman's definitive, if somewhat overwrought, biography, *Ladies and Gentlemen, Lenny Bruce!!* (Random House, 1974). Goldman includes a description of the paddy wagon encounter between Bruce and Carlin, though Carlin provided me with a fuller account. Many of the biographical details of Bruce's life and career are drawn from Goldman's book, though supplemented by the following:

The Trials of Lenny Bruce: The Fall and Rise of an American Icon, by Ronald K. L. Collins and David M. Skover (Sourcebooks, 2002), the definitive account of Bruce's legal cases. ("I'm a surgeon with a scalpel for false values . . .")

Seriously Funny: The Rebel Comedians of the 1950s and 1960s, by Gerald Nachman (Pantheon, 2003). The chapter on Bruce was the source for the quotes from Kenneth Tynan and the unnamed columnist. ("He airs the lowest thoughts . . .") Nachman's book also provided good background on Bruce's stand-up contemporaries in the new wave of the 1950s and early '60s.

Going Too Far: The Rise and Demise of Sick, Gross, Black, Sophomoric, Weirdo, Pinko, Anarchist, Underground, Anti-Establishment Humor, by Tony Hendra (Doubleday, 1987).

How to Talk Dirty and Influence People, by Lenny Bruce, with Paul Krassner (Simon and Schuster, 1963).

Funny People, by Steve Allen (Stein and Day, 1981), which includes an interesting chapter on Bruce.

The account of Dick Gregory's reaction to Bruce's "nigger" routine comes from liner notes by Grover Sales for the two-CD set *Lenny Bruce Originals* (Fantasy, 1991). The excerpts from Bruce's routines were taken largely from those CDs, as well as from *Lenny Bruce: The Carnegie Hall Concert* (Blue Note, 1995) and the boxed set *Lenny Bruce: Let the Buyer Beware* (Shout! Factory, 2004).

Chapter 2: Rebellion

George Carlin and I met for a two-hour interview in his office in West Los Angeles, and we followed up with several phone conversations and e-mails. Carlin is close to an ideal interview: he has a colorful story, talks about it articulately, and seems to remember everything. In addition, he kept a journal for most of his career, which he would consult for me when the occasional specific date or detail eluded him.

Relatively little of much depth has been written about Carlin, at least compared with many of the other comedians in this book, but a few articles proved useful:

"Carlin: Lenny Bruce Was His Idol," by Judy Stone, *New York Times*, May 28, 1967.

"George Carlin Feels Funny," by Mark Goodman, *Esquire*, December 1974.

"Golden Side of Comedy LPs," by Will Tusher, *Variety*, December 15, 1978.

"George Carlin: He Made Comedy out of His Fondness for Dope, But Today Drugs Are No Joke—They're the Eighth Dirty Word," by David Sheff, *People*, January 11, 1982.

"*Playboy* Interview: George Carlin," by Sam Merrill, *Playboy*, January 1982. ("If you want to see a cokehead . . ."; "For the entertainer, part of the thing you do is just style . . .")

Details of the legal fight over Carlin's "seven dirty words" routine are drawn from *New York Times* and *Variety* accounts of the case's progress in the 1970s. And the story of Carlin's experience on *Saturday Night Live* is described in both of the two major books on the show:

Saturday Night: A Backstage History of Saturday Night Live, by Doug Hill and Jeff Weingrad (Vintage, 1987).

Live from New York: An Uncensored History of Saturday Night Live, by Tom Shales and James Andrew Miller (Little, Brown, 2002).

Chapter 3: Race

When I began this book, Richard Pryor was still alive, but unable to do interviews. I had a pleasant meeting with his wife, Jennifer Lee Pryor, though she gave me only limited cooperation on the book. Many other people involved in his career, however, provided important background, especially Sandy Gallin, Pryor's first agent, and David Franklin, his manager for several years in the '70s. Pryor's old friend Paul Mooney was a bit more of a project. He and I spoke twice in person, but only following his sets at Caroline's in New York City, when he would field my questions while greeting friends and fans in the club's bar area after the show. Still, with the help of several follow-up phone calls, he was a valuable resource.

The literature on Pryor is, not surprisingly, more extensive than for most of the comedians in this book, and I depended largely on the following sources:

Pryor Convictions and Other Life Sentences, by Richard Pryor, with Todd Gold (Pantheon, 1995). Most of the account of Pryor's early life is taken from Pryor's own readable, though perhaps not entirely candid, memoir.

Tarnished Angel: Surviving in the Dark Curve of Drugs, Violence, Sex, and Fame, by Jennifer Lee (Thunder's Mouth Press, 1991).

If I Stop I'll Die: The Comedy and Tragedy of Richard Pryor, by John A. Williams and Dennis A. Williams (Thunder's Mouth Press, 1991).

Jokes My Father Never Taught Me: Life, Love, and Loss with Richard Pryor, by Rain Pryor (Regan, 2006).

"Beyond Laughter: Zany Comic Seeks to Solve His Own Enigma," author unnamed, *Ebony*, September 1967.

"This Can't Be Happening to Me," by David Felton, *Rolling Stone*, October 10, 1974.

"The New Comic Style of Richard Pryor," by James McPherson, *New York Times Magazine*, April 27, 1975.

"Black Comedy and the Pryor Commitment," by Dennis Hunt, *Los Angeles Times*, April 11, 1976. ("I was doing material that was not funny to me . . ."; "I was working very hard and wasn't making great money . . .")

"Berserk Angel," by William Brashler, *Playboy*, December 1979.

"Healthy and No Longer 'Ba-ad,' Richard Pryor Is 'Bustin' Loose,' " by Lois Armstrong, *People*, June 29, 1981.

"The Last Time We Saw Richard," by David Handelman, *Premiere*, January 1992. (Wayans quote: "Pryor started it all . . .")

Chapter 4: Improv

My first encounter with Robert Klein was in Los Angeles, where he was staying in a rented house while shooting a CBS sitcom, *The Stones*, one of the many TV projects over the years that didn't do a lot for his career. We met again a few months later for lunch in New York and talked several more times in person and on the phone. No one is more passionate or knowledgeable about the art and craft of stand-up than Klein, and he talked enthusiastically and volubly, not just about his own career but about the entire stand-up comedy scene. For some details of his early life and career, I also drew on his memoir, *The Amorous Busboy of Decatur Avenue* (Touchstone, 2005).

David Steinberg and I had lunch at a Hamburger Hamlet in Los Angeles and had a follow-up conversation on the phone. He too was entertaining and eager to reminisce about a stand-up career that isn't much remembered today.

A few other published sources contributed to the chapter:
Something Wonderful Right Away: An Oral History of the Second City and the Compass Players, by Jeffrey Sweet (Avon Books, 1978).

"Gospel According to Steinberg Is Strictly from Old Testament," by Dan Sullivan, *New York Times*, July 15, 1968.

"So Here Am I, David Steinberg, with My Big Gorilla Foot," by Charles Higham, *Los Angeles Times*, July 16, 1972.

"Robert Klein, Middle-Class Child of the Fifties," by Judith Sims, *Rolling Stone*, June 21, 1973.

"Wooo-ooo-ooo, It's Robert Klein," by Anna Quindlen, *New York Times*, July 29, 1977.

"For Robert Klein, Real Life Is a Laughing Matter," by Esther B. Fein, *New York Times*, December 15, 1985.

A good account of the Smothers Brothers' battles with the CBS censors is contained in "Mom Always Liked Them Best: The Smothers Brothers Story Revisited," by Jon Krampner, *Television Quarterly* 29, no. 3 (1998), and also in the chapter "Death by Committee" in Tony Hendra's book *Going Too Far* (Doubleday, 1987). Details of the Billy Crystal incident on *Saturday Night Live* are recounted in both of the *SNL* books cited above.

Chapter 5: Clubbing

I conducted two face-to-face interviews with Budd Friedman in Los Angeles, one in his photo-adorned office upstairs at the Improvisation, and the other in a restaurant near the club. His recollections were, of course, key to telling the story of the birth of the comedy club scene in New York. I also had many talks, both on the phone and in person, with Rick Newman, his counterpart at Catch a Rising Star. He was incredibly helpful, not just in recounting the great years of Catch a Rising Star, but in getting me in touch with several other sources for this chapter. (He got me into a couple of great Friars Club events to boot.) I met Bob Wachs, cofounder of the Comic Strip, the third of the comedy club triumvirate in New York, almost by accident in Easthampton, New York, and he became a great resource as well.

In addition, I drew material from the following:

Leading with My Chin, by Jay Leno (HarperCollins, 1996).

The Other Great Depression: How I'm Overcoming, on a Daily Basis, at Least a Million Addictions and Dysfunctions and Finding a Spiritual (Sometimes) Life, by Richard Lewis (PublicAffairs, 2000).

"Richard Belzer: If He's So Funny, How Come He Ain't Made It?" by David Hirshey and Jay Lovinger, *Rolling Stone*, November 12, 1981. ("I'm the kind of guy who tells the truth . . .")

"Breaking in the Bananas," by Thomas Meehan, *New York Times*, August 1, 1976.

"Tomlin, Pryor and Midler—and a Lot of Dogs—First Got Their Feet Wet at Budd Friedman's Improv," by Roger Wolmuth, *People*, November 17, 1978.

"Having Tagged Such Talent as Kaufman, Benatar and Kaplan, Rick Newman's Getting off the Ground," by Toby Kahn, *People*, December 29, 1982.

Chapter 6: Put-on

Albert Brooks was a bit wary at first—"I just don't want to be a paragraph in a book about George Carlin," he told me on the phone—but once we met, at the Brentwood Hills house he was using as an office during the editing of his movie *Looking for Comedy in the Muslim World*, he was a delight. Far from dismissing his early stand-up work as long-forgotten juvenilia, Brooks seemed quite proud of it, and his re-creations of many of his old bits made me laugh as hard as I did the first time I saw them. We had one follow-up phone conversation, and his manager Herb Nanas was also exceptionally helpful, as were his other friends, former colleagues, and two brothers. The chief articles about Brooks that I drew from included the following:

"Comedy's Post-Funny School," by Richard Corliss, *Time*, May 25, 1981.

"Albert Brooks Is Funnier Than You Think," by Paul Slansky, *Playboy*, July 1983. ("The funniest white man in America.")

"Albert Brooks," by Bill Zehme, *Rolling Stone*, April 18, 1991. ("The interesting thing is that he *finished* . . .")

"Reflections on Himself," by Bruce Weber, *New York Times Magazine*, March 17, 1991.

"*Playboy* Interview: Albert Brooks," by Bill Zehme, *Playboy*, August 1999.

Chapter 7: Some Fun

Steve Martin initially did not want to talk for this book, which was in keeping with his general aloofness from the press. After my numerous entreaties, he finally agreed to a relatively limited phone interview, from which most of the quotes in the chapter are taken. I was also able to see an early copy of his recently published memoir, *Born Standing Up: A Comic's Life* (Scribner, 2007), a candid and perceptive account of his art and his ambiguous relationship with fame, and I used it mainly as background to corroborate my account of his career and to fill in a few gaps.

One character notably left out of his memoir is Morris Walker, a high school friend who wrote an entire book about their school pranks together, *Steve Martin: The Magic Years* (SPI Books, 2001). Even allowing for the possible embellishment of a high school friend seeking some reflected glory, the memoir has some interesting anecdotes, and it is the source for Walker's quote. John McEuen, another high school friend, was also a major source for this chapter (in lieu of his brother Bill, Martin's former manager, who declined to talk), and so was Mason Williams, an unsung hero of Martin's early career. I was also happy to track down Maple Byrne, Martin's road manager during most of his stand-up years, who was an old junior high friend of mine in Kansas City (in the days when he went by the name Kenny).

I also utilized the following articles:

"The, Uh, Madcap Wasp Comedian," by Janet Coleman, *New York*, August 22, 1977.

"Bananaland's Top Banana," by David Felton, *Rolling Stone*, December 1, 1977.

"Comedy's New Face," by Tony Schwartz, *Newsweek*, April 3, 1978.

"Steve Martin: He's Off the Wall," by Richard Corliss and Denise Worrell, *Time*, August 24, 1987. ("As I studied the history of philosophy . . ."; "To spend time with him . . .")

Icons: Intimate Portraits, by Denise Worrell (Atlantic Monthly Press, 1989), whose chapter on Martin includes the complete interview with Martin she conducted for the *Time* article.

The comment about Martin by David Letterman comes from an interview I conducted with him in March 1980 for an article in the *Atlanta Constitution*.

Chapter 8: Chasing Carson

Mitzi Shore was ailing—frail and shaking with a nervous disorder—but after an appeal on my behalf by Argus Hamilton, she agreed to meet with me for an interview. On a hot June afternoon, she arrived in the parking lot of the Comedy Store on Sunset Boulevard, in the passenger seat of an SUV driven by one of the club's employees. She needed help walking and was in some discomfort sitting at one of the tables in the darkness of the club, where the streams of light seeping in from outside competed with the neon signs representing the major comics who had appeared at her club over the years. (Gallagher's light was out, which bothered her.) Even in her enfeebled state, her mind seemed clear, her grievances fresh, and I could still get a sense of the charm and charisma—and the willfulness—that made her such a dominant figure in the L.A. stand-up world of the 1970s.

David Letterman turned down my requests for an interview for more than a year, which was a disappointment but hardly a surprise, given his virtual estrangement from the press in recent years. At a fairly late stage of my reporting—perhaps after hearing about the book from the several friends of his I had spoken to—he finally agreed to an interview. We met in an office on Fifty-seventh Street just following the late-afternoon taping of his CBS show. Dressed in baggy shorts and sneakers—the same attire I saw him in nearly fourteen years earlier, when I wrote a cover story on him for *Time*—he talked far beyond the thirty minutes he had promised me, expressing his desire to go on the record about a period of his life that clearly meant a lot to him. His contribution to the book was invaluable.

Along with the many others who added their recollections to this chapter, I depended on these sources:

The Warm-up: The Autobiography of a Number Two Man, by Sammy Shore (Morrow, 1984).

The Late Shift: Letterman, Leno, and the Network Battle for the Night, by Bill Carter (Hyperion, 1994).

King of the Night: The Life of Johnny Carson, by Lawrence Leamer (Morrow, 1989).

Here's Johnny! Thirty Years of America's Favorite Late-Night Entertainer, by Stephen Cox (Cumberland House Press, 2002, revised edition).

"The Other King of Comedy," by Lawrence Christon, *Los Angeles Times*, April 17, 1983, a profile of *Tonight Show* booker Jim McCawley.

"Echo of Laughter," by Paul Brownfeld, *Los Angeles Times* Calendar, June 22, 2003, a profile of Mitzi Shore and her sons.

Chapter 9: Extremists

Robin Williams and I met for one interview, in a windowless conference room in the basement of the Trump International Hotel on a cold Sunday in January, when he was in New York shooting a movie. He was thoughtful, soft-spoken, and gracious in praising the contributions of his fellow comics—among them George Carlin, whom he lamented had not yet been awarded the Kennedy Center's Mark Twain Prize for American Humor. "Carlin *is* our Mark Twain," he said. There is no shortage of articles and quickie books on Williams; these were the most useful:

"*Playboy* Interview: Robin Williams," by Lawrence Linderman, *Playboy*, October 1982.

"In the World According to Robin Williams, It's Time to Drop Out of Mork's Orbit," by Salley Rayl, *People*, September 13, 1982.

"More Than a Shtick Figure," by Joe Morgenstern, *New York Times Magazine*, November 11, 1990. ("He has this incredible ability to recognize the most basic human truths . . .")

Robin Williams: A Biography, by Ron Givens (People Profiles, Time Inc., 1999).

Without Andy Kaufman around, I depended largely on the reminiscences of his friend and partner in crime, Bob Zmuda, and his longtime manager, George Shapiro, along with the other people quoted. Several other books and articles also made contributions to the story:

Lost in the Funhouse, by Bill Zehme (Random House, 1999), the definitive biography of Kaufman, and one of the most entertaining of all books written about stand-up comedy.

Andy Kaufman Revealed! Best Friend Tells All, by Bob Zmuda (Little Brown, 1999).

"The Identity Crises of Andy Kaufman," by William K. Knoedelseder Jr., *Los Angeles Times*, December 10, 1978.

"Laughter from the Toy Chest," signed by "Tony Clifton," *Time*, May 28, 1979.

"Andy Kaufman: Beyond Laughter," by David Hirshey, *Rolling Stone*, April 30, 1981.

Andy Kaufman: I'm from Hollywood (Shanachie Entertainment, 1992), a video that has the best account of Kaufman's wrestling years.

Chapter 10: Women

There were few enough women who were prominent in stand-up in the 1970s that I was especially hopeful of hearing from Elayne Boosler, by far the most successful woman to emerge from the New York comedy clubs during those years. Her decision not to participate, despite many requests, was my greatest disappointment in reporting this book.

Her intransigence, however, forced me to dig even harder for a few less-well-known women who were pioneers alongside her in the early days of the New York clubs, such as Nancy Parker and Emily Levine. Several other women comedians I spoke with were gracious and helpful as well, especially Joan Rivers, with whom I had an entertaining dinner in New York following one of her stand-up performances at the Cutting Room in Chelsea. I also drew on her lively memoir, *Enter Talking*, written with

Richard Meryman (Delacorte, 1987). Other sources for material on Boosler and other women comics of the period:

"Funny Girl: New, Hot, Hip," by Mark Jacobson, *New York Magazine*, March 22, 1976.

"Elayne Boosler Cuts Up at Pace," by Anna Quindlen, *New York Times*, October 12, 1979.

"Laugh Bargains for a Summer Night," by Stephen Holden, *New York Times*, July 24, 1987. ("Lenny Bruce had already made a fissure in the status quo . . .")

"Cable and Movies Calling, Comic Elayne Boosler Finds Her Place in the Fun," by Leah Rozen, *People*, October 12, 1987.

"In the Abrasive, Competitive World of Stand-up Comedy, a New Generation of Women Is Making a Go of It by Not Pulling Punches," by Phil Berger, *New York Times Magazine*, July 29, 1984.

"Johnny Carson: The Rolling Stone Interview," by Timothy White, *Rolling Stone*, March 22, 1979.

"Lily . . . Ernestine . . . Tess . . . Lupe . . . Edith Ann . . ." author unnamed, *Time*, March 28, 1977.

"Mork, Gabe and Dy-No-Mite Came from Her Comedy Showcase, So to Top That, Mitzi Shore Opens an, er, Women's Room," by Suzy Kalter, *People*, April 16, 1979.

Roseanne: My Life as a Woman, by Roseanne Barr (Harper and Row, 1989).

"Why Women Aren't Funny," by Christopher Hitchens, *Vanity Fair*, January 2007.

Chapter 11: The Boom

The Comedy Store strike still elicits strong passions on both sides. And both were well represented by Tom Dreesen, the leader of the strikers and the labor dispute's unofficial historian, and Argus Hamilton, the comedian who acted as Mitzi Shore's representative. Shore herself also spoke with me about the strike, the feelings still obviously raw. I also depended greatly on the thorough coverage of the strike and its aftermath by William K. Knoedelseder Jr. in the *Los Angeles Times*. Calvin Trillin's article a few months later, "Not Funny," in the *New Yorker* (January 7, 1980), is also an excellent and balanced account of the whole episode.

For the section on the comedy club boom and eventual bust, I drew mainly from these sources:

"New Breed of Stand-up Comics," by Fred Ferretti, *New York Times Magazine*, December 5, 1982.

"Stand-up Comedy on a Roll," by Richard Zoglin, *Time*, August 24, 1987.

"The Clubbing of America," by Duncan Strauss, *Rolling Stone*, November 3, 1988.

"Take My Nightclub, Please," by Annetta Miller, *Newsweek*, August 2, 1993.

"The Last Stand for Stand-up," by Chuck Crisafulli, *Los Angeles Times* Sunday Calendar, January 9, 1994.

I Killed: True Stories of the Road from America's Top Comics, compiled by Ritch Shydner and Mark Schiff (Crown, 2006).

Brother Sam: The Short, Spectacular Life of Sam Kinison, by Bill Kinison with Steve Delsohn (Morrow, 1994).

When Stand-up Stood Out, (Velocity/Thinkfilm DVD), a video record of the Boston comedy club scene.

True Story, by Bill Maher (Random House, 1994). Though fictionalized, Maher's novel based on his experiences in the New York clubs and on the road gives a good picture of the scene in those years.

Chapter 12: Mainstream

Jerry Seinfeld was one of the first comedians I interviewed for this book, and he set me on the right track. When we met at a coffee shop on the Upper West Side of Manhattan, he sat at a corner table but faced the crowd, seemingly unconcerned about being recognized, and he talked amiably and articulately about his stand-up days. He remains a "professor" of comedy, full of insight not only into his own work but that of the people who influenced him, such as Robert Klein and Bill Cosby. His documentary *Comedian* (Bridgnorth Films, 2002) also provided excellent background into his thought processes. Other major sources included these:

Seinfeld: The Making of an American Icon, by Jerry Oppenheimer (HarperCollins, 2002).

"How Does Seinfeld Define Comedy? Reluctantly," by Glenn Collins, *New York Times*, September 29, 1991. ("Anyone who's seen what I do knows I'm revealing how my mind works . . .")

"Jerry Seinfeld, and That's No Joke," by Tom Shales, *Washington Post*, April 22, 1992, in which Seinfeld discusses his brief flirtation with Scientology.

"Friends Recall the Freddie Prinze of West 157th Street," by Joyce Maynard, *New York Times*, February 4, 1977.

"The Good Little Bad Little Boy," by Richard Corliss, *Time*, July 11, 1983, cover story on Eddie Murphy.

Index

A Note on the Author

Richard Zoglin is a senior editor and writer at *Time*. For twelve years he was the magazine's television critic and is currently its theater critic. He has written *Time* cover stories on David Letterman, Bill Cosby, Diane Sawyer, Arsenio Hall, and *Star Trek*, among others. He lives in New York City with his wife, Charla Krupp.